Conversations with Top Achievers

With contributing authors
Jack Canfield
Dave Seymour & Peter Souhleris
Craig Golightly
Victoria Mason Acree
Rachelle Chase
L.M. Christenson
Christian Appiah-Knudsen
Marième Faye
JoAnne Kell
Kathleen S. McGowan
Annette Mease
Marc Frank Montoya
Maria Olson
Liz Phalp
Gerald Rogers
Derek Rollins
Matt Schultz
Rebecca Yates

Warning—Disclaimer

The purpose of this book is to educate and inspire. This book is not intended to give advice or make promises or guarantees that anyone following the ideas, tips, suggestions, techniques or strategies will have the same results as the people listed throughout the stories contained herein. The author, publisher and distributor(s) shall have neither liability nor responsibility to anyone with respect to any loss or damage caused, or alleged to be caused, directly or indirectly by the information contained in this book.

ISBN 0-9785802-8-1

Table of Contents

Introduction

Have you ever wanted to be a sitting in the room while someone you admired was being interviewed? Have you ever wanted to be the "fly on the wall" just to hear what they are really saying about success, happiness and life? I too have always wanted that and this is why I developed *Conversations with Top Achievers*. There are so many books out there that are too polished and do not get down to the nitty gritty on how to succeed. With this book series I structured the book so it would feel as if you were right there in the conversation. It is not overly polished or perfected but it is real and true.

Join with me as I interview some of the top achievers of our time. Some are *New York Times* best-selling authors and some are just like you and me.

I hope you enjoy these conversations and I invite you learn more at our website, www.DUPublishing.com.

Sincerely,
Woody Woodward

Jack Canfield

As the beloved originator of the *Chicken Soup for the Soul®* series, Jack Canfield fostered the emergence of inspirational anthologies as a genre—and watched it grow to a billion dollar market. As the driving force behind the development and delivery of more than 123 million books sold through the *Chicken Soup for the Soul®* franchise (and over 500 million copies in print worldwide), Jack Canfield is uniquely qualified to talk about success.

Jack is a Harvard graduate with a Master's Degree in psychological education and one of the earliest champions of peak-performance, developing specific methodologies and results-oriented activities to help people take on greater challenges and produce breakthrough results.

His proven formula for success reached global acclaim with his most recent National Bestseller, *The Success Principles: How to Get From Where You Are to Where You Want to Be*. This new standard in self-improvement contains 64 powerful principles for success utilized by top achievers from all walks of life and all areas of commerce. *The Success Principles*—and the entire empire of *"Principles"* books, products, coaching programs and branded retail merchandise—is Jack's most recent offering to the more than 100 million readers he currently reaches worldwide.

Website: www.JackCanfield.com

To book Jack Canfield call Teresa Collett, VP Sales, Corporate Training and Events 1-805-937-1199

Woody Woodward:
Who has influenced you in your career when you got started? Who were the people that affected you?

Jack Canfield:

Well, I think the people that affected me most—I was fortunate to work in the same building as Og Mandino when I was very young. I was in my 20s, and I worked for W. Clement Stone, who was a contemporary and friend of Napoleon Hill. And so, Stone was publishing Success magazine at that time, and I was working for W. Clement Stone's Achievement Motivation program, and it was magical. I mean, the guy was magical. He made me believe in myself. Dr. Billy Sharpe, who was the president of the Stone Foundation, he believed that everybody was smarter than him, and he would encourage you to bring that intelligence out and use it. Jesse Jackson. I went to his church when I lived in Chicago, and I saw the power of somebody holding a room of thousands of people, and how he would just go like that, and the band would stop, you know, and just watching that whole thing, which was very educational. And then I think from Mark Victor Hansen, I learned how to use overhead slides and then, now PowerPoint, which has been very fun to play at that level. You know, there have been so many people—psychologists, speakers, who have been influences to me.

One of my highest inspirations is Mother Teresa in India, just the fact that she could start with nothing. I have a quote on my computer from her. She was told when she left the monastery, "Mother Teresa, you have two cents to your name. What can you possibly do?" when she was going to start her own order. And she said, "Father, with two cents, I can't do anything, but with two cents and God, I can do anything." So, my favorite story about her is she decided she wanted to start a school. She had no money, and she had no agreement. So she goes to this street in Calcutta where she wants her school, and she sits down, and she opens up a book. She's on the sidewalk, just sitting there, and she starts teaching to the air. And all of a sudden, some kids come by and they go, "What are you doing?" "I'm teaching people how to read." "I don't see anybody." "Well, would you like to learn how to read?" "Yeah!" So these two kids are sitting there. The next day there were ten kids, and the next day there were 20 kids. About the third or fourth day, one of the people really wanted their kids to learn, and he was a carpenter. He made a table and a chair for her to sit on. A few days later, someone found a chalkboard and some chalk, and within a year, she had a school. But she just started because she was committed to it. That's inspired me to know that no matter what it is, no matter how much we don't have, that it's possible, we just start, and out of that starting comes the manifestation.

Woody Woodward:
What was one of the major turning points in your business, that you look back at your successful career and say, "You know what? This happened because, and that's why this happened." Is there a time that you can remember?

Jack Canfield:
Well, I think the biggest shift in my career was when I went and did the first *Chicken Soup For the Soul* book. What was happening was I was out giving speeches and seminars and workshops and trainings, and people would constantly come up and say, "That story you told about the Girl Scout, the puppy, the guy at the beach, whatever, is that in the book anywhere?" And I'd always have to say no. And so, one day, I was like, you know, it's like I should've had a V8 commercial. I went, "Oh gosh! I should've written a book about all this." So I made a list of all the stories I knew, and there was about 70 of them. I said, "I'm going to write one every three-and-a-half days, two a week, and you know, in a year, I'll have 100 stories." So that was what I started to do. I think a key for everyone in this world is you've got to have a book. It doesn't even have to be all that relatively new to everything else, but it's like a credibility piece. And so once we wrote that book and it took off, which it did and created a whole phenomenon—

I think *Time* magazine called it the publishing phenomenon of the decade—it shifted everything. A book can go where you can't. I mean, I meet people in the airport who come up to me and say, "Are you Jack Canfield?" And I go, "Yeah." And they say, "I read your book and it changed my life." And they start telling me how, and I'm going, my gosh, I couldn't believe that would happen as a result of a book. So I think that's the critical thing that took me from being an average guy to being, you know, a celebrity and someone that's really had the level of impact I've been able to have.

Woody Woodward:
What's one of your favorite quotes?

Jack Canfield:
Probably my favorite quote is one that a lot of people talk about, which is Napoleon Hill, which is, "Whatever the mind of man can conceive and believe, the mind of man can achieve," and I literally live by that. You know, if I can make it up and believe in it, we can create it. I mean, our publisher—we were rejected 144 times before *Chicken Soup* got published. Our publisher said we'll probably sell 20,000 copies. We said we want to sell a million-and-a-half in a year-and-a-half, and he laughed. Have you ever shared your dream and someone laughs at you? I'm sure you've had that experience. And now he laughs all the way to the bank as he travels around in his $35 million personal jet. So, the reality is that you just have to say, "I'm more committed to my vision than I'm committed to your doubt or my fear," and just go for it.

Woody Woodward:
What was the publishing company (Health Communications) doing before you and Mark came along?

Jack Canfield:
They were doing recovery publishing like, you know, alcoholics and co-dependents. Their best year up until then had been $17 million

in gross sales. When we were there, they were at $6.8 and they were going downhill. The trend line was totally down. And I'll tell you a quick story that most people don't know. We went to New York to sell *Chicken Soup for the Soul* with an agent. We went to five meetings a day for three days. Every publisher said, "You're nobody; the title's stupid; people don't read short stories; blah, blah, blah." So everyone rejected us. On the last day, Mark and I get up. We always walk in the morning for at least an hour just to get exercise. We walked by St. Patrick's Cathedral in New York City so we said, "Well, let's go in." And we went in and we meditated for about 15 minutes. I knew you could light a candle and ask for a prayer, so I said to Mark, "Let's pray," and we lit a candle, and we prayed that we would get a publisher for our book. Well, it took us another 14 or 15 months before we actually found a publisher. We found out two years later, after Health Communications signed the contract, that Peter Vegso, the owner of HCI, had actually been in New York almost on the exact same day we were there. He had gone into St. Patrick's and prayed that God would send him an author or some authors that would save his company. We were blown away. We had just come over for cocktails one night before dinner and we heard this. We both found out we had done that. So the next time I was in New York, I bought this glass etched design of the church, and we each have one of those on our desk right now.

Woody Woodward:
What is one of the greatest challenges you had overcome to get to do what you do now?

Jack Canfield:
I think the greatest challenge any of us have to overcome is, and certainly for me, was a fear of I'm not enough. Who am I to be speaking and teaching? What do I know that's so special? Fear of rejection is certainly a big one. I had low self-esteem when I started out. That's why I became a self-esteem expert. We always say you teach what you need to learn. And I think the other thing was, I realized, proba-

bly too late in the game, but it wasn't too late, later than what I would have liked to have learned, about the importance of team. I was kind of a solo entrepreneur for way too long, and then we began to create alliances and hire more people and co-author books. I mean we have 225 *Chicken Soup For The Soul* books, and every one of them is coauthored with Mark Victor Hansen, or many times a third person, a fourth person. We've even had five authors on a book, and we split the royalties five ways, but you've got five people out there promoting the five different groups or networks and so forth. As soon as we started doing that, my success just rocketed. I mean, everyone who's ever been successful has a team.

Woody Woodward:
Jack, you are a ferocious learner and reader. When you attend seminars how many pages notes do you take?

Jack Canfield:
Well, when I went to S.A.N.G. (Speakers, Authors Networking Group), I learn probably more than I can implement in the year or the six months. I think the first SANG I went to, I took about 150 pages of notes. It's about a year-and-half later, I'm still working on some of those things. I had so many business cards I had to staple them to the side of a page, make notes, put them in a three-ring binder, and then work through making those contacts over the course of the year. This year, we're just at the beginning of the third day, and I think—I counted up last night, I had 72 pages of notes, and I'm sure I took 5 more this morning. So far, we've only had one speaker.

Woody Woodward:
What is the power of them having a mentor?

Jack Canfield:
Well, I've both been a mentor and have had mentors, and I think that basically, you can't become an expert at everything. To go the next level, you've got to find people who've already been down that road you want

to go, or at least have done the level of impact of the thing you want to do. I always teach people to find mentors who have already done what you've done or want to do and ask them how they did it. There are certain things like the first time we went to the moon. No one had done it, but you get together with all the other people who want to go there and you form a mastermind alliance and work together. I've had numerous mentors in the financial world, selling from the back of the room, bringing humor into my talks, publishing, both from the level of creating a book as well as how to market and sell a book. I've had mentors of being on television, having my own show, being an interviewee. Tiger Woods, I think, has something like three or four coaches. He has a short game coach, a long game driving coach, a putting coach, a physical coach, a nutritional coach. So, if you want to be successful, you don't become an Olympic athlete without a coach, and so I think we all need mentors. We need colleagues. I have a phrase I teach which is, "You want to be a teacher to those below you, a fellow traveler to those on the same level, and a student to those that are above you." And I think it's saying I've had an opportunity to be all three of those in different areas, you know, in terms of who you're talking to.

Woody Woodward:

How do you deal with all the people who want something from you? How do you stay so giving in this world of takers?

Jack Canfield:

Ivan Misner, who started Business Network International, said, "Givers get." And so you've got to be a giver in order to be a receiver. It's a balance of 50/50. You know, one hand gives, one hand receives, and if you're only a taker, then it dries up the giving. Someone has to prime the pump, to go first, if you will. Everyone I've met over the years has just been incredibly generous with their information, with their time. Other speakers and authors will say, "Talk to my staff, you can have my manual, whatever it is you want." We want to support each other in being more successful. So, as they say, you know, as the ocean goes up, all the boats rise equally. So it's an unlimited pie, and when people get that it's about attraction, it does not have a limit. Someone said the other day, you can go to the ocean with a thimble, a cup, a gallon jar, a tanker, or a pipeline, the ocean doesn't care, because the ocean's infinite," and I think we find that the amount of information available, the amount of giving and sharing and cooperation is infinite.

Woody Woodward:
We all have that moment where we feel like we've made it. When you hit that moment? Did you buy something—a toy, a car, a trinket? Did you do something to commemorate your success?

Jack Canfield:
I think I had two moments of making it. I remember when I started, my first speech was $25. I drove through a blizzard to get there and a blizzard back. This was in Connecticut and Massachusetts, and I was so excited that I actually got paid to teach this stuff I was passionate about. And then I remember I went to $100, $300, $600, $800 for a day, and I remember my first $1,000 day, and I'm driving back from Pasadena to Pacific Palisades, and I stopped at a liquor store, and I bought a $100 bottle of wine, and I said to my wife, "We have made it. If we can make $1,000 a day when I speak, we're home-free." I can get $65,000 a day now for speaking overseas, but that was huge. The second big "we've made it" was when *Chicken Soup For The Soul* really took off in our third year into it and we got a $6 million check, it took our breath away." And so we actually moved from L.A. up to Santa Barbara, and we bought a $2 million home. We were living in a 1,700-square-foot home in L.A. We moved into a 6,000-square-foot home. All of the furniture we had in our old home fit into the living room of the new home, and I remembered thinking, "Oh my gosh, we're going to have spend a lot of money just to furnish this place," but being able to drive up a driveway instead of into an alley into a garage into a little tiny neighborhood and go, "This is ours," you know, and then walking into this amazing house, beautifully landscaped, six acres, barn, guest house,

office space, I just thought I'd died and gone to heaven. And for a little kid who grew up in West Virginia whose father made $8,000 a year to be able to have the kind of home I have and the kind of life I have is just extraordinary. So yeah, I definitely celebrated the success.

Woody Woodward:

In closing, any last inspirational thoughts you have?

Jack Canfield:

I go back to what Napoleon Hill said, "Whatever the mind of man can conceive and believe, the mind of man can achieve." With the right vision, drive and passion you can make any dream a reality.

Peter Souhleris & Dave Seymour

Peter Souhleris

Meticulous, detail-oriented and wildly creative; when it comes to finding small, measurable ways of making a big difference there isn't anyone better equipped to handle the job than Peter Souhleris.

Peter likes quantity, but he loves quality. After all—it takes a lot to satisfy this kind of entrepreneurial appetite!

Peter's process-oriented approach to developing properties was instilled with in him during his time working for several architectural firms in historic Marblehead, MA. That same approach carried over into house flipping when he took a leave of absence to work on his first house. Today, he handles just about everything from finding, funding, designing, managing, marketing and selling properties.

His diverse experience in commercial and residential Real Estate allows him to develop and renovate a wide range of projects. Producing beautiful, high quality and functional space is his vision whether the project is an apartment building, restaurant, office building, single family or condo conversion; Peter Souhleris consistently creates desirable end-products that leave his clients and consumers satisfied to every extent.

Over the years Peter has cultivated his creative side by DJ-ing at some of Boston's hottest nightclubs. Peter has been spinning records as a DJ since the 90's. Spinning has always been a passion of Peter's and allows him to feed his creative side in ways outside of the real estate & design industry. Peter still makes it a priority to be active—and continues to make guest appearances today.

His architectural background has honed his intense desire for precision. His love for his family motivates him to stay grounded and focused on what matters.

When he's not doing any of those things, he's helping to give back to his community as the co-founder of the Christian Angel Smile Foundation—a non-profit organization with a mission to feed and provide gifts to needy families over the holiday season.

From crossing the T's to dotting the I's, Peter appreciates the value that can be found in the smallest of details. For Peter, the attention to those details is what makes all the difference.

Dave Seymour

A Life changing commitment to Real Estate Investing is not a game, nor is it for the faint of heart. In this industry, success manifests itself in those who think big, believe big, and have the courage to act on both.

Dave's philosophy on the current market place parallels a Warren Buffet quote, "When everybody is greedy be fearful, and when everybody is fearful be greedy," or as we see it, when the rest of the world is running out, Dave is running in. It's a character trait he picked up while serving as a Firefighter and Paramedic in New England, and you can see it in everything he does.

Dave is the consummate leader. From the first day of demo all the way through to the cashing of the check after the sale, Dave can be found moving the proverbial ball down the field at breakneck speed—managing, positioning and keeping everything on track, on time, and on budget.

Dave's never been one for details, but boy—does he think BIG! Armed with British wit and unwavering persistence, Dave keeps the team motivated, he demands massive action and in return he produces massive results.

His greatest joys come from being a husband and father, both of which are the true motivation for all he does. The ability to see others achieve the success they never believed possible has been one of the most rewarding experiences in Dave's life.

For more information on training and education from Dave and Pete visit www.citylighthomes.com

Woody Woodward:

Dave and Peter, both of you are very successful. You two have the hit show on A&E, Flipping Boston. *You came from other areas of business and formed a partnership with the* Flipping Formula. *How has it been working with a partner in your business?*

Dave Seymour:

Working with a partner has been instrumental in my success mainly because of the fact that it's allowed me to leverage the things that I'm very, very good at against the things that I'm either not so good at or I don't have the time for. Our relationship was born out of a mutual respect, first of all. From there, it developed into what you see today with not only the *Flipping Formula*, but also *Flipping Boston* on A&E, the hit house flipping show on TV. What happened was that I was a student of the seminar world. I had come out of real estate training and education programs myself.

Born out of necessity, I was broke. Part of the instruction that I was given was to find likeminded people—and I actually met Peter on Craigslist where I found an ad that said something to the effect of "looking for investors or likeminded people." Peter and I had an opportunity to meet, and it was a couple of guys who had the same real core values, believed in doing what was right, and that was evident in our first meeting. Also, two guys who were hungry, who were animated and infused with the real estate business. I was coming from a place of financial weakness, but I was also coming from a place of being very motivated, very educated and could bring time components to Pete that maybe were not there for him in the beginning. Our relationship grew on that basis. I would put in a lot of legwork and time, and he would bring finances. It was one deal, and then another deal, and we continue to work off of each other's strengths, motivate each other's weaknesses, and it was trust.

There was a huge amount of trust there, and—which, let's be honest, is a rarity in a lot of relationships in life, but the trust factor that we brought to our business relationship has, obviously, been a huge component of our personal friendship at the same time. And it's powerful. It's very, very strong, and when you've got double the power, double the strength, double the motivation, it makes it a very formidable force in the business world. I think that's a big part of what has brought a lot of the success that we have not only in our real estate business, but also in our training and education business with the *Flipping Formula*.

Woody Woodward:
Peter, what's been your experience with that same question?

Peter Souhleris:
Of course, I agree with everything that Dave is saying. I would say, as silly as it sounds, that's how we did meet, on Craigslist. I posted an ad, like Dave said, something to the effect of looking for an investor.

Dave responded to that ad, and it was a conversation that we still talk about to this day. I knew immediately that I just connected with him. I clicked with him. He sounded like a guy that was loyal, had integrity, he appeared to have all the good, core fundamentals that you would want in a partner. I was not looking for a partner when we began that conversation; I was just looking for investors. I don't think Dave was either. We were just having a conversation. I was telling him what I was doing in my business. At that time, we were at different points in our careers.

I was a little more seasoned because I had been renovating and flipping for about 10 years give or take, and Dave was just starting to get into it. What I instantly saw in Dave, were good qualities that would allow for the fundamentals of something to continue. The value Dave brought to the table as time went on like he mentioned, was the freeing up of my time. For me, this was a great way to expand my business. I was doing it all myself, everything from finding the deal to funding, designing and selling it. When Dave came along he was great at as we call it "turning over rocks."

This is where I see Dave's biggest strength even today. Dave has an uncanny ability to talk to people and just keep on turning over rocks to find opportunities. When we first met, he was turning over every single rock you could imagine and fortunately, had enough energy that he could do that. Anyone else would have burned out.

His percent ratio today is so much more lethal and efficient. What I mean by that is that there's much more opportunity in the rocks he turns over today than ever before because of his experience. I'd have to say that was the beginning for us.

Seriously, he just had that personality, and there's a few times in life that I can remember where I've had relationships start from there. You just kind of know. I'm a firm believer in listening to my gut, and at that moment in time it told me that he was a good guy. I knew that I wanted to do business with him.

Little did I know at that moment that our conversation would start with one deal and land up getting us a national TV show and an education company that teaches people how to successfully do what we do by putting it all into a system. The Flipping Formula is the foundation and process that I started practicing over 15 years ago. Today, we have simply converted that same formula into something that can be duplicated to allow anyone that wants to go out and do it too.

Woody Woodward:
True partnerships are built by using our strengths and our weaknesses in helping one another. You guys have done that very successfully. You've got this amazing coaching company. You have one of the most success-ful shows on A&E. As reality stars, as celebrities, if you will, how has the fame and the fortune changed you, or has it not changed you at all?

Peter Souhleris:
I would say it hasn't. Well, I'll say for me, and I'm sure Dave is in agreement, it hasn't really changed me at all, as weird as that may sound. Look, it is cool when people come up to you and say, "Hey, we love your show," but we stay humble and feel blessed to have the op-

portunity. We're a couple of guys that actually do this stuff. We are not just in the reality TV show business; we live and breathe real estate. We're guys that get up and go for it every day.

We find deals. We fix them. We sell them. We're in the trenches. For us, it's just another day at work with a camera following us. Both of us kind of have that personality where we don't care if the camera is on us. We just do our thing. I remind myself everyday how blessed we are with the opportunities that have been given to us from the big guy upstairs, and feel very humbled by it.

So, we really don't have this aura or this swagger of celebrities. It's funny, because people look at us like that, and I get it. We certainly see that, but we don't act like that at all. As a matter of fact, one of the first things Dave and I said to each other was, if either of us ever act like that, we'll smack each other in the head, and so far we haven't had to do that. I don't see us smacking each other in the head anytime soon.

Dave Seymour:

I agree with my partner but what I will tell you is that the changes that have occurred have been subtle. First of all, Pete and I made a commitment at the beginning, which he just alluded to, is that we would never let pride and ego get in the way of this process no matter how successful this TV show thing was or wasn't. I have a saying that I've used for 23 odd years in my life now, and it's an acronym for ego, and I always said that ego stood for "ease God out." The day that I think I'm better than anyone else is the day that I need to go back to school and start all over again.

So, it's funny. I'm doing this interview. I'm sitting on a deck. We're looking at a beautiful marsh here in South Carolina on vacation with my family, and we went out yesterday and we did a little shopping at one of the malls, and I'm walking into one store, and this gentleman's going in and he says, "Hey, you're that guy from *Flipping Boston*. Love your show."

And then, another couple mentioned it to us when we were in a restaurant yesterday. Other than those acknowledgements of people saying, "Hey, I like the show," I'm, like Peter said, very humble and very grateful. There is no real, real change in our personalities. What I will tell you, which is nice, is that the added attention has allowed us to do things that we maybe couldn't do or get that much attention on before, and one of those is the ability to do some philanthropic works on a bigger scale. As you know, we're from the Boston area, and we recently went through some pretty horrible tragedies up in our own neck of the woods, and we were able, as a result of being TV guys, to get some exposure for a fund that Peter and I put together to raise money to help the folks who suffered the consequences of the bombings at the Boston Marathon.

Our goal is to be able to go in and either donate funds directly or be able to do some modifications to the homes of people who suffered injuries in that tragedy. If we hadn't been the TV guys, we wouldn't have been able to get that kind of national exposure, so for that we're grateful, you never know what blessings are coming down the pike or what good works you can do as a direct result of, like my partner says, turning over rocks, and I am an avid rock turner. That is for sure. We're doing this book interview with you right now, Woody, because I turn rocks, man, so we're blessed.

That's the bottom line. We're both very blessed.

Woody Woodward:

Will Smith said, "Money just magnifies our true personality." You guys have made money, lost money, made money, and with the TV show success, with the book success, with all the homes you get to flip, the money hasn't changed you. Now, that's a really rare thing. Usually, money or fame can destroy someone. So you talked about being humble. What do you do to stay humble because there are many people reading this book who are going to make money or lose money in the future? What advice would you give to staying true to your roots?

Dave Seymour:
Change diapers.

Peter Souhleris:

My son Athan, is 20 months old and my wife Desi and I compete of who's going to go pick him up and change his diaper and hold him whether its in the middle of the night, or during the day. As silly as that sounds, we actually enjoy that magical moment on the changing table as he giggles, smiles, and just does all his cute little stuff. Don't get me wrong, there's times when he is a handful, but it all reminds us how blessed we are to have these little miracles.

With my daughter Christiana, Desi and I also compete with who gets to read her books and tuck her in bed. It's just a day in, day out routine as we were before the show, as we are with the show and as we will continue after the show. And if you take a different approach to that, I think you are being very unrealistic, and that's just setting yourself up for failure, we both kind of have that vision, and we've always had it.

We put on our pants the same way everyone else does. Nothing's changed, man. Seriously, change a diaper or two, and if you remember that you're just the same dad, same husband, same brother, same son, same friend to everyone you always have been, and that can never change. And if it does, I think that's when failure kicks in, and sadness follows. That's what I believe.

Dave Seymour:

That's an awesome quote from Will Smith, and I've seen destruction firsthand when money is made and success is created, and I believe that there are some certain personality types that are just destined for tragedy. I've addressed my own demons from way back and today I'm able to look in the mirror and be okay no matter what the situation and that's an ability that I believe is rare. A lot of people can't look in the mirror and be at peace, and if you have that then wealth manifests in many, many forms, and it's not always coin. It's not always cash in the bank.

It's definitely the ability to be present, and it's a challenge, man. It's not easy. It's not a walk in the park. Life on life's terms can be problematic sometimes. Pete's right. Change a diaper or two to stay grounded. I have a one-year-old, a three-year-old, and an 18-year-old, and they will keep you humble. They will keep you honest, and they will teach you over and over and over again that you are only human.

Woody Woodward:

Dave, I like what you mentioned about taking care of your demons. We all have challenges, and I'm sure, Pete, you would agree as well. We all have those issues that keep us from reaching our full potential. Along your road of success, what books or what mentors did you seek after to help you overcome your challenges?

Dave Seymour:

My demons were 23 years ago. I stopped drinking, and one of the books that I read was some basic self-help books.

I looked at causes and conditions for my behaviors in life, and as far back as I could remember, I had an inability to be right size is the best way I described it, the inability to fit in society and an inability to fit in my own skin. If I had not learned how to address that and work on it, then I would have been of those guys that I refer to as having a personality type which was doomed for failure if financial success came down the pike. So, I worked on myself, a lot of reading, a lot of introspective teachings. One of the books that I love is *Who Moved My Cheese*.

It's such a simple story, and yet it's so adequate. We live or tend to do things over and over again through repetition and wonder why we don't get different results. And it's such a common mistake for so many people on the journey to success. Just because you want something, it doesn't mean it's going to come. You have to put the traction in place to get the results that I believe everybody deserves.

Everyone deserves good things in life, so that was definitely a book that had a big impact on me, but I would assume, if I had to be honest, the biggest impact for me was actually *The Secret* by Rhonda Byrne, which took the laws of attraction and delivered them as a science.

And I'm a living testimonial to that, I really am, that what you think about, you bring about. The belief in what can be, if you put the effort in, if you believe, it's just a testimonial to where I've been and where I am and, more importantly, where I'm going. That was a huge gift for me. It was a lot of study, a lot of, like I said, introspective thinking, and those were definitely two books that affected me a great deal.

Woody Woodward:
Peter, what about you? What books have influenced you the most?

Peter Souhleris:
I would say one of my favorites is *The Richest Man in Babylon*. Not only does it teach the core values of knowing how to earn money, but also how to live on a portion of that earned money while also allowing for a percentage of it to earn you more money giving you the financial strength to help others as well.

It expresses a belief of "get the knowledge of earning and it will instill a confidence within that allows you to also share that knowledge with others." It says that we should live a confident life of abundance, receiving all the fruits of our labor, saving a portion of it, spending a portion, as well as giving a portion away. Once you have the knowledge of knowing how to bake a cake, you can duplicate it again and again, thus instilling in yourself the natural God-given trait of sharing without worrying if you can bake another cake. Like with everything else in business, you must have a system and knowledge combined with discipline to save a portion of your earnings. Invest in areas where you have knowledge in or attach yourself to others that are successful in that arena.

Have the knowledge and power to be a type of person that self-educates, earns money, and then gives back to the community. I believe the message in this book truly has influenced me. I believe that it has had a huge impact on how I perceive things today. It's a nice combination and balance of the principles of money management and giving back by sharing your knowledge.

Let's also not forget a little book called the Bible which puts you in check and reminds us of what our purpose is here as we walk this earth.

Woody Woodward:

Tell me the experience of getting your own TV show. A lot of times that's way beyond people's idea of what's possible. When you guys met, you became partners. You created great programs. How did the A&E opportunity come about?

Dave Seymour:

I had been very fortunate in that I had the opportunity to represent some other real estate trainers and educators for a couple of years, so I was kind of entrenched in the infomercial/entertainer/educator arena. One of my peers, and to this day I still don't know who it was, had sent me a link or an e-mail saying that the film company who put the show together was auditioning for a new version of a house-flipping show and to send in an application. So, for me being the way that I am, the rock turner that Pete refers to, I downloaded an application from the Internet to go to the production company, and it was very vanilla, very black and white, name of your company, number of properties you flip, average prices, blah, blah, blah, blah, blah, blah. During this time, I had served 12 years as a firefighter and a paramedic in New England, as well as executing on my real estate business.

What I knew was that everything we do in life is marketing, and if I wanted to separate myself from the what I presumed would be hundreds of applicants for this TV show, I had to do it through my marketing skills. So, what I did was on the application that was downloaded, I totally ignored every question that was on it and every blank that I had an opportunity to fill in, I filled in with profanity, expletives, expletives beyond comprehension that my grandmother would never want to hear. And I explained to these people in no uncertain terms that there were no other choices than Dave the British Bulldog and Pete the Greek. I explained that this is where *Rescue Me* meets *Flip This House* and that you all had definitely some mental challenges in your lives if you just didn't get on a frigging plane and come to Boston and just sign us up, because you're wasting your time with anyone else.

Peter Souhleris:

And then, he forged my name on the application and stole my picture from Facebook and sent it in.

Dave Seymour:

Yes, I forged my partner's signature, stole his picture from Facebook, sent in the application, and my phone rang within half an hour of sending in the application. And long story short, they liked the dynamic.

They did a pilot for a day. It was just like a little half-hour thing that they put together to show to the A&E network, and then we were chosen out of 400 applicants, the only one chosen by this particular film company. They liked the big British guy. They liked the banter with the smooth Greek, and we fit very nicely into the format that they were looking for, so that's how it started. Actually, our debut was the highest-rated debut ever for a lifetime release on a Saturday afternoon in the lifetime category, so we were blessed, very humbled.

And we've just been going ever since, so that's kind of how we got it, and if I had ever told Pete I was turning that application in, none of us would have been here today, because there was no way he would have let that one go through.

Woody Woodward:

With marketing, the vanilla doesn't sell. We want the Chunky Monkey. We want those unique things. We want be out and different. So, why do you feel most people never stand out on a ledge? Are they afraid to be kicked off? Are they afraid of falling? Why do you feel that so many people fall into that vanilla category and never stand out?

Peter Souhleris:

I would say fear because people just want to fit in. They're afraid of being different, so they become complacent, but you can't have those fears. If you have those fears and if you follow the pack and if you do everything the pack does, you're going to be complaining just like the pack does. Well, we kind of have an attitude that's contrarian. I'm almost wired that way. When I see a herd going in one direction, I stop and go the other way. The direction that the herd is heading in doesn't always mean it's the wrong direction, but I am wired to just stop and look around and reevaluate. I think that's the biggest problem that people have today. They're just so comfortable in following each other and saying, "You know what? If this one's doing it, then I should do it." And it's a comfort zone. It's like a feel-good thing, and when we're too comfortable, when I'm comfortable, that's when I start getting itchy and I know something's wrong. I have to, once again, get uncomfortable, because I know that as soon as I get uncomfortable, I'm going to have that breakthrough and then turn it up a notch.

I will tell you it's not easy every time we challenge ourselves, but if you don't challenge yourself, you'll never grow.

Dave Seymour:
I think marketing is in your DNA. Let's think about it for a second. Whether you're marketing yourself as a teenager trying to find a prom date or whether you're marketing yourself as a real estate investor trying to find some lead generation or whether you're marketing yourself as the latest deodorant company, it's all in that DNA, and that DNA right down at the core goes to the basics. And Pete just touched on it.

It's fear of rejection, and this powerful motivator is in all that we do. If you are able to look in the mirror and be okay with what is looking back, then you can go out on that ledge and jump, guess what? You might fly.

Think about it for a second: that core necessity for safety can be such a hindrance in personal relationships, in business, in finance and in life, in general. I believe you have to take a risk. Every three to four to five years in my life I get itchy, I have to scratch something, and I have to mix it up. I have to do something different. It's the same whether it's marketing or the next move for City Light Homes, our real estate company, or the joys of watching something in its incipient stage going to a free-forming stage, as is the case with our education company, watching the idea, then watching it grow, watching it become a reality, watching it be free flowing, watching the successes of it. Stuff like that would never happen if we didn't have the chops and the guts to just step out a little bit and say, "You know what? What have I really got to lose at the end of the day?" DO IT.

If you weigh out the options, there's no risk without reward without a little bit of risk, and you take that calculated risk and you just go for it. And if you just go for it, I believe you get rewarded. I've always rewarded action rather than inaction, and I've always rewarded somebody who wants to do something rather than do nothing. And it's just a core value in everything that we do.

Peter Souhleris:

And it keeps you alive, man. It lets you know you're alive when you're active.

Woody Woodward:

Peter, you talked about going the opposite way of the herd. In 2007-2008, the housing bubble implodes and you guys are building the coaching company. So, you did everything that was opposite of what other people were doing. Now you have a hit show on A&E. Your coaching practice is growing exponentially across the country. Would you give your clients the same advice?

Peter Souhleris:

Yes, I would. But I would also say this, those that are seeking to change have to first change their daily routine. I mean its common sense. If you want change, you have to do something different; it's a no-brainer. I look at it like this: when you see that everyone is going in one direction and they've got that attitude that we're all going to die, it's all doom-and-gloom and you stay in that doom-and-gloom pit, you're just helping it to grow more and more. When I sensed that in 2007 the real estate market crashed, I just knew I had to change. Seeing this, I had to adapt. I could not just sit there and listen to all that.

Even the best of the best were calling me up and saying, "Hey, what do you think? Doesn't this suck? Isn't this horrible? Are we all going to die?" I just tried to avoid that nonsense.

I would shut myself off from that, far away from it, and I would focus my attention in different directions. We talked about turning over rocks; that's when you're turning over rocks like a madman. This is when you have to reinvent yourself. This is when you have to change things and have the qualities that are needed to change. I believe that one of those leadership qualities that you have to have is vision. Even if you don't know exactly where you are going, you have enough vision to know that staying stagnant and following a pack is clearly not the place you want to be.

Even though it was a few years ago, it really feels like yesterday to me. I remember just changing gears and re-educating myself and consistently seeking knowledge and looking ahead—having vision, thinking three steps ahead. I avoided negative people. That's the only thing, in my opinion, that's going to get you out of something like that. Stand tall. Keep your chin up, and persevere. Be a leader. You cannot give up.

Dave Seymour:
I was taught and continue to teach myself to be a contrarian investor, and contrarian just means opposite. If you look—I think it was Warren Buffett, and I'm not 100 percent, but Warren Buffett was quoted as saying a being a contrarian investor is really one of the foundations of what he does and is, and yet he continues to change all the time with regard to what the masses are doing. It's important to understand that fundamentals are fundamentals, and they don't change. But if you are just on somebody's bandwagon, then what are you really doing?

I've never coached a student to say, "Be at the breaking point of a wave." That's not where I want them to be because there's a little danger out there. We want fundamentals, so be just on the cusp of that wave. Be right behind the lead surfer, and let guys like Peter and I forge a way for you to be successful, and that was what took a lot of the pressure off of me was the fact that I could follow Peter's examples in the things that he was doing, bring my own sauce to the table and be able to add to what was already in play.

And in doing that, we just forged our own way through. When everybody else was running out, we went running in. It was what I called the firefighter mentality. As a fireman, my training and education was to go against everything that my core survival instincts were telling me. So, how do you do that? You do it through training, through education, through mentorship, and then you do it through action, and if you take those four components and you do that in investments and business, as far as I'm concerned, success is guaranteed.

Woody Woodward:
You guys are amazing partners. You're philanthropists. You're TV show hosts. You're successful entrepreneurs. What advice would you give to a budding entrepreneur, someone who wants to go out there, but is just too afraid to pull the trigger? What would you tell them?

Peter Souhleris:
You know what one of my favorite terms to say is? Just do it. I would say just jump right in and have an almost childlike attitude, and when I say childlike, I mean have fun and be fearless. And I always say, celebrate when you mess up because remember that means that you're getting closer to your success. Again, failure is the biggest fear that people have, and entrepreneurs just starting out are no different.

You have to be passionate about what you're about to get into as an entrepreneur. If you're not passionate about what you are doing and all you are doing is chasing the money, I would say stop, rethink and focus on why you're making this move. If you're just chasing the money, you're not going to be happy, and if you're not happy, you're not going be a successful entrepreneur. So remember, you will make mistakes. You will have failures, but these failures will help you to get to where you want to go. When these mistakes come about, when the failures come about, that's when I want you to celebrate because every mistake gets you closer to your goal.

I use the analogy sometimes of how in those old western movies you've got a guy getting close to being released from jail and he's, crossing off the days. Think of the mentality of that person as he's crossing out day seven, right? He's celebrating because he's seven days closer to getting out. That's the way I look at failures. Get them out of the way one at a time and you'll soon be closer to your success.

That's what entrepreneurs have to think about. It will put a smile on your face. It will change your complete mindset and you will get there a lot faster. More importantly, know that making mistakes is part of the formula and is part of becoming a successful entrepreneur. Be fearless. Have fun. Smile all the way there.

Dave Seymour:
I would add to that, too, and just in my own verbiage, show me somebody who's never failed and I'll show you somebody who's never tried. And that's the core—I mean, it's the core of what we do. You have to give it a go. What is the point in all of this if you don't go for it, if you don't give it a run or give it a shot? Passion is critical. Mediocrity doesn't breed success, so find out what that thing is that you're passionate about. It's the number one question that every entrepreneur has to ask.

Pete and I are fortunate in the sense that we have a number of different passions, and they're all aligned. We have passion in real estate. We have passion in giving back. We have passion in having fun. We have passion in our families, and we are able to take those passions and live in them and with them and for them every day, and as a direct result, the money comes.

And Pete's absolutely right. If you're just doing it for the cash, you're doing it for the wrong reasons. It's not about the money. It's about the service, and if you're of service and if you're an entrepreneur who can develop a widget or bring a service or do something that has an impact on another human being's life in a positive way, then learn how to monetize that. And what I would tell any entrepreneur out there is find out what you are exceptionally good at and do it as often as you possibly can, and learn how to monetize it. And if you do that, you're going to be successful. You're going to have great joy in your life.

Woody Woodward:

You two have accomplished a lot in your life, in your relationships and in your career. What's on the horizon? What's the next thing coming up that keeps you up at night that you're so excited to participate in?

Dave Seymour:

For me, I always love the hunt of the deal. I love hunting down the deal. I love working a deal, bringing it to the table, watching it come to fruition, getting Pete's input on the deal. I love the idea of expanding the philanthropic works that we've done.

Pete has a charity called the Christian Angel Smile Foundation. I'm excited to watch that expand and grow over the next couple of years, what we can do to put more time and energy and effort into that. I'm also excited about doing other TV shows. It's funny, after being a part of the TV business, I immediately became a student of the industry. If it's something that excites me and entices me, I become an avid student, so I'm excited to be able to bring some new genre to the screen. Hopefully bring some of our relationships that we've been able to work on in the past couple of years in the TV biz and leverage some of that out for some really good shows, some shows that can highlight the good in people and also give them all of the drama and the action that they're looking for as well.

I know we have got some unbelievable ideas in process that will be like nothing anyone has ever seen before.

Peter Souhleris:

I would say for me that the business of real estate, whether it's rehabbing or new development, what I think is really cool about it is that no two projects are the same. Every time you get into a brand new project, it's all bricks and mortar, sheetrock, flooring, tile and so forth. That's all there, but they're never the same. It's like every time I walk into one of these buildings, I get so excited. I get so passionate about going in and taking this ugly duckling and making it look beautiful and then creating spaces that people come into and appreciate. So, I don't know what it is. You never know what it is. Every day, like Dave said, a new deal comes out and we're scratching the surface, and we're looking at it. We are looking at doing some newer development opportunities and some larger projects.

The challenge we always have is they have to kind of fit in line with the TV show requirements, and that can be tough because we can't easily commit to certain projects while we're filming the show. We can part-time it, but our whole focus is on producing episodes right now with respect to real estate for our production company and for A&E. Dave nailed it on the head for me—my wife, my daughter and I started our nonprofit organization around six years ago called the Christian Angel Smile Foundation. The mission of this foundation was to basically feed people during the Thanksgiving and holiday season, provide toys and food and clothing for the less fortunate.

The inspiration was actually my daughter being born, and my wife and I just wanted to be able to give back to others for being blessed with our little miracle. That's what I call my kids Miracle 1 and Miracle 2... We both believe in raising our children to see that doing philanthropic work is natural. It's not wait until you're 16, wait until you go to college or wait until you make your first million. It's not. It's now, as soon as you open your eyes, you can have that will to want to give back, and I'm excited to see that grow to another level. As Dave said earlier, what is exciting about having a TV show is that it allows us to kind of put that out there a little bit more and gain more awareness and momentum for our charity.

We started off the first year feeding ten families, and we're up to thousands right now that excites me a lot. I love giving whether it's to my kids, to my wife or to my family. I love giving a gift 10,000 times more than receiving a gift. To be able to have a foundation that started a few years ago grow and watch that passion being passed on to my kids, too, that really ignites me.

Woody Woodward:
How do you define failure?

Peter Souhleris:
For me, the way I define failure is the first step to success, and if someone can just sit on that for a second and think about that, it changes their whole mindset. That's the way I look at it. I'm aware that it usually takes a series of failures to become successful, so, again, as I said earlier, when I fail, I'm excited that I'm getting that much closer. That mindset has to be in place. It makes for a much better journey. If people can get their head wrapped around that, the rest of it is easy. They should have a smile on their face knowing that failure is the first step to success.

Dave Seymour:
It's funny Peter, listening to you I'm going to write a book called the seven steps to failing the right way, how to fail seven times safely. You going to fail over and over again, but do it safely. So, how do you do that safely? You do it through mentorship, by following somebody who can help you and guide you and show you the way through.

Woody Woodward:
What's the difference between giving up and failing at something?

Peter Souhleris:
I love that question, man. For me, it's simple;

Giving up means that all your efforts went to waste, and that's seriously powerful. If I did everything I needed to do, everything, and I just said, "I give up," then everything I did from the moment I started to the moment I gave up was worthless. Failing, as I said, is the beginning to accomplishing what I started out to do in the first place. I think that's the best way for me to summarize it.

Woody Woodward:

How do you channel your fear into productivity?

Dave Seymour:

For me, every time I reach a moment of fear—it's interesting. I've used this analogy many times. The human body goes through fight or flight, and it's a natural response. It goes all the way back to the caveman days when we were being chased by dinosaurs. The physical things that your body goes through in both fight and flight are exactly the same, exactly the same, so why am I bringing this up when it comes to channeling fear for productivity?

Because when I have butterflies in my stomach, when my heart rate is up, when my peripheral circulation is diminished because all the blood is moving to my lungs, my heart, my kidneys, my liver, I know that I'm on the verge of something, all right. And nine times out of ten, I'm on the verge of something really good, because the dinosaurs aren't here anymore. The dinosaurs are gone, so I don't have to worry about getting eaten by a dinosaur, so my body is reacting exactly the same way. So, when I get that feeling and that sensation in me, I know that when I take that next step incredible things will happen. It's as simple as that. It really is that simple.

Every time somebody said, "You can't," I believed I could. Every time somebody said I won't or I wouldn't, I believed I already had, and as a direct result of that, I'm sitting here today on vacation in the sunshine doing this interview for a book with my buddy, Pete, talking to a guy like Woody, and life is good. So, that's what I do with fear. I laugh at it, I acknowledge it, and then I move forward and through it.

Peter Souhleris:

I guess I look at fear as fuel and energy, and I take that energy and I create something good out of it, and I know that I must be productive. I know that if I don't have a productive day that it falls into the next day. I am very well aware of what fear can and cannot do, and if I let it freeze me up, then, in essence, I become unproductive. When fear is in charge, it feels like you're going backwards. I ask myself, Can I make it? Can I make it? Can I make it? I know what's going happen if I stop fighting. I'm going to roll all the way backwards and fall, and that's not an option. So, I use that fear as energy and as combustion fuel, whatever you want to call it, and I just keep on pushing because "no" is not an option.

I think of worst-case scenario, and that is the fear. The fear is worst-case scenario, fear kicks in, and then it's danger. It's problems. It's chaos. That motivates me to push one more step, to do one more mile, one more foot, one more inch, whatever I need to do to be productive.

Dave Seymour:
I'll tell you what else you've done, Peter, as a direct result of those fears. You create systems to eliminate them, and that's something I've always admired in you.

Peter Souhleris:
Yeah, I'm a systems guy, because when I have that fear and I play it, I say to David, "I've played this video game before," so I know how to win

Dave Seymour:
You create a system.

Peter Souhleris:
When I've got a system. I walk into any situation a winner.

Woody Woodward:
Beautiful. Last question, what do you want your legacy to be?

Dave Seymour:
At the end of the day for me, it's simple, "He was a good guy. He was a good guy. He did what he said he was going to do. He took care of his family, and he tried to be of service." And if I leave that simple thing

as a legacy, then I'm happy with that. I hope my sons understand that I wasn't superman but that maybe I had some super qualities.

I just want to be known as a decent guy who did the next right thing, who never went out to hurt anybody and just showed up to his best and if you do that in life then it's all good. It's all good.

Peter Souhleris:

For me it would be to be remembered as a great father, a great husband, a caring, loving and thankful person, a great friend, a man of his word, a man that played hard and left it all on the field.

In its simplistic definition, "A good man," a man that was innovative, creative, a guy that loved to laugh but furthermore, loved to make people laugh even more, a man known as a good Christian, a guy that adored his family and did anything and everything for them with a smile.

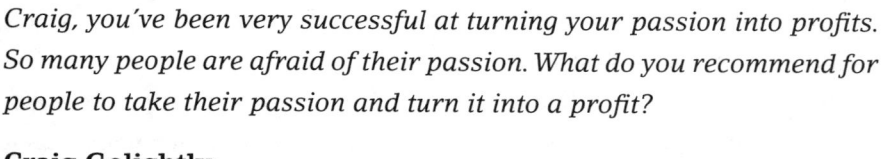

Craig Golightly

Craig Golightly is a software consultant, presenter, and trainer. He has provided software solutions in various industries for over 10 years and has a knack for identifying problems and finding solutions. He is also a dynamic presenter and loves to connect with people and teach them new things. Craig has a Master's degree in computer science and continues to stay on the cutting edge with software technology as well as communication skills and how people work. He also enjoys mountain biking, percussion, and woodworking. Most of all Craig loves to experience life with his wife and four children.

Contact info: go@craigdgolightly.com

Woody Woodward:

Craig, you've been very successful at turning your passion into profits. So many people are afraid of their passion. What do you recommend for people to take their passion and turn it into a profit?

Craig Golightly:

For starters, get uncomfortable! I'm against people staying where they're at, staying where it's comfortable. Fear often comes from the unknown and sometimes, people are actually afraid to succeed so they just stay where they're at and keep doing what they've always done, even though they are capable of more.

For people who are ready to move up to the next level, I recommend four steps. First, decide what you want. Second, find a mentor. Third, take action. Fourth, involve others.

Woody Woodward:

What do you mean by 'decide what you want'? So many times people can't decide what they want. How do you figure out what you want to do?

Craig Golightly:

I learned early on to make a decision. When I was about six years old, my parents were asking me something and I gave the standard answer, "I don't know," or its close cousin, "I don't care." So my dad sat me down and said, "Craig, just decide something. Most of the time, you will get exactly what you ask for because no one else cares. No one else wants to decide." Indecision is one of the most costly mistakes a person can make. When people don't decide, they're sending the message that any direction is OK because they don't know where they are going.

I vigorously oppose indecision in all areas of my life. That includes putting off a decision. We could save a lot of time by using the words "yes" and "no." Instead, people are too worried about hurting someone's feelings by saying no, or they are altogether non-committal with phrases like, "Maybe I'll be there, if you call and remind me," or "I'll let you know," when in reality the person has no intention of engaging their brain in the decision-making process. They're merely avoiding the decision. Make a decision and commit to it! Don't let indecision rob you of opportunity.

When I'm deciding what to do next, I ask myself what gets me excited? What am I interested in? What makes me feel more energized after doing it? Making a decision allows you to focus your efforts effectively and get on with making it happen.

Woody Woodward:

Well, number two you mentioned about finding a mentor. How did finding a mentor help you with aspects of your life?

Craig Golightly:

This is an interesting one that took me a while to figure out. There are two ingredients here. The first is hard work. Once you've made your decision, you have to work hard and bump your head a little. You need to fall on your face. Those experiences will help you be more open to suggestions from your mentor. You can only get so far by working hard and then you have to work smart. Now, I'm not saying you can leave out hard work. Some people feel they are entitled to something just because they are breathing and have a pulse. You have to add value by doing some form of work. This epidemic of entitlement and laziness is killing innovation. Nothing amazing happens by chance, and nothing new happens by merely showing up. Throughout history, great accomplishments and breakthroughs were preceded by hard work and repetition. Thomas Edison made over 1,000 light bulbs before finding one that worked.

The second ingredient is finding a mentor. Most of the time, there are people who have already done what you're trying to do, so save yourself some time and find a mentor. When I was in high school, I enjoyed percussion. In my junior year, I entered a state solo contest and didn't even place. I fell on my face. That woke me up to the fact that I needed to find a mentor. I found a great, experienced percussion instructor, Pat Flaherty, and he gave me the tools to actually get where I wanted to be. In my senior year, I won the state solo in not just one, but two different categories.

That same lesson applies in business and in life. As you decide what you want to do, even though you're excited about it, and you're passionate about it, you don't always have all of the answers. If you're OK with learning the hard way and you like to fall on your face, go ahead and do it by yourself. However, if you want to save some time and get up to the next level more effectively, find a mentor.

Woody Woodward:

After you've gone to that next level, what do you do?

Craig Golightly:

That's where step three comes in: take action. You can meet with your mentor, talk about things and feel good about it, but at this point, it's just an intellectual exercise. Meeting and talking is not a magic wand—you have to actually do it. Complete the assignments, practice the skills, and put in the work. You don't just meet with your mentor and then things fall into your lap. You have to take what you've learned and go apply it.

After you've met with your mentor, you've learned how to work smart at a new level, but you still need to work hard. The difference is subtle—are you working hard using knowledge that is experimental, or are you working hard using knowledge that is effective? The first will leave you banging your head against the wall; the second will help you climb over the wall and up to a higher level. Both require effort. Some people meet with their mentor and things don't work out because they never actually did anything to apply their knowledge. Knowledge found but never applied is quickly lost. If all you do is listen and learn, but you never take action, you're going to stay in the same place.

If you feel like you're working too hard on something, we're talking the banging-your-head variety, there's usually a better way to do it. You might figure out a better way through trial and error, or you can find a mentor and learn from their experience. Let's say you had an 8-hour task and you learned a way to do it in 6. So you kick back and do nothing with the extra 2 hours. Congratulations! You are average and will stay on the same level. Average people take the time savings and just leave their mind on auto-pilot. They haven't decided what else they want to do. If you want to move up to the next level, take what you've learned, work smart, then use the time you've gained to learn more and go even further. Now that doesn't mean you live at work or only do one thing all of the time. I believe in a balanced life and will often use savings in one area of my life to enhance another.

People also hold back because they're afraid to do "too good" of a job. Some say that the reward for good work is even more work, so people will sandbag and operate at their lowest allowable capacity. Holding back is harmful. The problem is that half-hearted attitude spills over into other areas of your life. If you only give 50% in one area of your life, that prevents you from giving 100% in another. You are the same person and your attitude is, well, yours. Doing just enough to slide by and "fly under the radar," so to speak, is going to shortchange your overall happiness.

Take action and don't hold back! If you don't, then you've wasted your time in finding a mentor. You've let your passion and energy for what you decided to do die off. You'll soon forget anything new that you learned, and you will be stuck on the same level.

Woody Woodward:
That reminds me a lot of the film industry. They can spend tens of millions, hundreds of millions of dollars getting ready to do a movie. They get the actors on board. They can get the stage built. They can do all those things, but until that director says, "Action," nothing happens. It's a colossal waste of money, time, and resources if people don't take action. After someone has taken action, step four you mentioned about involving others. How do you get other people to believe in your dream?

Craig Golightly:
One of the key ingredients here is passion. Are you excited about what you're doing? Does it keep you up at night? Do you really feel like you can dig in and learn what needs to be learned and do what needs to be done? You have your idea, you've got a mentor, you're working on stuff, but you can only get so far by yourself. There comes a point when you have to involve others. A key I've found with involving others is having the right communication skills. Whatever industry you're in, you have to be able to communicate with others effectively. You have to help them come onboard to what you're doing. Show them how it will help

their life get better, and how it will be exciting for them.

I'll give another falling-on-my-face example of involving others. I was the drum line leader at my high school. I was also very, very committed to what my percussion mentor was teaching me so I would practice 3-4 hours a day. One lesson that I didn't learn until later in life was that everybody on your team doesn't have to have the same level of passion and commitment and drive that you do. I would get after people because they weren't practicing as much as I was, but guess what? They were excited at their level and they could still make a contribution to the team. It was my job as the leader to see what level they were at then find ways to motivate them and help them to get up to the next level. I had to be on higher ground to help them move up. I also couldn't go out and do a show by myself; it took everyone working together as a team.

People who complain about or blame their failures on their team need to look in the mirror. Your poor teaching and training skills are the real problem. Stop using other people as an excuse. Everyone doesn't have to be at exactly the same level. They can all make a valuable contribution to the overall cause and it's your job as a leader to find out what drives them, what gets them excited, and what part of the project they could best contribute to. Leave the excuses about other people behind. Can you assemble a team and create something? Can you help your team members become better people in the process? Master that skill and people will come to you in droves to help you create your dream.

Woody Woodward:
What are you passionate about now? I know that you've built many teams, you've worked with IBM, you've been a software consultant for years making a huge impact everywhere you go, but we all have those things that we're passionate about that keep us up at night. What's keeping you up at night right now?

Craig Golightly:
The thing that brings me the most satisfaction is when I help people

save time, increase revenue, improve consistency, and add intelligence to their organization. The best is when I help them solve a problem they thought was impossible. Sometimes, the solution involved creating new software or improving existing software. Other times, it was a people or process problem solved through training and mentoring.

Technology can be a cumbersome burden or a distinct advantage. Too many people are still following an inefficient, manual process and the old software they have perpetuates the problem. Some people have tried to upgrade or replace their software only to run into roadblocks and failures that cost time and money. That bad experience has frozen them with fear in the headlights of indecision and they're stuck at the same level. They are missing out on innovations in technology.

Others are stuck due to people issues. Their processes and policies are outdated. They are not communicating effectively so they become their own biggest problem. You can have the best resources and technology, but if you lack Emotional Intelligence, you will continually hit walls in your organization and drive people away from you.

So there are two areas that keep me up at night right now. On the communication front, I've been learning about body language and how much of a difference it can make. I've always heard that actions speak louder than words, but I didn't realize how much our subconscious picks up on and reacts to those actions. You can't hide it! Less than 10% of what we communicate is actually our words. I have been amazed at the results I've achieved just by changing my body language.

The other area is turning sunk costs of compliance into valuable intelligence. Many organizations are required to record phone calls and meetings or collect comments from clients and customers. This data usually sits in storage doing nothing. I've been working with some text and speech analytics software lately that has really been a game changer and provides new insights of customer patterns, preferences, and how an organization can improve its service. We're talking the ability to process trillions of documents, or take 100 hours of audio and transcribe it in 1 hour!

Woody Woodward:

This type of technology sounds amazing, but for the layperson such as myself or an entrepreneur, how could they use this technology to increase their revenue or to save time?

Craig Golightly:

Yeah, don't let the fancy names scare you away. It really boils down to finding hidden value in the conversations and interactions you are already having with customers by using some amazing software tools. Take previously idle data and turn it into valuable intelligence. It can also automate some of your manual processes such as transcription of audio and reading and classifying customer comments or other text documents. Automate the repetitive, error-prone tasks so you can focus on what you're really passionate about and what value your organization really adds, not in all of the repetitive details. Sometimes, you can use software to completely replace a process; other times, it will do 80% of the work, then you come in and correct the other 20%. The key is knowing what makes sense for a machine to do, and what makes sense to leave in human hands.

Woody Woodward:

One thing I like that you said is using technology to free up our time to follow our passion. Yet sometimes, we're afraid to follow our passion. What experience have you had with people who are too afraid to follow their passion?

Craig Golightly:

You're just fishing for another falling-on-my-face story, aren't you? Well, I once worked at a company that required prior approval of any outside activities to make sure there wasn't a conflict of interest. So there I was with 5 or 6 other software developers and we had these great ideas but we were too afraid to ask for permission because they might say no and then we'd be on the radar. We let this cycle of fear hold us back for over 2 years. Finally at lunch one day, 2 other guys and I decided we would go for it. Well, they gave approval and we were able to have a great experience bringing that idea to life.

I don't believe it when people say, "That's just the way it is; I can't change anything." The fact is you're never stuck anywhere; you just need to turn on your brain and find new options. Fear can prevent someone from leaving a job they don't really like. Fear can keep people from speaking up when they see something that could be done better. "They won't listen to me," or "I never get time to do this or that," are another two excuses I just don't buy. If I find a problem and I have the solution for it, I do it. It's not always on the schedule. Sometimes, I have to risk my own time to do it, but most opportunities have opened up because I found something that was valuable to the organization. I took action and did it. Too much time and energy is wasted by whining about the problem instead of doing something about it.

If you wait to be asked, if you're just coming in and putting in your time, then you're going to continue on the same level with the same results. If you want to go up to the next level and have bigger results, then you have to take the initiative. You have to show that you can be innovative and do things that people aren't asking for. You may be the only one who sees the problem and the solution. Stop flying under the radar! Stand up and get noticed.

The other key is to talk to other people. Someone else may see the same problem and each of you hold a different part of the solution. As you come together and start working, you will have the whole solution. Don't be afraid to try. Don't be afraid to ask. Don't be afraid to go ahead and do it. Risk your time. You can never receive a bigger reward without putting some effort into it. It just doesn't magically appear. It takes time, effort, innovation, and results; the reward comes after.

Woody Woodward:
On your road to success, you've had many mentors. I know a lot of times people refer to books that have been great mentors. What books have

you read that have stood out, that gave you those "Aha" moments that kind of set you on the right path?

Craig Golightly:

The Jackrabbit Factor by Leslie Householder really changed my perspective of things. I also had a lot of "Aha" moments reading Dale Carnegie's *How to Win Friends and Influence People. Linchpin* by Seth Godin is another good one. *Perfect Phrases for Negotiating Salary and Job Offers* by Matthew and Nanette DeLuca is a great reference as well. I also learn a lot from history since it repeats itself so often.

You don't need to be online 24x7. Unplug and take some quiet time to ponder each day and reflect on things bigger than yourself. I've found that reading Scripture opens my mind as I work through problems.

Woody Woodward:

Your second step you talked about finding a mentor. Where would you recommend someone go to find a good mentor?

Craig Golightly:

Many mentors hold events and seminars, so start there. You can get a feel for what they are all about and what they have to offer. There's nothing like a live event or conversation to see the real person. Sometimes, fancy websites can be deceiving. Some also have books, CDs, or other programs, so that's another good way to check them out. Look at their results and the results of the people they are mentoring to decide if what they have is effective. You can learn from their successes and failures. There is also a lot of bad advice out there, ways to get success by taking shortcuts or being dishonest or doing activities that aren't going to bring a lasting satisfaction that you've succeeded so be careful where you look.

Some mentors that have made a big difference for me lately include Kirk Duncan, Woody Woodward, Garrett Gunderson, and Dave Ramsey. Mentoring is just this whole new world that can help you move up to the next level and once you start, you'll find many new connections.

Woody Woodward:
What inspires you right now?

Craig Golightly:
My family. I have a beautiful, supportive wife. She is very focused, positive and she really inspires me by the way she pursues her goals with such discipline and energy. She is musically talented, a great teacher, and very witty. That comes in handy with our four children who range in age from 10 to 4. One of my favorite parts of the day is when I walk in the door and they yell, "Daddy" and run across the room to give me a big hug. You know, I follow the things that I enjoy doing for work and it all comes back to the fact that I want to provide a good experience for my family. I want to have flexibility and time to be with them and do things that we enjoy together.

Earlier this year, we took a vacation to the beach and I went surfing for the first time in my life. It was something I decided I wanted to do so we made it happen and it was just fun to spend that time together and have an experience as a family. I didn't know how to surf so I found a mentor. Where are you going to find a surfing mentor? Well, I looked up places along the beach that we were going to go to, scheduled a lesson, and I was able to get up.

Now I could have just rented the gear and tried to do it myself. I could have even watched videos and read books, but nothing can replace the experience of having another person there with you who knows what they're doing, who can coach you and give you that real-time feedback of "Do this, watch out for that." It was well worth my investment of hiring a surf instructor because I was able to go and safely enjoy something I had wanted to do and I achieved the desired result.

Woody Woodward:
You mentioned this, and I don't think you realized it, but you talked about how you invested in a mentor. Mentors aren't free and they're not cheap a lot of times. Now there are some great men and women out there who will donate time and mentor you a little bit here and there,

but you do need to double down sometimes and put some real financial investment in finding a mentor. Has that been the experience for you?

Craig Golightly:

Absolutely. It's a mental filter. Are you willing to invest in yourself? People will spend a lot of money on a car, which goes down in value, but they are unwilling to pay at that same level for a mentor, which can raise their own personal value. I paid thousands of dollars to go to college, then thousands more to get a graduate degree. Who made the rule that you have to stop spending money on education as soon as you graduate? Or that college is the only source of education? It's a myth!

A good mentor has already walked where you want to go and they can help you avoid their mistakes and leverage their successes. Their experience is the result of all of their hard work, investment, and loss, sometimes millions of dollars. To give it away for free sends the message that their experience has no value.

I've found that when I make a sacrifice to hire a mentor, it raises my level of commitment. My mentor is also committed to me and that exchange allows your mentor to focus on you. It also causes me to really absorb what they are saying and take action. If there was no exchange for the knowledge, a person might not listen, or they might take it, write it down, and think, "Oh that was nice." But it never really sinks in and they never do anything with it.

Woody Woodward:

What do you want your legacy to be?

Craig Golightly:

First off, I want my family to know that I love them and I want to be someone who passed my knowledge and experience on to them. I want everyone I come in contact with to be a better person because they knew me, because I was able to do something to help or lift them. I also want to be known as someone who could solve the problem and who was also fun to work with. Too often, we pretend that we're all impersonal business people, but we're not. We are all real people, with talents, abilities, dreams, and problems. As we make that human connection, we achieve more than was ever possible on our own.

I want to be known as someone who stood against fear of success, indecision, laziness, entitlement, personal isolationism, inaction, idleness, holding back, settling, excuses, whining, bad software, inefficiency, poor communication and being stuck. Finally, I want to be known as someone who never stopped learning and who never gave up.

Victoria Mason Acree

Victoria Mason Acree B.A., CPC, majored in Business from Concordia University. She is a Certified Business & Life Coach and does so by the Enlightened Path. She is the owner of three businesses, the latest of which is 'Voice of Victoria' which started out a series and has further developed. As a business woman Victoria enjoys having several acknowledgments from her peers and top associations such as the Nation Association of Professional Women, and has been included in *The Cambridge Who's Who*.

Victoria is a native of Scotland and has traveled extensively over the world; she has lived in three continents and currently resides on the edge of the Rockie Mountains in the USA.

Victoria@VoiceofVictoria.com • www.VoiceofVictoria.com
www.Blog.VoiceofVictoria.com

Woody Woodward:
Victoria, your story is very inspiring. You've gone from tragedy to triumph. Share with our audience how you've gone from tragedy to triumph and what other people can do to turn their lives around.

Victoria Acree:

Yes, Woody. There was a time when I thought I had a bad start in life; convinced a good life would never work out for me. Those thoughts came from a childhood of domestic violence, with physical, psychological, and sexual abuse which resulted in my father being sentenced to prison thirty years later. My mother took me out of school at age 15 to work in a factory; she wanted more money. What it took me to earn in a week, she drank in a weekend; I never saw a penny of my earnings. With that kind of childhood, I grew up with low self-esteem. I never felt worthy of quality relationships, so I settled. Never get a good job, that I would never have a high school diploma let alone a university degree. The death of my 10 year-old daughter only intensified my misery. The good things in life would never be for me but for other people; for people with a healthy start in life. How wrong I was, Woody!

I love the words of Socrates who is famous for arguing that we must Know Thyself to be wise, that the unexamined life is not worth living.

It all boils down to "Know Thy Self." Examine your life! These words are also inscribed on the Temple of Apollo, and spoken of by William Shakespeare. We all have been conditioned, or rather programmed, since birth that we are a body and mind. One of the big highlights of parents-to-be is the choosing of the name for their baby. At the birth, we are focused on counting to make sure that there are 10 fingers and 10 toes. During the formative years, the focus is on physical and psychological development, and hitting those milestones. Yes, we are a body and mind, but something essential is often overlooked and that is the source or spirit essence that we truly are!

Woody, we are the most magnificent trilogy in existence! It is the omission of source or spiritual awareness, that higher state of consciousness, that gives rise to struggling throughout life. We have bought into that we are our name and that we have to be worthy of greatness. Hello people, you are that greatness! You do not have to be found worthy of that which you truly are! We are that divine essence. It was never lost. It does not need to be found, but uncovered from the false identity of the body-mind. When we stop looking outside of ourselves, and look within, we will experience Self. When we live from Self, that higher state of consciousness, we will experience the miraculous magic of life.

The great turnaround point starts with Forgiveness and Gratitude. I have long since forgiven my parents for their blind choices; they were both running on false programs. Forgiveness is not about letting the other person off the hook; it is releasing ourselves from the chains that bind us. Express gratitude for all that we have and are; we are limitless beings and I am grateful to know this and have it be my experience. Without Forgiveness and Gratitude we will continue to be stuck in an unhappy and unfulfilled life. Or worse still, co-dependence, being dependent on others for our happiness.

Over several years now, I have gotten into the study of Epigenetics; this has assisted me tremendously. We are not a 'read-only' format; we are reprogrammable, we can rewrite the programs. I did, and it is our personal responsibility to do so. Let's do it!

Woody Woodward:
So how does someone learn to know thy self?

Victoria Acree:
In 2001, due to personal agony, tragedy and suffering, I had what is described as a Near-Death Experience. "I" saw the body of Victoria in her bed and her mind was there also. I took a 'trip' that took me home, to the source which we all are, and back again. In coming back, I know the reality of this life is like a game and everyone can be the winner! It was due to this experience that I Know that I AM something other than what is seen in the mirror. For me, it was an instantaneous experience.

To know thy self is much like the process of Michelangelo when he chipped away at a large block of marble; David was inside.

It is by going beyond the exterior that the inner Self in witnessed. When we live our lives from the inside out, life just flows.

Woody Woodward:
I like when you talk about life as a game. When we know the rules of the game we can play a game better. So what are the rules of this life that we need to know so we can play a better game?

Victoria Acree:

I like to use the game Monopoly as an analogy, Woody. 'Mono' we are all the same Oneness; some call this Oneness god, source, the divine, etc. The label used to describe source is of no great importance. It is neither an "it" nor an entity, which would put a frame around Oneness which cannot be done. Oneness is all there is, there is no place Oneness is not! Playing the game, there are rules to winning. Knowingness of the Oneness is the #1rule. On experiencing Oneness, there can be no anger, competition, no sense of loss, no greed or violence. In this state of Knowingness, a higher consciousness, life can be looked down on much like a board game. The dice is thrown and we move around the board, this is life. In doing so, we are allowed to make choices. When a player has played their game to the best of the abilities, they may be 'out'! We do not get devastated when we are 'out' of a game! This can be like the experience we call death, the body maybe 'out' but who and what we really are lives on.

Rule #2, we are here to create, and learn by the action of creation.

It could also be described as having a big Lego Land in which to experience life, there are endless block of different shapes and color, as in life we are unlimited beings. It is when we buy into the false sense of 'me' as an individual, separate from the one source, that we live life backwards. The greatest and only true wealth is within.

There are individuals that get their sense of self-worth from their money and other possessions, or who they know. They have allowed themselves to be fooled by the ego-mind. You can never be your money or possessions; these are merely toys of the game. Nice toys, indeed, but not true wealth; the joy of true wealth makes all those toys very trivial. Knowing how to play the game will give wealth beyond measure with the least effort.

Woody, I could talk to you all day on this subject on Knowingness, but our conversation does not allow for full expression, and accessing Knowingness.

Woody Woodward:

Having gone through so much tragedy in your life, how do you coach someone else to have hope when they feel all is lost?

Victoria Acree:

I first acknowledge their pain, I express genuine empathy. There is much I can personally relate to thanks to my own past experiences; and I do mean thanks! When a client feels lost, it is because they have become so by their false identification with their limited belief that the body and mind is all they are; they are still running on a mistaken program; their negative thoughts hold them prisoner. It is a very painful state to be in.

Most importantly is the question "are you willing to take on and be responsible for the creation of your own life experience?" Hopefully, the answer is yes.

I offer a prescription to lift people out of the mud.

One: Write out three full sentences for things that you are grateful for. Do this 3 times a day for 30 days.

Two: Do 3 acts of kindness three times a day for 30 days.

This is a drug-free prescription for depression and it works! The pharmaceutical industry cannot match this. It will lift a depressed person up to a point that they are ready, willing and eager to do more self work to bring about wholeness.

I invite my client to be in stillness. This is not always easy to experience; there is so much chatter going on in our heads. With practice of meditation, the mind will become quiet. In the stillness, there is space to experience the oneness that we are, in this state worry and fears will dissolve. It is in the space that the opportunity to rethink can take place, but it is inspired thought that comes through.

Before we can determine in which direction to go, we first have to know where we are. At this point, we may become aware of all the wrong programs we have installed in ourselves over a lifetime. We don't have to replay them again, just identify them, and let them go.

Letting go is also a process.

Gratitude for what is already at hand and the art of forgiveness is a discussion. Encouragement and support in the wisdom of letting go of blaming and accusing. All these topics are covered.

Developing knowing awareness doesn't happen overnight, Woody. For some, it's a process. Again, while it's good to maybe understand this conceptually, what I share is not a concept. But understanding conceptually is not a bad place to start. By going deeper inside the Self, we will find the divinity that we are all Oneness. Once a person realizes that—and when I say realize, I mean the realization of that true reality—there is only one and we're all that! This realization uncovers our ability to receive our dreams.

Woody Woodward:
When you look back on your life, what is the greatest risk you have ever taken and was it worth it?

Victoria Acree:
It was in 2006 and I was an employee. I enjoyed my work and the pay was OK for what I was doing and carried a good benefits package. However, my employer changed my shift to that which I was not hired. This change in shift meant that I could not see or spend time with my daughter. Being a single mother at the time, this situation had turned into a personal dilemma. Pointing out to my employer that I was hired for my original shift fell on deaf ears. After a couple of weeks of suffering being an absentee mum, I realized that I had to make a change as my employer refused to.

I sat there in my cubicle and prayed for wisdom to bring a resolution to the predicament that I found myself in. Quite spontaneously, and without much thought, I found myself typing a one sentence notice of termination to my employer stating that I was resigning immediately and without notice. I printed out the notice and collected my few personal belongings together. On heading to the door, I handed my notice to my boss and then left the building. As I had done so, it was as if a higher energy was carrying me across the parking lot. The first thing I noticed was the birds singing in the trees and how alive they were. I got into my car and rolled down the window, the air felt wonderful. I turned the volume of the car radio up high and drove home to my child whom I had not seen in several days.

On the drive home, I was conscious of the fact that in firing my employer, I would have no paycheck or benefits the next month. Still, all felt well and I was in a profound state of peace. All that mattered at that time was that I could be home for my child; motherhood for me takes precedence over a selfish employer. I was not company property, nor was my home life. I was not for sale and I can't be bought.

Time spent at home was wonderful; I felt more myself. I did spend time pondering on what I would do next. It was while driving on the interstate that I turned on the radio and an advertisement came on from Concordia University, they were announcing a new program for adult student attending only one night per week. Before I knew it, I steered into the exit lane and made a U turn and headed straight for their campus. On meeting with an advisor, she said to bring in my college transcript from the local community college that I attended some years previously. I handed in my transcript and filled in all the application forms. Within ten days, I got the letter saying 'accepted'.

I had by this time secured a job locally, it didn't pay a lot, but it was an income with benefits and I was given a work schedule that would accommodate my schooling and family life.

I was undecided about my major, and just went with 'Business' as it seemed like a broad subject. My first semester, I was on the Dean's List and I graduated at an honors level. Years later, my degree in business with its associated knowledge has served me well in my own business endeavors, including starting and operate businesses, and as a business consultant.

I have long since acquired the wisdom of letting go of that which no longer serves me. Yes, it was a risk to walk away, and yes, it was worth it.

Woody Woodward:

Do you feel if you would have stayed at that job you never would have graduated from that college and got a business degree?

Victoria Acree:

For sure! My having a university degree in business was not my employer's goal, it was mine. Today, in retrospect, I recognized the role in which that employer played in my life path. Had that regrettable situation not occurred, had I not been given a cause to walk away, I would probably be still sitting in that cubicle working on my employer's goals instead of my own. There are others who are currently in such situations. Because they do not recognize the genius within themselves, they put their goals and dreams on the back burner. My own situation ultimately worked in my favor or I would not be where I am today.

Woody Woodward:

I know a lot of people who are reading this chapter who might be in the same situation and be afraid and scared to death to follow their dream and quit their job. And we're not saying quit your job, but what we're saying is look at what it is going to take for your dreams to come true. Like Victoria, she took the risk that was necessary for her. You need to look at what necessary risks you need to take.

So Victoria, now that you are a leader in your community and in your business, how would you define leadership? What is a leader to you?

Victoria Acree:

Speaking as a professional Business Consultant, Life Coach and Mentor, the characteristics of a good leader apply to all endeavors. The characteristics of a good leader are many. They include integrity, honesty, self-awareness, intelligence, as well as emotional intelligence, knowledge of their business and the needs of their clients, self-confidence, desire and motivation, drive, creativity, diversity, self-monitoring, and a sense of humor. While the list is lengthy, it can be divided into two, personal characteristics and professional characteristics.

The most important characteristics are the personal ones. Good leadership starts with the personality of the leader. While the leader may have skills and knowledge of the project at hand, it would be an unfruitful endeavor if there were a lack of personal integrity. Personal integrity and the honesty in dealing with others are what provide a basis of trust. Followers or subordinates need to know that they can trust the one who leads them. The self-awareness of the leader is important. A good leader knows his/her strengths and weaknesses. She/he also knows if he/she is task or relationship oriented.

Emotional intelligence is another important factor worth mentioning. The leader of teams in the workplace requires their ability to control personal feelings and moods. Successful interpersonal communication can be both a trait and a developed skill. The need for empathy and understanding of the feelings of clients and team members are a component in the cohesiveness of a successful team or a group, or individual for that matter.

To instill motivation and drive in a team or client, the leader must lead by example in these areas. Motivating team members, especially when the going gets tough, with words of encouragement can ease the stress of many situations.

Intelligence is another factor that attributes to good leadership. Subordinates often look to their leader for knowledge and support when in doubt.

Creativity can keep the work exciting. A good leader will be open to creative ideas from their team, allowing for input and new ways of being effective.

Embracing diversity is another attribute that is part of the good leader's toolbox. The team or clientele will most likely be made up of individuals from different lifestyles and cultures. A particular approach in dealing with one team member or client may not work for others. Being mindful of the differences and similarities among all parties can give positive contributions to the project which can result in a receipt for success.

Of course, knowledge of the job would be a good contribution. Knowing the functions of each component of the job to reach the desired outcome will give understanding to the leader in decision-making and contribute to the strategies and any paradigm shift that may be needed to reach the goal and mission of the organization.

The Big Five personality dimensions of conscientiousness, extroversion/introversion, open to experience, emotional stability, and agreeableness are the personal qualities that are found in a good leader.

Woody Woodward:

You've been a leader, and you still have times when life seems difficult and challenging. What do you do to keep yourself up when times get tough?

Victoria Acree:

This brings to mind my favorite quote by Albert Einstein: "You cannot solve a problem from the same level of consciousness that created it."

The art of dwelling inside 'the eye of the hurricane' is something that I have cultivated over time. Within the eye of a hurricane, there is a calm and peacefulness. It never ceases to amaze me that once again Mother Nature shows the way. We have all seen the weather reports that show the size of an approaching storm and the likelihood of damage and destruction. The eye of the hurricane is only mentioned as a reference point and as the center, rarely is the environment of the eye mention.

Should there be an occasion in which I sense any frustration, I will recognize it immediately as a feeling of discomfort and that is indicative that I have wondered too far from my core center, of the truth of who a really am. I had stepped into the chaos of life and allowed the negative energy which is to be found there to attach to me, therein lays the pathway to tough and challenging moments.

Having experienced hurricanes in my life some years ago, I empathize with those who still experience that destructive damage that is the result of stress and anxiety; feeling battered by personal and professional tough challenges are wrenching. These are exactly the stressors in life that lead to ill health.

My cure: I go for the eye of the hurricane and know that in doing so I will have a safe harbor and the opportunity to refocus. I do this by allowing myself to become still and just breathe for about twenty minutes; the breath of life is a cure for many ailments. In that stillness my noisy mind will become still eventually. This, for me, is getting back to the core of Self, and it is in this state, a higher consciousness state, that inspired thought comes through. So often, ideas will come to me that will be the answer to a situation that was once frustrating, where I couldn't previously see a clear way. It is as if a way is opened up. It could also come via a phone call or unexpectedly meeting someone who will provide the missing piece I was looking for. This is like the eye of the hurricane for me; while all else is chaotic around me, I can be still and have the most ideal answers pop into my mind.

Obviously, Albert Einstein had a Knowingness of the different levels of consciousness that can be used to shape our lives to meet our desires. I have his quote posted in several places in my home and on the dash of my car.

Life is all about creating, and the creations will provide lessons to be learned by being in the process of the required action. Don't be too troubled if you hit a bump in the road; everything is a learning experience. With a different mindset and mental attitude to the approach of life's challenging and tough situations, know that there is a way out. The way out is to focus within.

Woody Woodward:
As you've had a lot of success in your coaching business and in your personal business, how do you define success?

Victoria Acree:
Yes Woody, I have been awarded life-time membership in the National

Association of Professional Women, the NAPW, and was included in *The Cambridge Who's Who*.

Success means different things to different people. Success for me is a process, and it starts each day by waking up to another opportunity to evolve to the next best level of myself and my chosen accomplishments. I am a natural goal setter and my goals are stated in my own hand writing, and I carry a goals notebook with me everywhere I go. I still use a vision board and have fun filling it up and spend ten minutes each morning studying it; I do enjoy carrying these pictures as mental images throughout the day. I dress the part and walk my talk. I'm a people person and love to mingle with others and have the confidence to extend my hand and introduce myself; shyness is not an option.

I am sincerely comfortable being more interested than interesting. I am interested in hearing the news of others, and sharing my own news follows naturally. Success truly is a journey and some stop off point on the journey can appear to be unwelcoming, I've learned that these are just learning point along the way and that is often the best way to learn, by being in action and doing. There are many components to my success journey, namely the other people that I meet and connect with along the way, visiting with them in beautiful places and experiencing all the diversity that comes with it.

The main contributor to my success is my ability, which took time to cultivate, is to accept any given situation AS-IS. By being in an attitude of acceptance, I can look at the given situation in the present moment and either it is my preference or it is not my preference, in which case I call it my present project, never a problem, I no longer use the word problem. Projects can be fun if approach with a positive mental attitude. It has often been my experience on reworking a project that a more successful option has resulted than was first anticipated; these are an A+ for me.

I have long since realized that by not getting frustrated and just seeing the situation as it is, there becomes a greater clarity of thought, inspired thought, that I never had before, and all just falls into place perfectly.

Of course, there is planning and strategy structuring. I am both the product and the service; walking my talk and mingling with others draws opportunities for me to share with the company with whom I spend time. These occasions afford me to mentor and coach. Business consultation quite naturally follows.

I hold myself accountable for all occurrences in my life; there is no blame game. With the right mental attitude, and the absence of procrastination, success is available to all. This is my life journey and I captain my own ship, and nothing can be more successful than knowing that I am assisting others to be, do, and have the same.

Woody Woodward:
So for someone who has gone through a lot of tragedy like yourself, and let's say they have been very inspired by this chapter and they want to help other people. How should they go about it?

Victoria Acree:
First, make sure the person in question wants the help that is being offered; it is never a good thing to intrude in the lives of others with our own opinions.

Having said that, have you ever seen a coach at a gym, Woody? They do not do the bench presses for the one who wants to get in shape. They stand to the side and support, encourage and hold accountability for the progress made and will applaud all efforts. This is the way to help others.

As always, in assisting others, gentleness and empathy should be expressed. Should the person who is stuck in the mire of life need to do so, give them the space that is needed to 'get it off their chest' and be a good listener while they do so. However, I would like to point out that this should never turn into a 'pity-party' as this is detrimental to healing; acknowledging their situation is all that is needed.

Everyone has their 'story' to tell, but should be reiterated for the purpose of healing only. Joining in the retelling of stories can only harden the situation like cement. I have read on social media the same story being retold for over a year with well-meaning friends joining in on the unfairness of the situation; this is of no help at all.

The person to be helped must want the helpful healing and assistance. Assisting others may require Socratic questioning that will naturally bring answers out of the person being assisted. It is not for the helper to tell others what they should and should not do, but to allow the other the space to realize the best answers for himself. Ask the one being helped if they would be willing to have an accountability and support partner.

Woody Woodward:

We all have people in our lives that have helped us. Maybe it was an individual or possibly a book that helped you. How have mentors helped you overcome your challenges?

Victoria Acree:

My mentors are like two sides of the same coin, Woody. On the side of heads, there are the names of Napoleon Hill, W. Clement Stone, Henry Ford, and my fellow Scotsman Andrew Carnegie. I have studied all these men for over a decade. While they may have different genres, or different industry focus, they all have common threads, more importantly the same mental attitude. A positive mental attitude is the gateway to success. It makes no difference what a person's goals and abilities may be, if a positive mental attitude is not employed then there is every likelihood that their goals won't get off the drawing board, leaving them to be unaccomplished dreams that will never be realized. Many of these men have lived a 'rags to riches' life. It would have been so easy for them to say 'I can't do it because....' But they didn't.

I, too, like some of them, came from a less than perfect background and grew up with little to no self-esteem. Studying these men has greatly assisted me in cultivating and developing a positive self-esteem and to require of others that respectfulness be part of the relationship, both personal and in business. I know for a certainty that we do come into this world with gifts and talents, however, many do not believe in such and readily buy into the 'poor me' attitude because of a less than perfect start in life was their plight.

In my study of such men and others, I identified pattern of behavior, some of these patterns happened quite naturally, while others cultivated a pattern. The lives of these men are worth taking time to study. These men left behind legacies that were obscured for a time until there was a global boom on the birth of the technology and communication arena; now their works are easy to access. The words spoken by these great men are as pertinent today as they were when first spoken back in the day. I have studied them in book form. My books are all marked by me in the margins, highlighted, underlined, dog eared, and well thumbed. Yet these are my masters.

My latest 'great master' to study is the works of Bruce H. Lipton, PhD. Studying Lipton's research on Epigenetics only confirmed that Knowingness of which I mentioned earlier in our conversation. While it is easier to understand 'reprogramming' I would venture to suggest that we just delete the old false programs and the true information is what is left to experience.

The tails side of my mentor coin I describe as "the tormentors who were my mentors." There have been life circumstances and people in my life whom I had blamed and cursed, including God. When I did eventually get over my pity party and looked back, I saw that I learned much from those life circumstances and relationships that have contributed to my success.

The most important thing I learned from these situations was about myself and the role I played in all of them, almost like sitting in the audience and watching a play in which I was also a member of the cast, sometimes playing the role of the protagonist and sometimes the antagonist. In retrospect, there were occasions where I should have said yes, and in others a definite no. These tail mentors have been as helpful to me as the head of the mentor coin in propelling me forward.

Woody Woodward:

In your business what has been your greatest "Aha" moment? When did you realize I'm in the right place, in the right time, making a difference?

Victoria Acree:

I recently moved to Utah; the move happened quite spontaneously, before I knew it I was driving a large moving truck through the Rocky Mountains with my car trailing behind on a dolly. I found the perfect place to live at the perfect price. There is energy here in the mountains and my writing, and seminars have taken off. There will possibly be three publications before the end of the year; and the phone keeps ringing. Speaking nationally is a joy as I do love to travel. In addition to that, I have had the opportunity to talk on the radio also.

After having moved to Utah, and in February 2013, I had the opportunity to talk to an audience of more than 150 people. My sharing was well received and I had a greater opportunity to mix with some of the attendees after the event answering many of their personal questions. I gave out my contact information. The next morning, I got a phone call from a woman who was at the event the night before. Bless her heart; she could hardly speak for crying. We spoke for almost an hour, she expressed thankfulness for what I shared at the event, she had many of her questions answered there, but she had some more. By the time we had finished talking she was feeling better than she had felt in years. The event had generated many notes of thanks which I will always treasure.

The last three lines of a poem by Ralph Waldo Emerson reads: "To know even one life has breathed easier because you have lived; this is to have succeeded."

Yes, I'm in the right place at the right time; I'm living my life's purpose to assist and benefit others. Every day has an "Aha" moment for me.

Woody Woodward:

As a top achiever there are times when we have fear. How do you channel your fear into productivity?

Victoria Acree:

Fear is stated by many as 'False Evidence Appearing Real,' this I know to be true, however, this statement is cold comfort for those who are currently experiencing a state of fear. 'Paralyzed by fear' is another adage that comes to mind, and this too is true for many people. Fear is like a welder's torch, it will powerfully bond all worries together and only intensifies the situation. Fear can take such a grip on a person that it will cause them to become frozen on the spot, many preferring to stay in bed and pulling the covers over their heads, feeling as if by doing so that their situation and the corresponding fear will go away. It won't! All they are doing are keeping them warm.

The very best antidote for fear by far is ACTION! Action is the opposite of frozen paralysis. Many heroic deeds have taken place in our neighborhoods by a burst of action, there was no time to think of all the possible dangers that may befall the hero, he was in there and out again and then didn't realize just what great deed he had done. Had he taken the time to ponder all the possible dangers, he would have been paralyzed with fear and no rescue would have taken place.

Not all, but many fear-filled situations arise out of procrastination, the number one killer of success. The longer the delay in action, the more looming the fast approaching deadline becomes. These situations can make a person feel like their back is to the wall and out comes the fear like a bully in your face. Many wonderful opportunities may come along, but are you in the position to reach out and grab them? Or have you been putting off the necessary preparation and therefore lose the opportunity? And whose fault was that? Possibly the wonderful opportunity is right there in your hands, but still putting necessary action off, then regretfully, it is like your fingers just part and the golden egg falls to the floor. Get rid of the procrastination! Procrastination can be banished by getting passionate and enthusiastic about you goals and dreams.

Get up! Get a notepad and pen, make a to-do list, make the phone calls, write the e-mail, make the appointments and attend them, ask the pertinent questions, request the answers you need. In the process of action, the feeling of fear dissipates and the situation will be resolved one way or another. Where required, reach out and ask for help!

I love my day planner, an inexpensive one works well, and the month-at-a-glance page is great for all that is coming up; keep on schedule and on top of the responsibilities. Don't let life control you, stay in control of your life!

Woody Woodward:

Another acronym I heard for fear is forget everything and run. When we feel fear, we do forget everything and we run away from our problems. I agree with your solution. The solution of fear is take action.

Victoria Acree:

Absolutely.

Woody Woodward:

What inspires you the most?

Victoria Acree:

What inspires me the most is inspiration, my experiential Knowingness that I am more than my body and mind! My false sense of self, the ego-mind, is no longer in the driver's seat. The drama queen in my head has been silenced; she has been dethroned, so to speak. Inspiration comes from within not from without. It is like the wind beneath my wings; it lifts me higher.

In this life plane, nature is very inspirational. Many years ago, I would have taken a short cut through a park and never even notice its beauty. Now I will pull over to the side of the road to look at a beautiful tree. I love walking in nature and it is very therapeutic. Just pay attention and watch how nature evolves. We are the greatest part of nature; the divine source energy seeks to express itself through us. By getting out of my own way, great energy does come through, often with better answers that I could ever have come up with.

Woody, there is nothing that I have done or can do or accomplish that others cannot do also. As humans, it is an equal playing field for 95% of us, the other 5% being those who come into this word with lesser abilities and are for the 95%ers who are blessed to assist them in this life. I invite you to join me on the phenomenal life journey. Be Inspired!

Rachelle Chase

Rachelle Rasband Chase is an inspirational and motivational speaker, teacher, mentor, and writer. Her passion and purpose is to share the truths she has learned that enabled her to overcome a 22-year-long eating disorder. Her greatest desire is to help others create the same peace and joy in their lives that she has created in her own. She is grateful for the opportunities she has had to speak at several events and highly values her role as a Mind/Body/Spirit Wholeness mentor. She has a blog in which she writes in greater detail about the essential truths people need to incorporate into their belief system and way of living if they desire to be freed from addiction, self-sabotage, or any crippling negative behavior that is affecting their relationships, their ability to deal with life, and their peace and happiness.

Her greatest success is being married to her sweet husband for over eighteen years. Her greatest achievement is her five beautiful children.

Blog website: www.rachellerchase.blogspot.com

Woody Woodward:

Rachelle, you had an eating disorder for 22 years that hurt you and affected your success in life. What have you done to overcome that challenge?

Rachelle Chase:

Throughout those 22 years, I found myself going from pits of despair and depression that would last for months and months to points where I felt driven to find something that would pull me out. I tried everything—prescription drugs, diet programs, exercise programs, therapy and counseling, self-help programs, and several different alternative methods of physical and emotional healing. My goal was always to find something that would make me happy again. I would say to myself, "I'll be happy when I weigh this much" or "I'll be happy when I can fit into this size of jeans" or "I'll be happy when I am in control of my eating." Happiness was always the destination.

I would work extremely hard to be successful at whatever it was I was trying in order to reach that destination. I did succeed at times with losing weight or fitting into that pair of jeans or controlling my eating, but I would still be unhappy. Every program I tried failed to provide me with the permanent and lasting relief, peace, and happiness that I was looking for. Why? Because in everything I tried, I was going into it with the attitude of "You better fix me. You better make me happy."

In January of 2012, I was led to a mentor who helped me realize that the only way to find the peace and happiness I was searching for was for me to fix me. I was the only one that could make me happy. I love quotes and one of my favorites is "Most folks are about as happy as they make up their minds to be." Happiness really is a decision. Another quote I love says, "There is no way to happiness. Happiness is the way." It is something we create moment by moment, not something we finally find one day in the future.

I also realized that my problem was not about the food or my weight. My problem was with the negative thoughts, feelings, and beliefs that I entertained in my mind which drove me to the food. "We don't see things as they are. We see things as we are." My negative beliefs about myself were creating my negative reality. As soon as I was willing to accept that and then face up to those negative beliefs that I had buried and suppressed for so long, I started to find relief. As I let go of the negative, I created more room for the positive.

And that's when happiness became my journey, not my destination.

Woody Woodward:
There are so many people reading this chapter right now, who either

knows somebody who has some kind of addiction or disorder or chal-
lenge in their life, or they themselves may be going through one. What
advice would you give them to either help a friend or to help themselves?

Rachelle Chase:

If you have a relative or a friend that is suffering from an eating disorder or any type of addiction, my first bit of advice to you is to acknowledge that they are the only ones that truly have the power to fix themselves. I understand that forced measures need to be taken at times for severe, life-threatening situations, but I also believe that lasting, permanent healing will not take place until that individual wants it, is ready to look inside, and then do whatever it takes to make it happen. With that being said, they still need help. So encourage them to get help by finding a mentor that will assist them in the recovery process by providing guidance, accountability, and a safe place to talk. Recognize that you may not have all the answers because you haven't walked in their shoes, so help them find someone who has.

More than anything, love them. Accept them just the way they are even if you don't agree with what they are doing and even if it pains and frustrates you deeply that they are bringing upon themselves their suffering. As they feel your love and acceptance, they will gain more personal power to do whatever it takes to overcome the negative behavior they are dealing with.

For those of you who are suffering yourselves, please recognize that this isn't something you have to do on your own, nor do I believe it's possible to do it on your own. Please know that you are not alone! There are so many others that have suffered or are suffering as you are. There is help out there and there is hope. Find a mentor. Find someone who has been through what you have been through. Make sure that their tools and methods are based in truth because truth is the only real healer. "The truth will set you free!"

I have a blog that I created for the sole purpose of sharing the truths I have learned that enabled me to overcome my eating disorder. While I feel a mentor or someone to talk to on a weekly basis is critical in the healing process, becoming aware and opening your heart and mind to truth also plays a huge role. If you're interested in learning in greater detail about the truths that set me free and which can do the same for you, you can read my blog at rachellerchase.blogspot.com.

In recognizing that you need help, also recognize the help you need from God or your Higher Power. Because I believe in God, I also believe that no true healing can occur without His strength and mercy or without the help of your Higher Power. Access that power through prayer or meditation. Recognize that as mortal, imperfect beings, we need God or a Higher Power in order to overcome our human negative behaviors and weaknesses.

Finally, please realize that the only one that can change you is you. I believe that if you want to change the direction of your life, you have to be willing and ready to do the hard work. You have to be willing to face your fears and those hard feelings and experiences from the past. We keep pushing the hard stuff away or shoving it down through our addictions and self-destructive behaviors because we don't want to deal with it. The whole reason we have these addictions and negative behaviors is because they provide us an escape from the hard realities of life. I would go emotionally and cognitively unconscious when I would binge eat. Thus the behavior became addictive because it provided me an out from the shame, guilt, and pain I was feeling. What I didn't realize is that when I pushed those negative feelings down and out of my consciousness, I wasn't gaining power over them. They were gaining power over me.

It's like pushing someone under water. Just because we push the hard stuff down and out of our view doesn't mean it's gone. It's still there lurking beneath the surface and eventually it's going to come back up for air. In fact, the hard stuff will continue to resurface and cause us problems until we stop shoving it down and instead, face it and let it go. Only then will we finally be free of it.

"The best day of your life is the one on which you decide your life is your own: no apologies or excuses, no one to lean on, rely on, or blame. The gift is yours. It is an amazing journey, and you alone are responsible for the quality of it."

In the end, your happiness is up to you.

Woody Woodward:

I've realized, as I've interviewed people over the years, that every successful individual like yourself has had a mentor at some point in time in their lives. When someone is looking for a mentor, what should they look for specifically to find the right mentor for them?

Rachelle Chase:

Finding a mentor can be tricky in this day and age. There is a lot of ego in the world. Yes, there are many that are talented and knowledgeable in their field. But many who profess to be well-educated mentors do it for fame, power, and money. They mentor with an attitude of "I'm better than" as opposed to an attitude of "I've been where you are and I just want to help you in any way I can!" Look for the type of mentor that has the latter attitude. Look for a mentor that doesn't see himself as above you or greater than you, but rather equal to you. However, because they have navigated their own rocky roads successfully, they turn back to assist others along their way.

As I mentioned previously, another huge quality in an effective mentor is that their methods and tools are all based in truth. I have participated in self-help programs in which the truth was twisted in order to accomplish the program's selfish aims. Participants in the program were deceived into thinking they were gaining power and self-confidence when, in actuality, they were becoming prideful, egotistical, and ultimately destroying their family life. All truth comes from God or our Higher Power and we can know what is truth by the way we feel and by the actions that come as a result of believing it. The fruits of truth are peace, love, joy, humility, and goodness with a desire to then serve others.

Don't be deceived by an ad or a person that promises results and success fast. Success is built over time. It is not achieved in a day. It may appear that way sometimes, but most individuals achieved success because they were determined and patient with the learning process. Their success didn't come without failures. Their success came because of their failures. However, they viewed their setbacks and failures not as absolutes, but rather as stepping stones to their success. Giving up is the only true failure.

Permanent, lasting change and success takes time, patience and a willingness to learn from your mistakes and failures. So find a mentor who not only believes this, but who has done it themselves and who wants to assist you in doing the same. Find a mentor who is willing to go the distance with you, however long that distance may be, in order for you to achieve the success you desire.

After 22 years of my own personal struggle, I now have the privilege of being a mentor because I truly want to help people who are where I was get to where I am now. I want them to feel the same joy, peace, contentment and fulfillment in life that is now mine. Because truth is the only real healer, I am a seeker of truth and desire to teach those life-changing truths to others. The greatest joy I receive is watching someone I mentor have their own "A-ha!" moments that enable them to see their own beauty and greatness and which propel them into their brilliant future full of purpose, promise, passion and hope.

So listen to your heart. Be aware of truth and the twisted deceptions of it. Be patient in the process. And find the mentor who is invested in your long-term success, not their own.

Woody Woodward:
I know that you are a very successful mentor now helping many people overcome their challenges and reaching others worldwide through your blog. You have told me that you have identified five key truths to enable healing. Why don't you walk us through those five key truths?

Rachelle Chase:
The FIRST TRUTH of healing is becoming aware of your thoughts.

Many of us believe that if a thought comes into our mind then it must be true about us. This is false! Thoughts do not define who we are. Thoughts come from many different sources, both positive and negative. It's when we believe a thought is true about us, when we attach ourselves to a thought, that it becomes us. "As a man thinketh in his heart, so is he" (Proverbs 23:7). It doesn't say "as a man thinketh in his mind." A thought we believe in our heart to be true becomes who we are and our reality.

The thought cycle defines how this occurs. A thought leads to a feeling which leads to an action, which leads to a result, which leads back to a thought. Then the cycle continues, creating either an upward positive spiral or a downward negative spiral. This is a natural law of the human condition. James Allen states in his book *As a Man Thinketh*, "Man is made or unmade by himself; in the armory of thought he forges the weapons by which he destroys himself; he also fashions the tools with which he builds for himself heavenly mansions of joy and strength and peace. Man is the master of thought, the molder of character, and the maker and shaper of condition, environment and destiny. All that a man achieves and all that he fails to achieve is the direct result of his own thoughts."

If we are unaware of the thoughts we are accepting and believing, then we are powerless to stop the effects of them. Negative thoughts breed negative results. Positive thoughts breed positive results. It all begins with a thought. If we can change our thoughts, we can change our results. If we can change our results, we can change our lives.

So be aware of the thoughts that are coming into your mind. Don't automatically believe everything you think. Analyze your thoughts. Think about what you are thinking about.

The SECOND TRUTH is to identify the negative.

We are constantly being affected by negative influences. They come from negative experiences, negative people, negative thoughts and negative feelings. Sometimes we can't choose the negative forces coming at us from the outside, but we can absolutely choose how we deal with the negative from the inside.

As the Chinese proverb so poetically describes, "You cannot prevent the birds of sorrow from flying over your head, but you can prevent them from building nests in your hair. "   We get to decide if the negative birds of thought take up permanent residence in our minds.

By identifying untrue negative thoughts, we gain the power to get rid of them.

The THIRD TRUTH is to let the negative go.

By letting go of the negative, we make more room for the positive. By opening up space for the positive, we create an opportunity for positive change and progression. "Once you replace negative thoughts with positive ones, you'll start having positive results."

I have two amazing tools in my emotional tool belt that I use when I need to let go of the negative. One is for negative thoughts and the other for negative feelings. Both of these tools are physical representations of what happens mentally and emotionally. They are powerful and they work!

One is called the Little Black Book. This little black notebook acts as a prison for all of my negative thoughts. Negative thoughts are those one-liners that come into our mind which then cause feelings of depression and discouragement. "I am ugly." "I am fat." "I am worthless." "I can't do anything." "I'm not good enough." By simply writing these one-liner negative thoughts in my little black book, I lock them in prison and they can't get out. They stay trapped there. I don't revisit them and they no longer do me harm. I love this tool! I can promise you from experience that it works! It is one of the means by which I have experienced such a great change in my life over this past year-and-a-half.

The other tool I use is for letting go of my negative feelings. This tool is called the Write and Burn. When any negative feelings surface such as hatred, jealousy, anger, sadness, or frustration, I use this tool. I grab a blank sheet of loose leaf paper and write, "I feel ____ because…" And then I just write. I let all that I am feeling pour out onto that piece of paper.

Feelings are just feelings. We only cause ourselves unnecessary pain and grief when we judge ourselves for having negative feelings. We are not bad for feeling anger or hatred. We are mortal human beings and even the negative feelings are part of our mortal experience. However, if we don't let go of the negative feelings, they lead to negative actions which then lead to negative results which then plummet us down that negative spiral into that pit of despair and depression.

I believe the majority of us want to be happy. In order to be happy, we have to acknowledge the truth that negative only breeds more negative. You reap what you sow; holding on to destructive, negative feelings will not bring us happiness nor will it give us power over a situation or person. It actually gives those feelings power over us.

So let the negative feelings go. Write all that you feel. Ask why you feel that way and keep asking why. Get it all out. Feelings, just like thoughts, do not define us. What we do with our feelings is what defines us.

The last part of this tool requires you to burn the paper you just wrote on. Why the burning? Let's think about a forest fire. It's a scary thing and our first reaction to hearing about or seeing one is fear, shock, sadness and concern. Although a fire can be traumatic and destructive, it provides an opportunity for the earth to be renewed, cleansed and purified, allowing for new growth.

In Wyoming's Yellowstone National Park, when a naturally-caused fire ignites, it is watched but not snuffed out. It is understood that a fire is nature's means of rebirth. This is exactly what we are doing to our souls by burning that paper. It can be scary and hard to do, but it is worth it because it enables our souls to be renewed, cleansed, and purified, allowing new growth to sprout.

In my garage, I have a #10 can that I use for burning my papers. I first take all my anger out on that paper by crumpling or ripping it up. Then I put that paper in my #10 can. I believe in God and I believe that only by coupling my efforts to let go with His grace and mercy will my soul be completely cleansed of that negative feeling. So, I say a little prayer in this process. I ask for God's forgiveness of the negative feeling I was harboring in my heart. I then ask for God's help in letting this negative feeling go. By asking for these things, I recognize my humanity in having this feeling while also acknowledging His divinity and my need for His enabling power to let it go.

Then I burn that piece of paper. Every last bit. As that paper burns, it turns black which represents the blackness that was in my soul from that negative feeling. I watch that blackness go up in smoke and disappear, naturally releasing a sigh of relief. I end by saying a prayer of gratitude. I thank God for helping me let go of that negative feeling, preventing it from cankering and contaminating my heart, and rejoicing in the cleansing and freeing of my soul.

This is a beautiful, healing process. However, it may sometimes be very difficult and painful, just as it was for me. We may cry as we write. We may have a hard time burning the paper because we fear what we'll be or do without that negative feeling or behavior. But by releasing the negative, we are freeing ourselves from bondage to it. It's been said, "No matter what happens or how bad it seems today, life does go on, and it will be better tomorrow. You gain strength, courage and confidence from every experience in which you really stop to look fear in the face."

By facing and letting go of the negative, we gain back our personal power of choice. We then are enabled to fill that empty hole with the positive, with truth, propelling ourselves into positive action and results.

Yes, using these tools takes time. However, you've got to do the work if you want the results. Letting go is an essential part of the healing process.

The FOURTH TRUTH is identifying and believing the positive.

When we let go of the negative thoughts, beliefs and feelings, we create space for the positive. What is the positive? The positive is the truth of who we really are and any truth that uplifts and inspires us to be the best we possibly can be. Unfortunately, many of us are misled as to where to find that truth. We often define who we are based on how we measure up to the standards of the world. This pursuit of being acceptable to the world inevitably leads to a life devoid of peace and joy. Why? Because the world's definition of who we are is not based in truth. The world is imperfect, thus its standards are imperfect. The world is temporary, thus the peace and joy it offers is temporary. The only source of lasting peace and joy comes from the everlasting and eternal Creator of peace and joy. If we desire this kind of peace and joy, we need to stop defining ourselves according to the world and start defining ourselves according to God or a Higher Power.

We are each different, unique, and special with equally different, unique, and special purposes to perform. We need to pray and meditate to access the truth of who we are. We need to take time to identify our strengths, talents, and gifts. We also need to look at our experiences and trials, our weaknesses and flaws. Even the hard stuff in our life is meant to shape and refine us into all we were created to be. Identifying and believing these positive truths of who we really are allows us to then act positively.

The FIFTH TRUTH is acting on the positive.

Practice makes permanent. If we want to make a positive, joyful and peaceful life our new way of life, we have to practice it.

A great tool I use to act on the positive is called List It to Live It. Throughout my eating disorder, I used journaling as a way to cope. Even though it was therapeutic for me, I mainly used it to recount all the negative things that were going on in my life. Another favorite quote of mine is "The only reason it's a part of your life is because you keep thinking about it." I dwelt on the negative. Therefore, that's what I got back.

So next to your little black notebook and your stack of loose leaf paper for burning, have a colorful notebook in which you write the positive—the inspiration and blessings you receive from God. Record the things you are grateful for and the good things about yourself. When we write about and focus on the positive, it becomes more ingrained in our heart and soul. Then according to law, our reality and circumstances will respond in kind. By focusing on the positive, we'll get positive back.

Be who you truly are. Share your talents and gifts with others. Be real with the struggles and trials you have faced or are facing. So many of us are closed, locked doors. Though this may keep our fears and insecurities from getting out, it also prevents truth and love from getting in.

As you act on the truth of who you really are by letting go of the negative and embracing the positive, you open that door to your heart and soul through which love, joy and peace can enter. Others will then be drawn to you because of the light and warmth you radiate. You will become a source of hope for those who, too, want to be filled with love, truth, joy and peace. By living your truth and loving your fellowmen, the joy that comes as a result will be beyond what you ever imagined possible!

And that's the goal! The whole purpose of using these five truths is to create a life full of incomprehensible peace and joy. Isn't that what we are all searching so desperately to find? I know from personal experience that if we will implement these five truths into our daily way of thinking and acting, we will make this new, joyful and peaceful way of life the majority of our life.

Woody Woodward:

I love that statement. Take this new way of life and make it the majority of your life.

Rachelle Chase:

Yes, absolutely! It takes time and patience. We will continue to have our down moments, but it is truly possible to make this positive way of life the majority of your life!

Woody Woodward:

What is your focus and your daily routine? How do you stay on track?

Rachelle Chase:

That is another huge part of succeeding at this process. The key to making these truths work for you is to not only practice them, but to live in the moment. When we emotionally dwell in the past or the future, we put ourselves in bondage to it. We stop our progression. The only place in which we have agency and choice is in the now. The only way to progress and change is to use our present moment to act. However, living in the moment doesn't mean we don't take care of things from the past or for the future. It means that we use the moment we have to do something about it instead of wasting time fearing it.

Being fully invested in my present moment is what keeps me on track. Because I have practiced being aware and living in the moment, I now know what behaviors I slip into when I am trying to escape or distract myself from my present reality. I still don't always catch myself before my negative thoughts become negative action. But the sooner I become aware and bring myself back to the present, the sooner I can act by using my tools to shift myself from a negative to a positive place.

Woody Woodward:

It's very inspiring talking to you. Who inspires you?

Rachelle Chase:

The people who inspire me are those who are living true to who they really are. They inspire because they are being their authentic, real selves. They see value not in what the world can offer them, but in what they can offer the world. They use their talents and gifts, trials and experiences to help and benefit the lives of others. They recognize their own power, light and greatness, but they don't take the credit for it, giving credit where credit is due.

The majority of these inspirational people have overcome great hardships. They persevered and were determined to succeed no matter how many times they failed. They never gave up. They learned from their temporary failures and continued on. Now they stand as a beacon of light and hope to others. And because their ultimate desire is to help others while being true to their purpose for living, they are possessors of real peace and joy. These are the type of people that inspire me and the type of person I hope I am.

Woody Woodward:

What has been your greatest "Aha" moment in your business of helping other people?

Rachelle Chase:

I had just finished reading the book *Peaceful Warrior* which, by the way, is also a fantastic movie. This novel is all about recognizing and acting on the truth of who you really are by living in the moment. Near the end of the book, the main character had a remarkable experience of great enlightenment. It was incredibly inspiring to me and very powerful. That afternoon, my husband was driving us along the freeway. In that moment, the truth of what I had read sunk deep within my heart and soul. I was completely awestruck and spellbound. I couldn't speak or move. Tears welled up in my eyes and my heart burned within me because for the first time, I understood who I really was.

I have always believed in God and that He is not only the Creator of this beautiful world, but my Creator. However, the power with which this understanding hit me in this moment was greater than I had ever felt before. I realized that the order in which God created the earth and mankind had great significance. Mankind was His final creation. We were His crowning achievement. We were His master-piece. So in other words, because we were His final creation, all that He had created before us reached its masterful perfection in us. We were the grand total of all His previous creations. By understanding that truth, I came to the realization of my greatness and power. Not in a prideful way, but in a humble way acknowledging God for every-thing I am or hope to be.

I looked at the majestic, grand mountains and realized God cre-ated me to have a majestic and grand purpose.

I looked at the tall, strong, steadfast and immovable trees and I realized that God created me to stand tall, strong, steadfast and im-movable against the winds and storms of this life.

I looked at the great expanse of the sky and realized that my God created me to have a great, expansive potential.

I looked at the beautiful sunset, the brightness and light of the sun and realized that God created me to be a beautiful, bright light radi-ating warmth and the hope of a new day.

I thought of the powerful ocean and I realized that God created me to be a powerful force for good in this world.

In that moment, I realized that all of these characteristics were not only about me, but about every man and woman that have ever lived, are living or will ever live on this earth. Because of all the negative influences and voices in this world, we underestimate and even dis-believe the ability, potential, greatness, light and power that are with-in us. We are so much more than our finite minds can comprehend!

One of my absolute favorite quotes is by the inspirational author Marianne Williamson. She says, "Our deepest fear is not that we are inadequate. Our deepest fear is that we are powerful beyond measure. It is our light, not our darkness, which frightens us the most. We were born to make manifest the glory of God that is within us. It's not just in some of us; it's in all of us. And when we let our own light shine, we unconsciously give other people permission to do the same. As we are liberated from our own fear, our presence automatically liberates others."

I absolutely believe that is true about me and about every single one of us. We all have the glory of God within us and that makes us incredibly powerful. When we discover and live true to the purpose of our creation, not only are we happier and more at peace than ever before, but we become a powerful force for good in bringing light into this darkened world. "Your spark can become a flame and change everything!"

This "Aha!" moment has changed the way I look at and mentor others. I see everyone with more love and compassion because I see them how they are in the moment while also realizing who they can become. I understand that everyone has their hard stuff and they are doing the best they can with the knowledge they have. But despite our human, imperfect nature, each one of us is an incredible, powerful, divinely created being with enormous potential!

Woody Woodward:
There are a lot of top achievers who've gone through many challenges much like yourself. When you look back in your life, what is the one lesson you would love to tell your 20-year-old self today.

Rachelle Chase:
I would tell my 20-year-old self to "be.YOU.tiful!" That is my favorite word! It is the theme of my blog and when I speak, that is my focus.

I believe that all of us are our own kind of beautiful. The world wants us to believe that there is only one way to be beautiful so we are all trying to fit that mold. But God says differently. He says that for every human being He has created, there are that many types of beauty. We are each beautiful in our own uniquely special way—flaws, talents, weaknesses, strengths and all. The whole package is what makes us beautiful. So, I would ask myself, "Why are you trying so hard to fit in when you were born to stand out?"

I spent so many lost years looking outside of myself to fill the emptiness inside. But as it is said, "You'll never get enough of what you don't need because what you don't need won't satisfy." What I really needed was inside of me all along.

I just needed to be my own beautiful.

Woody Woodward:
What do you want your legacy to be?

Rachelle Chase:
I want my legacy to be one of faith, love, light, power, passion, and purpose. I want it to be known that I did go through hard times, but rose above them by believing who I really was as defined by God. I want to be known as someone who had faith, relying on God for strength to act on truth and to fill me with power to be who I was created to be.

As spoken of in Marianne Williamson's quote, I want to be the type of person that because I have let go of my fears, my influence helps liberate others. Because I let my own light shine, I help others to do the same.

My greatest desire is that I will be known as someone who loved others unconditionally and wanted to help them in any way I could to be their happiest, best, real, authentic self. I want to lead others to the source of all light, truth, love, joy and peace, even God, who will show them who they really are if they are ready and willing to see. If they choose to see that, they will be moved to act—going forward with power, radiating light, and fulfilling their reason for being on this earth. If they choose to do that, they will have greater peace and joy than they ever dreamed possible.

That's what is happening to me and that's all I could hope for anyone… everyone!

L.M. Christenson

L.M. Christenson is a 4 time author, Life Coach and motivational speaker. She began working in the world of healers over 23 years ago learning everything she could about the mind, body and spirit connection. L.M. used her Apocalypse of Light 9 step program to personally overcome the heartaches, trauma and darkness that came from the death of two siblings early in her life, being molested by a janitor in her kindergarten, the 8 ½ month long coma and subsequent death of her only remaining sister two weeks before L.M. graduated from High School, suffering the loss of one of her remaining siblings to drugs, alcohol and mental illness, and Apocalypse of Light has been invaluable helping her heal from an unusually difficult divorce. L.M. has learned to value the beauty of life without disregarding the darkness. She loves spending time with her family, painting, writing, exploring nature and photography.

Websites: www.lmchristenson.biz

Woody Woodward:

L.M., you had a challenging life yet you turned your life into quite a success. Tell us a little bit about your childhood and your adulthood and what gives you the strength to endure.

L.M. Christenson:

As a child and young adult I was blessed with good parents and a relatively peaceful upbringing; wandering through the woods, climbing trees, wading in streams. It was truly magical. But as is common with many of us, I also experienced dark and difficult things that prepared me for future challenges as a mother and a spouse and as a businesswoman that I never expected in my wildest dreams I'd ever experience. Through the light and dark times in my life, I have found nine principles that helped me face the darkness and reclaim the light I had as a child.

Woody Woodward:
So what are those nine principles?

L.M. Christenson:
Principle one is: We are born beings of light. Principle two is: We must live conscientiously to reclaim our light. Principle three is: Time is a precious gift. We must wisely choose how to use it.

Principle four is: Each of us came to this earth for a purpose and often multiple purposes but two are universal: Number one, each of us came to this earth to gain experience and grow into better beings of light. Number two, each of us came here to leave the world a better place.

Principle number five: Each of us is hardwired to our purposes in this life; we are on auto pilot so to speak. Principle six is: Other people are not programmed to support us.

Principle seven is: When we engage with people and things that are REAL, we consequently bring to our consciousness both our light and dark emotions. Principle eight is: There is a war between light and darkness going on inside each of us.

Principle nine: We have to ROAR at our dark emotions in order to create space for more of our light emotions.

Woody Woodward:
Before we get into the 9 principles, I noticed two acronyms among your principles. Can you explain what REAL and ROAR stand for?

L.M. Christenson:
Thank you for asking; yes these are actually really important to fully understanding my Apocalypse of Light platform.

Things that are REAL, stands for: Radiates peace, truly Educates, makes us feel Alive, and helps us find and share Light.

ROARing at the darkness stands for: Recognizing, Owning, Accepting and Releasing our darkness.

Woody Woodward:

What I love about interviewing people is everybody has had different challenges and different heartaches. I can understand that through your past and the challenges you've gone through that you created all nine of these principles from life experiences, things that you've personally gone through that you've suffered or that you have witnessed in the suffering of others. So let's go back to principle one and explain in further detail what that means and how we can use it.

L.M. Christenson:

We are born beings of light. I don't think anyone would argue that when we see a new baby, they are filled with light, they practically glow. This is because they are pure, innocent, and peaceful. I believe children are great teachers, especially helping us to remember our light. There is a very sad scene in A *Christmas Carol* by Charles Dickens, where Scrooge tries to smother the light of the Ghost of Christmas Past. You see, the light bothers Scrooge because he has too much darkness in him. His darkness consists of selfishness, anger and shut down emotions but underneath his cold façade, he is full of heartache. I think we as adults have a choice to either fall prey to heartache and the pain that comes to all of us or ROAR at the darkness and reclaim the light we had as little children.

As a life coach, I have found it beneficial to explore the light we had in the early years of our life. Pictures, happy memories, the things, activities and people we loved the most; the things that connected us to our light as a child. I won't necessarily encourage anyone to return to eating pureed squash but I will encourage the reclaiming of beautiful memories of light that we often bury under pain, heartache and dark emotions.

Some of my childhood memories of light are of sunlight falling through the leaves of trees, little ladybugs, dancing with my father around our house on his toes, finger-painting, and being safe with my family in front of our woodstove during a power outage. Even with the tragedy and heartache I have faced, I have reclaimed these precious sparks of light from my childhood and they help me feel peaceful especially when times are tough.

Woody Woodward:

Now I know all nine principles don't go in order, meaning that we experience them at different times. So what's number two? Say that again for our readers and explain how that applies to their life as well

L.M. Christenson:

We must live conscientiously to reclaim our light. Conscientious living means that we are aware of ourselves. We know what helps us and what hurts us. We evaluate what builds us up and what tears us down and make conscientious plans to remove what is tearing us down and embrace those things that build us up.

I remember when I was a young mom, I was struggling with—well, I was eating a lot of sugar. It wasn't alcohol, it wasn't drugs but I was feeling addicted to it. I had to have it. I needed to have more of it and the more I had of it, the less it did for me. I realized one day that the sugar was controlling my behavior, I was moody and had less energy and I was putting myself on a path to diabetes. But the thought of letting go of my sugar was like Bilbo Baggins's reaction when Gandalf asked to take the Ring. Inside of me was the classic war between my light and my darkness and I had to conscientiously choose which was going to win.

Fortunately, I began doing research and realized that I was probably low on B vitamins and began taking some tried and true supplements that actually made me feel better. I had more true energy and felt in control of my life. I conscientiously exchanged a "zombifying" addiction that was darkening me for REAL vitamins that would add to my light. I will talk more about zombification later.

Woody Woodward:

What's principle three again and how does that apply?

L.M. Christenson:

Principle three is: Time is a precious gift. We must wisely choose how to use it. There are many things we can do in this life. I mean we often run from one extreme to another filling every second of every day trying to do it all or escaping into our favorite addiction becoming "zombified." Unfortunately, as we become "zombified" by escapes and addictions controlling our lives, we feel less and less alive, less and less peace and happiness.

Often we do this because we are trying to avoid the pain of our dark emotions. Unfortunately avoiding pain by running from, avoiding or shutting down our emotions only truly shuts down our light emotions, leaving us with the very thing we are avoiding, our pain. Only ROARing at the dark emotions and reclaiming our light will fill us up with the happiness and peace we are truly after.

But we have to make choices in our lives about how we use our precious gift of time. We can literally fill our lives with virtual realities, virtual relationships, escapes and addictions that can give us very little back except for a desire to have more of what can't satisfy us.

We have to choose. I remember a time as a young mom when I was going to the gym. It would take 3½ to 4 hours to get my children and myself ready, go to the gym, exercise for 45 minutes, shower and get back home.

That may be doable or even critical for other moms but it was making it difficult for me to accomplish my other important life goals. But again, I didn't want to let it go because I loved it. Now going to the gym wasn't an addiction or an escape it was simply taking more of my precious time than was necessary. When I finally chose to exercise at home for 45 minutes instead of going to the gym, I saved myself nearly 3 hours a day!

Woody Woodward:

What is principle four?

L.M. Christenson:

Each of us came to this earth for a purpose and often multiple purposes but two are universal: Number one, each of us came to this earth to gain experience and grow into better human beings. Number two, each of us came here to leave the world a better place.

This principle is powerful. If we believe that we came to this earth for a purpose that purpose will guide us how to use our time. It helps us choose what brings light into our lives and what just fills the space.

Another powerful piece of principle four is to recognize that we came here to leave this world a better place. Serving others around us is so healing, so energizing. Selfishness is the opposite and a very destructive emotion to our souls and to those around us. George MacDonald, a man whom C.S. Lewis considered his mentor, said, "The love of our neighbor is the only door out of the dungeon of self." (George MacDonald, *An Anthology by C.S. Lewis*, section 49, 1973) That's huge—serving others is a healing principle for our souls and critical for the healing of this world.

Woody Woodward:

What about principle five and how does that help us?

L.M. Christenson:

Each of us is hardwired to our purposes in this life; we are on auto pilot so to speak. A good example of this is one of my children. She was born to sing and dance. I'm not kidding. Even as a three-year-old she would create beautiful dance routines with a gentle beginning, building up to the crescendo in the middle and then finishing with a finale. I'd sit and watch her in amazement. It felt so peaceful, so beautiful, so full of her light. She created her first song on the piano at age three. It was a beautiful piece. And she could sing just like an angel. In fact she had a little bravado.

It was interesting to watch her with different dance instructors, different piano instructors and different mentors. When she and I worked together, I built her up and gave her a lot of free time to create. I had some piano skills, some voice training and some music theory that I taught her until she progressed beyond me. I filled her environment with good music of all different kinds from classical to classic rock. I could feel that everything I gently placed in her path helped her develop her music and dancing skills and she'd just grab a hold of and embrace, truly just devour it, until it became a part of her.

A couple of her mentors continued to help her grow rapidly and healthily but some shut her down by their criticism and cattiness when at one point she stopped dancing and singing around the house for six months to a year. It was devastating for me to watch. I just missed the light that seemed to have been snuffed out by someone else's darkness, like Scrooge trying to cap the Ghost of Christmas Past's light. I could see that a piece of her soul was just shut down. Her hardwire purposes in this life were criticized to the point where she became so angry and depressed that she could not find her purpose easily during that time.

But fortunately, because she *is* hardwired to create music as one of her purposes in life, the opposition eventually helped her find her ROAR and strengthened her passion for music. And as she was given space and time and healthier opportunities, she built her light up again and is again creating beautiful music. She has written words and music to five or more songs this last year alone.

Woody Woodward:
A lot of us don't want to experience life the way we are currently experiencing it. So how do we overcome that challenge?

L.M. Christenson:
That is a challenge. That's a real challenge. And it goes back to recognizing our darkness, recognizing the things that created that darkness and removing those habits and those dark emotions from our lives and filling our lives with REAL habits and emotions. Often we have to go back through our life's experiences to find out how we created our dark habits, responses and emotions. I have found very often that darkness is created in us when someone didn't believe in us, or didn't understand us, or who hurt us, abused us, or discouraged us because they simply didn't know how to help us find who we truly are.

I got to a stage where I was experiencing my life in ways I didn't want to be experiencing them. My life was filled with relatively good things but I wasn't doing the things that I really loved. I was feeling smothered and frustrated. I had to go back to the REAL things in my life and reclaim my light. I went back to my childhood and remembered how I loved painting and writing.

I have a picture of me at age 3 or 4 in one of my dad's old shirts covered from head to toe in finger-paints. At age 10 or 11, my grandma gave me my first oil painting kit but life got in the way and this important piece of my soul was neglected. At this time in my life when I remembered loving painting, I finally took out my art supplies, studied art books and painted just to fill my soul and reclaim my light. I have some peaceful and fulfilling pieces of art that I have created but what is more, I have experienced hours of peaceful creating and reclaimed my light.

In fourth grade I won a writing contest. They asked for a 3 page story and I wrote 10 pages! It was thrilling to write a story. The reward for winning was to participate in a writer's conference but unfortunately someone made a mistake and didn't make room at the conference for my mother. When we got there, they refused to let my mother stay, stating fire codes as the reason. It made me so upset that I didn't stay at the conference. And sadder yet, I didn't write creatively again until this time in my life when I remembered the thrill that writing gave me as a child and I reclaimed my light. Now I am the author of four books with plans for many more!

Woody Woodward:
What about principle six?

L.M. Christenson:
Yes, other people are not programmed to support us. We can read about any great person, Leonardo DeVinci, Joan of Arc, Winston Churchill, or Elizabeth Browning and there's going to be people that support them and people that don't. Some stories are more tragic than others where the person has a lot of opposition, a lot of abuse, a lot of pain that they have to face in order to find and fulfill their purpose. But if we recognize and accept that even some of the people closest to us—our mothers, our fathers who may love us may not understand how to support us in our purposes.

There's a huge need to ROAR or Recognize, Own, Accept and Release those dark feelings of pain and anger that occur when we are thwarted in our auto pilot. But if we realize that other people aren't programmed to support us, we can stop blaming others for getting in our way or not helping us to fulfill our purposes. As we make peace with the fact that others won't always understand or support us, we can focus on our job of fulfilling our purposes.

Woody Woodward:

I know you coach a lot of successful people. When we've been hardwired to do something and we've been shut out by so many people—all the naysayers and all those dark emotions that you referred to, how do we find our own light again? How do we tap back into that hardwired program that allows us to really shine at our highest level?

L.M. Christenson:

You know Woody, that's a great question. The whole purpose of my Apocalypse of Light platform is to help us get back to our hardwired program and allow our light to shine at our highest level. We have to remove as many dark and "zombifying" people, places and activities from our life. And we need to replace them with REAL people, places and activities. We have to conscientiously accept our purpose and uncover the ROAR in us so that no matter what, we will fulfill our purpose.

When we truly accept our purpose those very difficulties that we face from others and from the war between our light and darkness can bring out the ROAR we need to become what we came here to become. If we don't find that ROAR, our dark emotions like fear, pain, bitterness and anger can crush us. Many great souls give in to the dark emotions and the naysayers and eventually self-destruct. It is why living conscientiously, ROARing at our dark habits and dark emotions and replacing them with habits of light and emotions of light is so critical.

Woody Woodward:

That's beautiful. I know you just covered multiple principles but for the sake of order, will you just explain principle seven real quick?

L.M. Christenson:

Principle seven states: When we engage with people and things that are REAL, we consequently bring to our consciousness both our light and dark emotions.

Principle seven is one of my favorite principles because I truly believe that REAL people, REAL things, REAL places help us to reconnect with the light we were born with, if we ROAR at the darkness that is also revealed as we connect with things that are REAL. As I stated earlier, REAL is an acronym for Radiates peace, truly Educates, makes us feel Alive, and helps us find and share Light, REAL.

For example, a REAL activity is standing in a windstorm and letting the wind just wrap around you and feeling the energy. I love to envision the wind helping me release pain and sadness as I stand there. I feel energized and alive. Another REAL experience happened one day when I especially missed my sister after she died, I went to her cemetery and found an ancient Cedar Tree and just sat beneath it. It was so healing and peaceful. Other things are REAL to other people like creating a beautiful painting, listening to music that enlivens you, watching a sunset or finding a solution to a problem, cutting wood or working hard, helping someone in need, giving or receiving love, taking a hike to a waterfall, photographing that waterfall, holding a baby, gardening, cleaning, fixing, building. What is REAL to you?

There are things that aren't as REAL. And while some of these next examples might have some REAL elements, like an inspiring movie or a fun afternoon with friends on Guitar Hero, zombification more often occurs in these settings. Sitting in front of the TV or video games for hours on end deaden our senses, even "zombifies" us. I consider zombification to be what happens to any of us who plug in so much that we can't utter a cohesive sentence or we become more impatient or even stop caring about the people closest to us. Because these virtual worlds are so much easier to deal with than REAL people with REAL emotions and REAL problems, going back to what is REAL becomes less and less appealing. It can be entertaining and there are positives aspects of being plugged in for short amounts of time but zombification is a real problem with our society when we are so apt to escape into the next virtual world, social media addiction, running in and out of unhealthy relationships, drugging ourselves with poor diets, medications, drugs, sex, pornography and alcohol.

The Zombie Apocalypse is actually what inspired me to launch my Apocalypse of Light to combat the zombification of our lives. In order to combat the zombification of our lives we have to get back to what's REAL. Things that Radiates peace, truly Educates, makes us feel Alive, and helps us find and share Light. We have to put our hands in the dirt and reconnect with the rhythms of nature. We need to play REAL games that challenge our minds and help us connect with those we love. We need to fill our lives with REAL music that enlivens our souls. We need to reclaim the color in our lives from all the black unless we are going to a funeral. We have to have REAL conversations with a REAL people. And we have to be willing to do the REAL work of ROARing at the darkness and reclaiming our light; in our own hearts, with our own families and in our work and play. If we do this REAL work we can have satisfaction in our REAL lives and no longer need to escape or zombify ourselves. My hope is that the Zombie Apocalypse will be healed by an Apocalypse of Light, one person at a time. We need one person at a time that is willing to connect with things that are REAL, ROAR at their darkness and reclaim their light.

Woody Woodward:
What's principle eight and how does it help us?

L.M. Christenson:
There is a war between light and darkness going on inside each of us. The struggle between light and darkness is a theme replete throughout history from religious books to Shakespearian plays to modern day Sci-Fi Fantasy novels, it's a principle that we as human beings have always been up against. One of the formative books in my youth was written by Orson Scott Card called *The Seventh Son*. In this book there is a Maker and an Unmaker. It is a fantastic analogy of the powerful Maker encouraging people to create and build while the powerful Unmaker encourages people to

tear down and destroy. Dark emotions, if left unchecked and "unROARed" at, tear us and others down; light emotions build us and others up.

Light emotions and dark emotions are like opposing magnets. Light repels dark and dark repels light. Light attracts light and dark attracts dark. One will win in the end. So, this war that's going on inside of us between the light and the dark is something we've got to face or fall prey to.

Woody Woodward:

How does someone face that? How does one challenge that because we all have it?

L.M. Christenson:

Absolutely. Let's look at principle nine: ROARing at the darkness. Recognizing our darkness, Owning and Accepting our darkness, and Releasing our darkness. ROARing is another acronym that I created from one of my special REAL experiences. I was on the roof of a hotel in Playa Del Carmen Mexico getting a massage; it was absolutely heavenly. It was 80 degrees with a soft breeze blowing. The massage therapist was using stones, Cranial Sacral, Swedish deep tissue and more techniques that I don't remember right off. At one point, she quietly commented, "A Toucan just flew by, that is significant." And with the ocean rhythmically creating a peaceful background sound—it was just so REAL.

The masseuse taught me a simple principle that I have thought about for years and has made a huge difference in how I deal with my light and darkness. She introduced me to the idea of recognizing, accepting and releasing my darkness.

I think one of the hardest things to recognize and accept is that we all have dark emotions and that it's okay. It's real. Emotions just "are" but we have been taught that dark emotions are bad. We feel ashamed of our darkness or use our darkness to rebel or hurt ourselves and others or we try to escape from our darkness. Anything we do with our darkness besides ROARing at it hurts us or others around us.

Fortunately, there are a lot of tools that I have found that can help us face our dark emotions. That's part of what I do during my coaching. It is really one of the toughest pieces of my platform, to recognizing our darkness.

One of the things we can do to recognize our darkness is stop and evaluate when we're hurting other people. It seems simple but often admitting that we hurt someone takes great courage. But if we rationalize or justify our anger we miss the opportunity to find out why we are angry, ROAR at our anger and the underlying emotions (anger always has underlying emotions) and reclaim our light. Another thing we can do to recognize our darkness is evaluate what is in another person that makes us angry. People often come into our lives that teach us about our darkness. They mirror for us our darkness and are usually the people that drive us the craziest.

Woody Woodward:
And finally principle nine?

L.M. Christenson:
We have to ROAR at the darkness. We already talked about this but I will add one more thought. So often I have heard the lie that just being positive is enough, or in my Apocalypse of Light terms, reclaiming our light is enough. The other piece of this huge lie is: Ignoring dark emotions protects us from dark emotions. The truth is that ignoring dark emotions simply allows our dark emotions to grow inside of us and eventually take over. ROARing at our dark emotions is the only way to make room for more light.

Woody Woodward:
You've been through a lot; I thank you for your transparency and honesty. For the reader who's at home right now, what's the first baby step that they can do to ROAR at the darkness, to take their life back into stepping into their own greatness, their own light?

L.M. Christenson:
We need to start where we are by ROARing at something in our lives that isn't necessary. Each of us has excess in our lives that needs to go, take this moment to remove one small excess, a toxic friend, a bad habit, a waste of money or time. Next, with the space we just created, we need to

add into our lives one thing we truly love; something that is REAL and full of light. It can be as simple as taking time to meditate, going on a regular date night with someone we love, reading a favorite classic, planting a favorite flower or reclaiming a childhood dream. Do one simple thing that we love, that we've been denying ourself, embrace it and let it fill our soul with that peace that comes as we reclaim our light.

I remember one day, final story, I was sitting in a parking lot waiting for one of my children in one of their classes and just felt an urge to go walk around the perimeter of the property. I thought it was a funny urge but it was the time of year when I like collecting herbs for different medicinal purposes and I thought well maybe there's something growing that I could harvest. After walking the entire perimeter of the property, I found nothing but a single daisy. And this little daisy had some drops of dew on it.

I picked the daisy with dew on it. This flower reminded me of my sister because she loved daisies. I brought the daisy back to my car and took pictures of it with my phone. It made my day. REAL things are often simple but their power to enlivened, bring light, happiness and peace to our souls is great.

Woody Woodward:
What projects are you are working on now that make you the most excited for the future?

L.M. Christenson:
By September, my Fantasy novel, *Beyond Trivar*, will be published. It goes along beautifully with my Apocalypse of Light. It is filled with powerful characters and the timeless plot of war between light and darkness.

Woody Woodward:
What do you want your legacy to be?

L.M. Christenson:
An Apocalypse of Light. My vision is that we as beings of light can continue to individually ROAR at our darkness, reclaim our light and collectively share and grow that light across this beautiful planet creating a powerful Apocalypse of Light.

Christian Appiah-Knudsen

Christian Appaih-Knudsen is a rare find. Christian became an ambassador for Power In You in 2009. As an ambassador he shares his story with students across the state of Utah. He has an inspiring message and vibrant presence. It is no surprise that at the end of every performance he is swarmed not only by students but also faculty members and adults.

Christian is a natural leader and mentor. His charisma radiates the moment he walks in the room. As an individual he is dedicated to giving his best in every aspect of his life.

Indeed, he is determined not only to achieve great things but to also help others do the same. In a world so preoccupied with getting to the top, it is refreshing to know someone like Christian who is concerned about helping others reach their potential as well.

In addition, he is among the most pleasant, light- hearted and honest individuals I have met. He possesses a brightness that seems unsurpassed. Christian has had significant obstacles in his life, yet he does not view them as such. He sees each experience as an important opportunity that has shaped him into the remarkable man he is today. This type of maturity is yet another rare trait that Christian possesses.

Already he has accomplished so much in his life. I will watch his unfolding career and future with great interest; it is certain to be impressive—in fact, it already is.
—Mary Kaye Huntsman, First Lady of Utah

Woody Woodward:

Christian, you have a very unique story. You've overcome vast adversity. Tell us a little about the beginning of your life and what led you to do what you're doing now.

C. Appiah-Knudsen:

I was born in West Africa, Ghana, in a very tiny village called Abesim. I was living with my grandmother, who was about 75 years old, and my younger brother, and sister. Growing up, life was extremely tough for us. We lived in a tiny house or a hut constructed with mud, sticks of twigs and dried grass. We were so destitute to the extent that we could hardly make ends meet. In fact, there were nights where my siblings and I went to bed hungry.

One day, my grandmother came up to me and insisted that I learn how to hunt so that I could help her support the family. Grandma's words caught me off guard because it came out like this, "You're going to learn how to hunt." I was puzzled and my first reaction was like "What?" I felt compelled at that specific moment to ask grandma why I had to be involved in such a precarious activity that was not common to kids at my age in village.

But then all of the sudden, I thought about our struggles and how my mother and father are around to lift some of the load off grandma. I was the oldest child and, therefore, I had to grow up quickly to fill in the shoes that our parents left empty. As I thought about it I came to the realization as why grandma would want me to learn to hunt at a very younger age. That gave me the courage to get involved. However, I still wanted an answer to the question of why my mother and father were not around. It was a perfect opportunity to get an answer as grandma had never said anything about my parents. I had the courage to ask and the answer she gave me blew me away. It was the complete opposite of what I was anticipating to hear.

She told me the reason why we were in the village, why I had never known who my biological father and, of course, why my mother was never around is that growing up, we had everything. My grandfather used to own a small gold field where he made a lot for himself. Though my grandfather was very successful, he had one major problem. He was not highly educated. He only had like a third-grade education which was a big problem because when the merchants from Europe, and Portugal, would come and buy his gold, they bought it very cheap. My dad, on the other hand, was a very well-educated man who has traveled around the world, and so he knew the value of the gold from when it has been shipped out of Ghana.

Because of my father's global knowledge regarding the value of gold, my grandfather saw it fit to bring him into the family business and asked him to literally be the middleman who does the bidding and everything. From that point on, the business flourished. As a result, my grandfather decided to expand the company and he became very busy trying to look for different locations to purchase. Unfortunately while he was gone for about a month trip, my dad made legal papers and sold everything my grandfather had—everything—and fled out of the country. Nobody knows where he is.

Due to this issue, two of my uncles who were going to school in Germany came home because my grandfather couldn't afford to support them. He was heartbroken. He grew bitter and angry with himself and, of course, with the man who literally robbed him of everything he had. It got to the point where he just could not deal with the pain and embarrassment that he committed suicide. My grandfather's death was by far the most painful tragedy that befell my family. This made my uncles very upset with my mother, and they went around saying that she had married an evil person. I still have vivid memories of my uncles beating up my mother so many times all because of bringing a crook into our family. My uncles despised me. My uncles despised me big time. As a kid, I didn't know what was going on at that time.

I didn't even know why somebody could have such hatred towards such a young kid like me. To make a long story short, my grandmother said to me, "You know, with the tribes that we live with right now, you are literally like the older male in the family. And right now we are in a very tough predicament, and I need your help."

Woody Woodward:
How old were you at the time?

C. Appiah-Knudsen:
At that time, I was already like six.

Woody Woodward:
Six years old and you had to start providing for your family.

C. Appiah-Knudsen:
Yes. I didn't understand why, but I didn't have any choice because in my country, if somebody's older than you, even for a day, you don't disrespect them. You give them respect, even if they older than you for an hour. This was very hard for me, and my grandmother took me to these two hunters in the village to give me lessons. They wanted to make sure that I was strong enough to go with them, and so I began my training by simply following them and observing everything they did while we were out hunting in the middle of the night.

I did everything I was told to do for my safety and experience. Often, I had to do training where they would put me in a middle of a big field with tree in the middle of it, and they would release like 5 dogs from each corner, about 20 dogs. And my job was to run as fast as I can and get on the tree in the middle, and to climb it as fast as I can so that in case we go to the forest and our lives are in jeopardy, I could find a safe spot. And so I did this for almost like few months, and then I started going hunting with these people.

I hunted so many things—you name it. I hunted elephants, antelopes, all sorts of dangerous animals, even lions. You look at my legs; I actually have a scar on my knee because my kneecap popped out from hunting a lion. I did this till I was almost 11 years old.

My entire life, all I really wanted to see was a car. And I remember as a kid, I used to walk miles and miles just to see a car. Sometimes, my grandmother used to get so upset with me because when I would leave, I would not tell her, because if I told her, she is not going to let me go. Most of the time, my friends and I would get together and go, and we still would not get to see a car which was always very disappointing. I always enjoyed hearing stories about cars whenever some of my friends would go to the city and come back. In spite of hearing all the fascinating car stories, my desire to see one for myself still lingered.

Ultimately, my desire became a reality when my mother came to the village one day and fulfilled a promise she had once made to me: to take me to the city to see cars. I could still remember her walking up to me and calling me by my African name, "Kojo" which stems from the day of the week I was born. I was born on Monday which is called Kojoda in Twi, "You remember I told you I was going to take you to the city to see cars?" The reply of course was "Yes!" She then said, "Today is the day."

Woody Woodward:
And you're 11 years old?

C. Appiah-Knudsen:
Yes. "Today's the day." I remember I was over at my aunt's house with my brother and sister. My brother and sister had to move and go live with my aunt at that time, and go to school. So I was the person who provided the money for school fees, books, medical, everything. Everything that I got from hunting in the forest, I would sell it, and whatever amount of money I made went directly toward my siblings' schooling.

I thought that if my siblings could go to school and achieve the best in life, they would help me to also achieve my goals and my dreams. So I was literally sacrificing my life for them. I remember borrowing my cousin's pair of shoes and a shirt in order to go to the city with my mother. I still have the shirt up to now. When my mother and I boarded a car for the first time, I was overwhelmed with joy. I felt as if I was on the top of the world. I could not even believe what was happening. My dream was to see one and here I was sitting in one.

A definite part of it was the very first time I saw lights. I was so terrified that I would not get close to it because I thought that I would get burnt. My mother brought me to the capital city of Ghana, which is Accra. I kid you not; there were thousands and thousands of cars. I was excited like even to see a traffic light, and my mom had to explain to me what a traffic light really was. But to make a long story short, my mother took me to this elderly guy who I've never met before.

These guys took us to a house, an apartment complex, where we stayed till almost 8:00 at night, and while we were there, there were these two men who came in with a taxi, and they put a handkerchief in my mouth and they tied it, and they told me not to make a sound, because if I do, they will kill me. As my mother led the way, we got into the taxi. I later went in a boat by myself where we stayed there for almost two weeks.

Woody Woodward:
You were trapped in a boat for two weeks.

C. Appiah-Knudsen:
Yeah. We stayed there for almost two weeks. And then when we got out of the boat, that was my very first time I saw a white person, and I freaked out—I literally freaked out. I was having a nervous breakdown. I had never seen a white person before. It's kind of funny.

Woody Woodward:
And where were you?

C. Appiah-Knudsen:
We were in Netherlands. We had landed in the Netherlands. We got into Amsterdam, and here we were in the midst of bunch of white folks. I remember clearly being so cold, and shivering, because it was in middle of the winter over there. My mom and I went and we boarded a train for Belgium. The very first time we arrived in Brussels, we went to somebody's house and we rang the doorbell. Nobody came out, and my mom told me, "Hey, let's go walk around.

We'll come back." And as we were going, I asked my mother, "Why are we here? Who are these people?" My mom was somebody that really did not like to talk. She would say, "Do not ask her questions, do not ask her questions." Failing to heed her warning could put you in a very uncomfortable problem. And so she was quiet; she kind of ignored what I was trying to ask, and at some point, I told her, "I'm not moving a foot unless you tell me where we are going and why we are here. Who are these people?" And that's when my mother and I have one of the most profound conversations that I will never forget. She looked at me, and she said, "Kojo, I admire everything you do. I'm sorry that I haven't been the mother that you wanted me to be, and I brought you here so that you and I can have a better life, so that we can go back home and help your siblings. You don't have to hunt anymore to do such a thing." I was beginning to believe my mom at that point, but then everything turned sideways.

I told my mom I was hungry and I wanted something to eat. I watched my mother walk across the street from where I was standing. She said I should stay there and she'd be right back. But my mother never came back. I was later taken into Juvie, because in Belgium, once you've given birth to a child, they pay the child to go to school. And so if you under 18 and you get caught doing school hours in the street, your parents will have to answer a lot of questions from the police. They will literally send you to the Juvenile until your family comes and claims you.

That's when the social workers get involved, everything. At this time, I have no documentation, anything that shows where I'm from, where I live, I did not speak French, I did not speak Dutch, no English, nothing except Twi. For over two and a half years, I stayed in Juvenile. The entire time I was in Juvenile, I was fed spaghetti every day. I got so sick and tired of eating it that there were days that I could not even force it the down my throat. This experience scared me so much that I don't like spaghetti. If you are going to ever invite me to your house, please don't feed me spaghetti. I have had my fair share of spaghetti.

I was later discovered by a former worker that was originally from Africa. He was retired but he came there often to visit his colleagues, and he used to be a caseworker. This man happened to come from Ghana, where I am from. I was from the south part of Ghana and he was from the northern part of Ghana. Fortunately, I could speak his dialect, because Ghana has so many different dialects. One day I was in my cell, and this guy walked by, looked at me, and did not say a word to me. Not long after our strange encounter, I found out that his name is Francis. He approach me one day and said, "Woho te sen?" which means "how are you" in my language. That was the first time in over two and a half years I have heard something that sounded familiar to me. So Francis and I quickly became friends, and he wanted to know what was going on, and I told him the story, what had happened. He couldn't believe it. He had a hard time believing it. And I said, "Well, why am I here, then?" And I remember he took me to his house to be able to investigate this case.

As I was sitting in his house for the very first time I saw these two sisters on TV playing against each other in a tennis match. I would later come to know the two sisters as the Williams sisters who still dominate the game of tennis today. And then came two gentlemen with a badge from his church, and did a small service for him. As they were leaving, one of them turned around and looked at me very strangely. I had no idea who these men were.

Right after they exited, Francis turned to me and said, "Hey, do you know what those guys just said? I replied, "No." I did not know the language to even understand what they were saying. Francis continued, "The one who was staring at you said that he feels like he needs to help you." In fact, at that time I was very negative about life. All I wanted to do was to go back to Ghana, and I do what I did to take care of my grandmother and my two siblings. It was very hard because I had no one to talk to. I could not speak French, or Dutch to converse with anyone besides Francis.

A few weeks after my strange encounter with the two men from the church, I started attending church with Francis. The first time I walked into the church, it felt very weird because it had been years since the last time I went in one. I did not know anyone and no one knew me. I felt kind of awkward. That all changed when Francis began to introduce me to the members.

One of the families that he introduced me to was the Knudsens, an American couple working overseas for the U.S government. Just like most of the families I met, the Knudsens were super friendly. The couple asked Francis about me and he gave them water down version of my story. The Knudsens were so interested in my story that they later got together with Francis where he told them the whole story.

He told them of how my mother and I had been smuggled to Belgium by boat, and how my mother had vanished leaving me on the streets of Brussels. Soon after hearing my story, the Knudsen's became heavily involved in my life. Over the ensuing months, they somehow were able to work with the Belgium government and miraculously got me out of Juvenile. They then became my legal guardians. Although I did not understand English very well, I was able to develop a very good relationship with the Knudsens. They moved into their beautiful home in the outskirts of Brussels. I looked to the Knudsens for everything and they always went above and beyond to make me feel loved.

They later ask me whether I'd like become a member of the family through adoption. I did not know what adoption meant so without hesitation I asked, "What is adoption?" They explained to me that being adopted basically means becoming their child. I was astonished beyond measure. Here I was thinking they are going to figure out a way to send me back to Ghana to reunite with my family and then all of sudden they want me to stay and become their son.

I loved the Knudsens and I still do, but I could not deal with the thought of living with them without my two younger siblings around. I had always fought vigorously on their behalf prior to coming to Belgium. Because of them, I spent many sleepless nights hunting so that they can eat and go to school. They were everything to me. I had not seen or talked to them for years and I always thought of what it would be like to have them around. However, I had to ponder the adoption proposal for many nights before I gave the Knudsens an answer.

Ultimately, I gave them an answer that they were not anticipating. The answer I gave them came out like this, "I have a brother and a sister back in Ghana and you cannot take me away from them. I do not want you to adopt me without them." The response they gave me surprised me. They said, "Okay, what about if we adopt all three of you so that you guys can stay together?" I replied with the question, "How is that possible?" That's when they sent somebody to Africa.

They found out where I was from. They went to my village, and that was when they met my birth mother who was in a very critical condition, dying from a breast cancer. And they asked for permission to adopt me, my brother and sister, and she gave the permission. But for all these years, I never really took the time to ask myself why all these things happened because my anger and disappointment in my mother had a great hold on me. How could this happen? Am I even any good to society? How can my own birth mother do such a thing?

But sometimes in life when things like this happen, they happen for a reason. I doubted myself. I thought I was not good enough. Otherwise, why would my mother bring me to this strange place and desperately leave me on the street? At the time of the adoption, I was 17 years old. For the first time in my life, I got to go to school. I spent the first 17 years of my life hunting to support my siblings and now I had to go to school to find out what school was all about.

While my peer group was out having fun, I would be having one on one study session with my tutor learning my ABCs. It was hard enough learning the basics of school; it was even harder not being able to relate to my peers. In spite of it, I managed to immerse myself in extracurricular activities. I joined the track team because I was used to running from all the hunting back in Ghana. My running ability not only gave me the opportunity to make friends, but it also gave me the opportunity to tour many parts of Europe.

That first year I was at the school, I turned 18, and was still struggling to learn to write. I could remember clearly the very first day my siblings and I started school. My younger brother and I were asked to write a short essay about ourselves individually and the only sentence I was able to write down was, "My name is Christian Appiah-Knudsen from West Africa, Ghana," and that was all I could write. My brother, on the other hand, wrote a three page essay in less than an hour. I was shocked. This experience diminished my confidence level so drastically. From that time on, I started to doubt myself and what I was capable of doing. I was glad that I joined the track and field team because it rekindled that confidence. For the first time at the school, I found something in which I could out beat all the kids. I wanted to be somebody so I exerted every effort to be the very best athlete. Do you know the expression "Whatever you do, do it well so that you can walk away feeling good?" That was exactly what I did.

My absolute commitment to track and field did not last that long because I got back from an event in France and my mother had already packed my belongings. As soon as I walked in the house, she came up to me and without even welcoming me home like usual. The first words that came out of her mouth were, "You are moving to Utah. I packed your stuff and here is $150.00 for expenses. Your flight leaves in three days."

Woody Woodward:
From Belgium.

C. Appiah-Knudsen:

Yes, from Belgium, "You're moving to Utah" was what she looked me in the eyes and said. She said, "Right now, I'm looking at you as a little eagle. You know the bird eagle?" She said, "I'm going to send you out there as a little eagle, but I want you to come back with strong wings as a big eagle." I didn't understand what she was trying to say. I was so furious about the sudden move because I did not know anything about Utah or where it is located on the map of America

All I knew was that one of my uncles was going to meet me at the airport. That was it. And I was going to live with my grandmother for some time until I could afford to find an apartment. However, here I was at the age of 18 about to fly on an airplane for the very first time. I remember she told me, "When you get in the plane and they ask you what you want to eat, you have to say, 'Rice.' I know you don't like most of the food that we have here because you're not used to it. If you don't specifically ask for rice, you will be offered something you are not used to eating."

I remember clearly sitting in the airplane, and a flight attendant came up and asked what I wanted to eat. She politely asked, "Coffee or tea?" The answer I gave her was "Rice" because that was what my mother told me to say. It was so funny everybody was laughing at me, because I said it so loud. That was an experience I will never forget.

When I got to Utah, I had to go to this place called Children's Club where I used to ride my bicycle about 20 miles every day to go learn my alphabet, trying to get my GED.

I tried to get my GED for five times in a row, and I failed all five attempts. There were so many times I wanted to give up, but I knew I have something bigger to live for, and I could not give up that easily. On the sixth attempt, I passed the GED. I told myself if I can get my GED, then I can attend college. I enrolled myself in classes at Utah Valley University in 2008. It was a very different atmosphere because the expectation was harder. Almost everyone I had the opportunity to meet knew precisely the major to pursue. I, on the other hand, I did not even know where to begin. With the help of my counselors, I started taking classes for my generals. It was intense and for me to keep up with everyone, I had to turn in my assignments in a week in advance. On the first day of every semester, I would go to the teacher and I would say, "Sir, I would like to know all the assignments that need to be submitted to you, so that I can start now." And that was what I did the entire time. They would give me all the homework. I would work on it at my own pace. So if I am to write a 20-page paper, I start on it maybe three weeks before the due date.

I did not put it off until the last minute because I am not one of those students who could write a 20 page paper from scratch in three hours and still turn in a very good paper. I do not have that ability. My ability was to do a small part of the work so every day, my goal was to write at least maybe a page. I would work on it and try to edit it, and sometimes, I finish it. I would take it to the writing lab. They would tell me everything I have written is garbage and I would have to go and start all over again.

I didn't even know how to do research. Regardless, I was determined to learn and I realized that it did not matter how long it would take me to get there. As long I turned in my 20 pages on the due date, then that was all that mattered. I became good at what I did. Starting from being a D-minus student to becoming an A student, to me, is a great accomplishment. Moreover, I never dreamed of having a car. I became interested in learning how to drive. I went to the DMV to take my test to just get a driver's permit. I did it five times, and I failed. My sixth time, I was in Virginia. I went in and said, "I'm not going to bow down until I get this." And I got my driver's license in Virginia. When I returned to Utah, I took another test to switch my Virginia license to a Utah license. Fortunately, I passed with no problem. Soon after getting my license, I embarked on a mission to get a car. After months of hard work and dedication, I finally purchased my first car. The reason why I said I believe in possibility is that I never thought that I would ever go to school. But I'm a junior in college, studying for my bachelor's right now. That is a great accomplishment; that is a great possibility in life.

Second, I had an opportunity to meet with the President, the former President of United States of America, and the former secretary of state, Condoleezza Rice, a good friend, and a great mentor. I went from living in a remote village to meeting the then President of the United States. It was a very moving experience and since then, I never underestimate myself.

All I want people to know through my life stories is that no matter our background whether rich or poor, small or big, we have self-value. Often, we compare ourselves to others and what they have accomplished and we feel like we are nothing to society. I am convinced seeing the value we each possess leads to many great accomplishments in life. I came to Utah with only $150 in my pocket and by the age 21, I owned my own home, and a car. Look at all the possibilities.

This is something that I never believed I could have. When I go to my country in West Africa, Ghana, I'm viewed to be one of the richest people. I'm viewed as the person with a success story because for somebody as young as I am to have a car, that is amazing. So yes, I do believe in possibility. No matter what happens in life, we can overcome it. We choose to decide what we want to learn out of it. Mine has been a great, long journey with a lot of different experiences. My long-term goal right now in life is to become a motivational speaker.

I have the goal of meeting with John C. Maxwell one day, because he's my hero and I believe in possibility. Even though I do not know as I'm sitting here right now how I'm going to do that, I know I will. I never thought I would have the opportunity to meet a former President of the United States and talk to him, and having him even congratulate me on becoming an American citizen. So everything is possible with me, and that is why I want to share my story with others, so that they can believe in possibility and try to overcome the obstacles.

Woody Woodward:
When you talk to other—let's just call it Americans, if you will—who have had an easy life, and they complain, how do you tolerate their complaining?

C. Appiah-Knudsen:
I just look at the opportunity people in America are given and every time I see people complain, I just want to say, "You know what? It is better if you go to Africa, see how little people have it there, and they

are the happiest people ever." Here a kid will be 16 years old and will have his/her first car. Some of them do not even appreciate it. When I see that, it hurts because some people here feel so entitled to getting things the easy way that they do not take a full advantage of the many opportunities available to them. Kids in Ghana will do anything to go to school even if they have to walk 20 miles to get to the nearest school. In Ghana, kids walk in early morning in the dark to go to school five days a week. Sometimes they go the whole day without even eating. Here, kids, they don't have to worry about what they're going to eat the next day because mom will have their lunch box packed for them before they get on the bus for school. On top of all these privileges, most people have a very negative approach to life and do not learn to appreciate what they have available to them.

A lot of people make fun of my accent. They have no idea how I even came to learn to speak English, and most of the American English and everything. I have a hard time understanding it but at least, I know my yes and no. If I go to Africa right now, I could be speaking my language perfect, and no one can understand that because they never took the initiative. That's why I see all these people come in from Africa, they're trying to get in and fit into the society and everything. To me, you don't have to. You just have to be you, and learn the best that you can.

And so that's why I started giving speeches and helping people to see what is possible—that everything can be a possibility. It doesn't matter if you're born with differences. It doesn't matter if you're born short. This reminds me of a story of a gentleman that I met while I was doing the speech for the former Governor of Utah, which is John Junior Huntsman, and his wife, Mary Kay Huntsman. And I met this kid, and he's about four, four-and-a-half feet, and the kid was so negative simply because he was short.

Everybody makes fun of him. Because of that, he already smokes and drinks. I looked at him and I said, "You know, you are underestimating yourself. Can you see?" He said, "Yeah." "Can you talk?" He said, "Yes."

"Can you run?" He said, "Yes." "So why are you making your being short stop you from doing everything that you supposed to? Because all these people that are tall and looking good and everything, they can talk, they can see, just as much as you can. You have the same ability."

"Don't look at yourself and feel bad because when you do that you bring yourself down every single time." And that's when I pulled out my hundred dollar bill, and I told him, "I want to give you this hundred dollar bill, but before I give you my hundred dollar bill, I want to do something with the hundred bill and then decide if you still want the hundred dollar bill." So I crumbled the hundred dollar bill, and I said, "Do you want this hundred dollar bill?" He said, "Yes."

I put the hundred dollar bill on the dirt, stepped on it, and I said, "Do you still want it even though it's dirty?" He said, "Yes." And I said, "Why do you want my hundred dollar bill so bad?" And he said, "Because it's a hundred dollar bill." It doesn't change in value, no matter what I did to the money. And that's when I told the kid, "Okay, I'm not giving you this hundred dollar bill, but I want you to look at yourself as this hundred dollar bill. No matter how much everybody will make fun of you, no matter how much people will think you're short, you're still worth this hundred dollar bill. I also want you to do something. Go home, look at yourself in the mirror and say, 'I'm still worth it.'"

Without self-value inside us, we cannot see our potential in life; and I hope that helps answer your question.

Woody Woodward:
You have such a gift because of your tragedy to inspire people and to change people's perspective. Going forward with the rest of your life, what do you want your legacy to be?

C. Appiah-Knudsen:
Woody, right now back home in Africa, I have some few people, few kids that I'm trying to help. I don't have much to give, but I want to be the person that one day, if I die today, or if I'm walking around and somebody will see me, I want them to know me by name, or I want

them to remember me. I don't need the world's money to create a greater legacy because I want them to remember me for who I am, like Martin Luther King.

We still celebrate his day because of his greatness and ability to influence people to do good. That's what I want to leave behind as a legacy. To be able to have somebody to look at me, or look at my statue, or one day, read my book, and say, "Because of this person, I changed my perspective." I remember I gave a speech to a young adult in high school around 12th grade level. There was this kid that was really having a hard time, and I didn't even get the opportunity to meet him one-on-one.

But after I share my story about possibility and what they can do to overcome obstacles in life, the kid started making some changes. And recently I was at the gym and as I was working out, the kid walked up to me and said, "You're Christian, right?" And I said, "Yes." He smiled, "You came to my school. I was there, and then I remember what you said touched me so deeply that I decided that I wanted to change. I graduated one of the top in my class even though I felt I wasn't even going to graduate. Now I'm going to college."

He's actually attending Brigham Young University (BYU) right now, and all the great things that this kid is able to do. He said, "Because of what you said that day, it stuck to me and I can't forget about it. So I want to say thank you." That is the kind of legacy I want to leave behind, you know, Woody, for somebody to get influenced to be good, and to do good in the society.

Marième Faye

Marième Faye, the "Wealth Creation Coach" is the founder of "The Enlightened Financial Healing Group" and the creator of "Wealthy Women Academy." She is passionate about helping women entrepreneurs break through their financial limitations, so that they can create lasting wealth doing what they truly love and making a positive difference in the lives of people around the world on a global scale.

Marième grew up in Senegal, West Africa She attended college in Boston where she majored in finance. She has worked as a financial advisor, mentor, a mortgage loan officer, financial strategist, and a speaker.

Marième strongly believes that poverty is a "disease" of the mind that can be cured with her Financial Healing Blueprint combined with proven wealth creation strategies.

www.mariemefaye.com
www.wealthywomenacademy.com

Woody Woodward:

Marième, you've had a very interesting childhood and adult life. You started out in a very affluent family in Africa, went through poverty, and then turned your life back to have what you have now. Tell us more about your life in Africa and about yourself?

Marième Faye:

I was raised by a loving father who treated me like his little princess and spoiled me most of my life, and a mother who was very strict, over protective, and wanted me to be responsible, which made me think that she didn't love me. I truly didn't know how much my mother loved me until after my parents' divorce, when we bonded and became friends.

I am the oldest of 7 children; I have 5 sisters and 1 brother. I also grew up with a half-brother and a half-sister. I have been like a parent to my younger siblings most of my life and consider myself their "second mother."

One marked event in my life was being sexually abused on several occasions by six different men between the ages of 5-12 and came to the conclusion that I unconsciously didn't want to be a girl anymore. So I decided to become a "man" and was pretty much a tomboy until I was in my twenties. Some of my childhood friends smile when they see me now because they knew me as a tomboy and are delighted to see me embrace my feminine side.

To this date, my parents still do not know that I was abused. Back then, I was too afraid to lose my father's "love" or to get beat up by my mother. I was too ashamed to talk about it because I felt like it was my fault. So I buried it in my memory. I never mentioned it to anyone until I turned 31 two years ago and started my inner healing process to free myself from that trauma with a coach.

My parents' divorce in 2003 marked the beginning of a new era in my life, which literally turned everything upside down. I remember being sick for 6 months because my mind could not accept what was happening to me and my family. The doctors gave up on me knowing that my illness was more psychological than an actual sickness. They knew that I was the only one who could heal myself, which I did when I got tired of being sick.

My dad married a girl who was a couple of years older than me, I wasn't happy it about because I knew she just married him because of his money; everyone knew that except him.

He slowly "abandoned" his whole family and destroyed the relationships he had with all his children. He found out the truth about his new wife 9 years later after she left him with her two kids when he lost all of his wealth.

When I was about 24, my father sent me to school in Boston to "get rid of me." He was encouraged by his new wife who didn't want me around because he still had a soft spot in his heart for me. About a year later, I received a call from my dad, courtesy of my stepmother; he told me that I needed to take care of myself and find a way to pay my school fees because he wasn't going to do it anymore. That was the greatest gift they have given me, even though it appeared to be my worst nightmare at the time.

I was already helping my mother financially to raise my six siblings who were still very young. I became my family's provider and my mother's "only hope" from that point.

I literally lost myself because I made my family my one and only priority and didn't care much about anything else that was going on in my life. So I went into a depression phase. I was on the verge of suicide and lived in lack and poverty so they could be taken care of. In 2011, I met two of my mentors who helped me discover my life purpose, find myself again, and reclaim my personal power and life.

Woody Woodward:
Is that why you're very passionate today about helping women with the right mindset and helping them get to the level of success they want to have?

Marième Faye:
Yes, absolutely! When I became a personal development student and started to study successful business owners and entrepreneurs, I found out that they all had things in common: a strong mindset, very clear goals, and a plan to achieve them. The mindset is often the missing link because we have been programmed from childhood with a belief system that doesn't always serve us in a positive way.

We have been taught to live from the outside in, to use events and experiences in the outside world as a measuring stick that we compare ourselves to and judge ourselves by. We always come up short and then we feel bad about ourselves in one way or another, instead of living from the inside out, and expressing our inner greatness, getting out of our comfort zone, and creating the life we desire. In order to create success and real results in our lives and our business, we must first change the way we think. That will change the way we feel and act so that we can get what we have never had. We literally need to break through our own limitations which sometimes can go very deep into our belief systems as it involves past traumas, anger, resentment, guilt and other emotions that are preventing us from succeeding.

I was my very first client, and made the decision to change my life and create wealth in all areas of my life.

We all have the right to be rich and to live an amazing life while doing what we truly love to do, and expand our greatness.

Woody Woodward:
What do most people not know about your industry?

Marième Faye:
Everything is connected! Creating financial freedom, making money or wealth has "nothing" to do with money; it is about managing one's emotional state and life. If you don't teach your clients about mindset and discover what their habits and blocks are, they will only experience short-term success, if any. That is why we focus on helping our clients break through their limitations first, and then we dive into systems and strategies to help them thrive in their businesses doing what they truly love and map out a long-term wealth creation plan to get them ready for the future.

No one really wants money; we all want what money can do for us, and we all want to have the ability to make choices without money being a limiting factor.

Woody Woodward:

You are a busy businesswoman. How do you juggle all that you do on a daily basis?

Marième Faye:

I manage my activities, not time. I create time blocks on my calendar with my daily activities and reminders. That's how I keep my sanity and give myself room to be spontaneous and do what feels right to me in the moment.

Woody Woodward:

What advice would you give to entrepreneurs, other top achievers about time management? What technique do you use? What do you prefer to do to stay on top of all your goals?

Marième Faye:

Plan your week or days in advance and make yourself your number one priority. You cannot give from an empty "cup" so take the time to nurture yourself and schedule it on your calendar. As far as using a technique, I find "the power hour" or "morning ritual" a very powerful way to start a day. It consists of taking the time to exercise, meditate, spend some time dwelling in the energy of gratitude and connect with God or your understanding of the higher power through prayers, journaling and read an inspirational book before you start your day. It will put you in the right space and allow you to be more productive throughout your day.

To stay on top of my goals, I first prioritize my activities, and then I schedule them by doing the most important and hardest things first. I would recommend using an online calendar to manage your daily activities like Google calendar, and set up reminders so you can stay on top on things and maintain harmony in your life and your business.

Woody Woodward:

You have a coaching academy called Wealthy Women Academy. What is the main focus of that academy and how does it help women?

Marième Faye:

I created Wealthy Women Academy to help women entrepreneurs break through their financial limitations so that they can create lasting wealth while doing what they truly love and making a positive difference in people's lives.

Our academy helps women who are struggling financially, stuck in their business, the women who want to take their business to the next level of growth. We first create a solid wealth creation mindset, then we apply our proven wealth creation strategies to help them get their desired results.

In the process, we help them create an empowering financial story, and fully experience life without financial limitations keeping in mind the present and also preparing for a comfortable retirement when the time comes.

We are about empowering and educating women entrepreneurs to live a rich and abundant life filled with joy and bliss. Women are givers and ultimately, helping them will create a ripple effect of abundance on a global level.

Woody Woodward:

From your experience, what's the number one thing that gets in someone's way from being successful?

Marième Faye:

A poor belief system filled with unconscious beliefs and habits that ultimately sabotage their success. That is why you see a lot of people experience short-term success when they have a goal in mind, but ultimately fail and fall short. You can make a conscious decision to pursue what you desire, and work towards creating new habits, but until you change your beliefs, you will only experience short-term success.

Woody Woodward:

How do you know if you have a bad mindset? So how do you correct your mindset?

Marième Faye:

Your current results will tell if your mind is your ally or your worst enemy. Results do not lie. Our minds work like a computer. When you have computer viruses, your computer doesn't work properly, so you need to use an anti-virus to get rid of the viruses. Then you can install a new program that is more in alignment with what you want to create and you learn to use the program by repetition.

Our minds work the same way. First, you diagnose or become aware of what your blocks and limiting beliefs are. Then you need to get very clear on your intentions, dissolve your unconscious counter-intentions, visualize yourself already in possession of what you desire and create simple daily actions that you can easily implement. Most importantly, have someone like a coach or a mentor to hold you accountable for your results and share with you strategies and blueprints that will accelerate your learning process and get you the results you desire faster.

Woody Woodward:
Is there a book that you've read that helps? Is there a book that you recommend that would help people with their mindset?

Marième Faye:
Psycho-Cybernetics by Maxwell Maltz.

Woody Woodward:
What is the greatest risk you've ever taken? And was it worth it?

Marième Faye:
The biggest risk I've ever taken was to change my mindset and my belief system. You see, I was raised as a Muslim and in a society that has certain traditions and a culture that we lived by. There are lots of things that I liked about my life growing up, but at the same time, I found myself in a self-made "prison," wearing a veil of success on the outside, while living a lie on the inside in an effort to look good or perfect, and preventing others from truly knowing the real me. I was afraid of being rejected by not conforming to the rules, traditions

and culture that I grew up with. Being vulnerable and publicly talking about my family issues, my sexual abuse and other unfortunate events in my life, not only was I "exposing" myself but my family's secrets and that is not acceptable in our society. Being vulnerable and authentic was a very big risk, the risk to lose my family and friends. Since I have changed my mindset, the comments I make on Facebook have changed, too. I remember my older half-sister calling me one day and asking me if I was part of a cult after seeing my Facebook posts. She reminded me of who I was, where I came from, what my religion was, and whose daughter I was. She warned me about being spiritual because for her, it was dangerous. One of my best friends called me once when I started dating my "white" boyfriend who wasn't a Muslim and asked me literally if I was ready to dwell in hell for eternity for the love of a non-Muslim white man. Shifting from fear to love was the biggest risk I have ever taken and the best blessing I have ever received. And yes, it was worth it because I freed myself from the prison I built for myself over the years the prison of my own mind. I became aware of the self-punishment I imposed on myself for years, being vulnerable with my past pains from sexual abuse to poverty, and sharing it with people. I fully accept myself as a child of God and not as a "slave" of God as I was raised to believe as a Muslim, taking a leap of faith to build a relationship with God and demystifying some of the things that I was taught to fully stand in my power and embrace my truth.

Woody Woodward:
With that vulnerability, did you find that people actually opened up to you more and your relationships became more real versus a fake scenario?

Marième Faye:
Yes, and it was liberating! People got to know and see the real me. As a result, I connect with people on a much deeper level. I love the fact that I'm not attached to their opinions of me anymore, and I'm

OK with them loving or hating me; it is their choice and none of my business. Vulnerability and authenticity definitely create meaningful and real relationships.

Woody Woodward:

You're like many other successful people I've interviewed; they all hired coaches or mentors along the way. You even coach people, but yet you still hired coaches. What does it take to be a good mentor?

Marième Faye:

A good mentor has their clients' well-being in mind. It is someone who knows how it feels to be in their client's shoes, someone who knows their deepest pains, sees beyond their fears, someone who believes in them, sees their greatness, sees their potential, and has the ability to educate and guide them to achieve the results they really want with clarity and confidence while holding them accountable every step of the way.

Woody Woodward:

You've hired mentors; you are a mentor; you've been around a leadership genre for a long time. What does it take to be a good leader?

Marième Faye:

A good leader in my opinion is:
- Courageous: Courage is the first thing that comes to my mind, courage to stand for what you believe, courage to keep going when you are prosecuted, courage to believe in your message and fully stand by your words no matter what.
- Inspiring: Have the ability to inspire others to greatness, inspire them to follow you if they resonate with you and your message.
- Authentic: Be yourself. People want to be lead by the real you not a fake copy or image.
- Vulnerable: Be willing to show them that you are human and have weaknesses too.
- Empathetic: Show empathy. Show people that you walked their path or a similar one and know how they feel and what they have

been through, this creates instant connection.

- Committed: Be committed to your goals, dreams, to your mission and your vision.
- Persistent: Be OK with failing over and over again. Keep going and don't give up, especially when you are down on your knees and have the whole world against you.

Woody Woodward:
You've been on both sides of the fence, from poverty to profit. How do you define success?

Marième Faye:
Success for me means having the freedom and the choice to use my time, money and energy as I desire at any given time while living in harmony, joy and bliss in all areas of my life.

Woody Woodward:
It's a great definition. If money were not an object and you could do anything in this world and you knew you would not fail, what would you do?

Marième Faye:
Two things:

1. I would take my business global right now and establish my coaching academy in all the major cities in the world so that I can empower and educate women to create thriving businesses and create lasting wealth. Imagine a handful of purpose-driven women entrepreneurs making a difference in people's lives, contributing to the economic development of their countries and empowering others to stand in their greatness and live an abundant life; that is where my business is going.

2. Create a nonprofit organization and build orphanages for poor "street children" in African countries, give them a chance to live a better life by empowering and educating them starting in Senegal, West Africa and expand it globally.

Woody Woodward:
What's the greatest "Aha" moment you've had in your business?

Marième Faye:
Realizing that my personal and business lives are "one," that every thought, every feeling that I have has an effect not only on my personal life but also on my business, and on my bank account. Once that clicked, I studied the mind and learned to make it my personal ally and not my worst enemy. I am at a point where I can "see" my thoughts through the language that I speak (I studied conscious language and that helped with this process) and catch self-sabotage before it happens. As a result, I can correct myself and get back on track so I can be more productive and BE in alignment with my goals.

Woody Woodward:
How do you channel your fear into productivity?

Marième Faye:
I allow myself to feel fear because it always shows up for a Reason; it is a great teacher. Always question your fear. I acknowledge it and I ask myself why it is there. When I get my answer, I address it and keep moving forward. Being still and meditating help with that process.

Woody Woodward:
What advice and encouragement would you give to a budding entrepreneur?

Marième Faye:
- Clarity: Get very clear on what you want to do. Clarity equals results, and this is what most entrepreneurs struggle with at the beginning of their journey. They feel passionate about what they want to do, but are not clear on how to effectively communicate their message, who to deliver it to, or how to do what they really want to do.
- Purpose: Know the reason why you want a business; this will keep you focused and persistent, especially when times are challenging.

- Plan: Once you are clear on your goals, set up a plan to achieve them. I love doing things in steps; it makes it easier to follow. It is very effective to work backwards when it comes to setting goals. You can break down your goals to weekly or daily actions and create marketing campaigns and sales funnels accordingly.
- Hire a coach or a mentor in your field, preferably someone who is already successful at what you want to do, so that you can accelerate your success and have accountability for your results.
- Consistently work on mastering your mind so that you can control your emotional state and your results.
- Be persistent and never give up!
- Have faith; believe in yourself and in your mission or purpose.
- Make gratitude a priority and always show up to serve.
- Always BE in Alignment (ABIA) Spiritually with God or your understanding of the higher power.
- Always build meaningful relationships and nurture them. Seek to give value rather than always asking what you can get.
- Join a mastermind group, which is a group of like-minded people who help each other succeed and support each other.

Woody Woodward:
What do you like best about what you do?

Marième Faye:
I love seeing the transformation that happens in my clients' lives. I love seeing them shift, get amazing breakthroughs, realize how powerful and amazing they are, and choosing to become who they want to be. My financial healing process changes my clients' financial story and has a positive effect on the rest of their lives. You can't put a price on that. It is very beautiful to witness and it is always an honor to be a guide in that process. Being able to see them fulfilled, happier and joyful in their life and business is absolutely priceless.

Woody Woodward:
If you could share any advice with someone what would it be?

Marième Faye:

Always BE yourself. Believe in yourself. Get to know who you truly are. Learn to be in alignment with God, your higher self or the universe. Master your mind. Build meaningful relationships. Be present. Have faith. Dwell in love and always be grateful. Always show up to serve and you will live a rich and harmonious life.

Woody Woodward:

What do you want your legacy to be?

Marième Faye:

An empowered world that believes in personal power, love, abundance, joy, freedom, and bliss. A world that believes in using financial wealth as a tool to serve, create a better life for others, as well as for themselves. A world that dwells in love, self-love, and unconditional love. A world that has faith, courage, gratitude, wealth, and infinite possibilities for everyone. A world that only speaks one language: LOVE.

The only limitations that exist are the ones we set upon ourselves. My contribution, using finances and wealth creation as a vehicle, fulfills me. I know that when money is not making decisions for people, then they will create a better life. They will make empowering choices instead of making decisions based on how much money they have in their accounts and settling for poverty, pain and unnecessary suffering.

Woody Woodward:

Any last words?

Marième Faye:

I am leading a worldwide financial revolution, and healing poverty from within. Please join me; let's all do our part and make this world a better one for future generations.

Be powerful, live with purpose, and believe in infinite possibilities!

JoAnne Kell

Joanne Kell is currently writing a book containing the life stories of five success-ful women who are survivors, not survivors in the over-used sense of the word, because, in her opinion, we are all survivors as humans to some extent. Rather, women who have not just lived to tell about it, but ones who have used their experiences to become strong, powerful and successful, living through many ob-stacle and tragedies. They are about helping others without enabling them. They live for their loved ones. These women will be given the opportunity to get their story on paper. Joanne will help guide the process by organizing a fundraiser for them to help cover the cost of their time away from work and family, help-ing them open up to some deeply protected experiences, ones that through the survival process, may have been stuffed away. Allowing them to heal in a way, which keeps them moving forward in life, not letting themselves succumb to the role of a victim.

She is a mother of two, a grandmother of three and she devotes most of her time to her family. She is a successful Real Estate investor.

Woody Woodward:

Many times when a person is reading a book like this, they often feel the author has no idea how they feel. Your story is different than most. You have gone down deeper than most people could imagine. Will you share with us your story?

JoAnne Kell:

My first memory is when I was about three years old. I remember being sexually abused by an uncle who had lived with us our entire childhood and he would do it on a very regular, daily basis. I remember being very close to him and I didn't know any different. There was nothing I could do to change my thinking because I was so young. But throughout time, he was not the only one. My father was on the CB radio a lot, and he would bring in different people, different friends into our home and they would end up being abusers to me as well.

As we got older, my brother began being my escort. He would take me to places that I would have to go, and somehow I just knew when I went there, that sex was going to happen. When I had told friends and they'd say, "Why didn't you stop it? Didn't you say no? Didn't you leave?" I mean, here I was 12, 13. I can run, but the thing is I had experienced it my whole life. There was nothing telling me to change it. My gut was distorted by then, and at that time I wanted to break free, but not sure how. Even though the abuser was someone I did not know, it's not like I knew I had a choice. It was always that way.

When I left home at 14, I didn't know that my whole childhood my father had been arranging these situations and using my brother to escort me there. I just thought that I was predisposed for sexual situations and that's just the way it was. When I finally left home, it was because my father had punched me and it caused my face to split open and blood was everywhere. At that point, I had to leave. I went to a person's home that I had met shortly after we moved into Portland. They took me to the hospital and there was a report made. When my father was questioned, he told them, "Keep her, She was an uncontrollable little brat." The crazy thing is the reason for leaving was my father's physical abuse, not for the constant sexual abuse he was causing.

We grew up in La Crosse, Wisconsin. When I was 11 years old, they sent my brother, sister and me to Minnesota to live with my uncle, who was my dad's twin brother. We believed our uncle was going to kill our father. We thought for many years because he had given up some information that caused my uncle to go to prison. By the time he got out of prison and found us, it turned out that I loved him more than my dad, for sure. I just thought he was great. My dad was very, very strict. We always had to wear dresses. We could never wear pants. However, my uncle let me wear pants. He actually took me to K-Mart, and that was the first experience I ever had going into a real store and buying something that was not leftovers or hand-me-downs.

We were only able to stay with him for three months. That was really sad. I did not want to go, but he sent us down to Oklahoma, where my parents had headed off to get some kind of place to live or get established somehow, get their welfare checks and Social Security checks coming in. Once we got to Oklahoma with our parents, we were there for about a year, and then they took their checks, bought us all Greyhound tickets to Los Angeles.

My parents' favorite thing to do was to go out for coffee. My father would meet different people that he would bring home, many that would turn into abusers. I didn't know until years later that my mom knew. My mom was very weak. I knew that even as a child because my father would spank her the same way he would spank us kids when she made him mad. My mom died probably 13 years ago. Because I saw her as her as very weak, I knew she couldn't really protect us. I don't know if she knew the extent of what was really going on.

When we got to Los Angeles, we ended up living on the streets for about three months. We were able to find a shelter and we stayed there for a couple weeks and then we got an extension for another week or so. Once we had to leave the shelter, we were back on the streets again. We would stay literally from one 24-hour restaurant to another. My parents would go in and they would get coffee so that we could stay off the streets and not just be wandering around when it was late.

To this day because of that experience, I don't take for granted going out to eat in a restaurant. It's my favorite thing to do. When I go out, I do not have a sense of entitlement. If they bring me something wrong, it's not a big deal. I don't make an issue of it. I remember these people would be sitting there and they would have waitresses and waiters bringing them food. I remember thinking, "Oh, my gosh, how lucky! These people are so lucky that they can just have people bring them stuff. Not only that, but then they can walk away and leave some of it still sitting on their plates." I wanted so bad to just go eat off these people's plates, and I don't care that they left it. I wanted to. I was starving as I would smell food going by and there was nothing, nothing, nothing that we could do to have any of it. We were so hungry most of the time. We rarely got to eat.

I would be so tired at times that the dishes clanking made my head hurt and I would just cry. To this day, I can't stand the sound of dishes clanking. I remember one time my mom would walk me across the street—we were literally in downtown Los Angeles—and there was a park where she sat down on a bench and I laid my head in her lap and I thought, "Oh, my gosh! That's so nice of my mom. She's just sitting here and she's probably tired too, but she's just letting me lay on her lap." I thought that was so nice of her. Then just as we got situated these police officers came up on their horses and told my mom that the park was closed. So we had to get up and walk back across the street to the cafe that my dad, brother and sister were at.

There were a few days that we were put up into a hotel in Los Angeles. It was the Cecil Hotel on Second Street, it was a dump. It had rats and roaches that were freaking HUGE! These roaches were so huge, and they were crawling out of the faucets in the sink that was in the room. I mean, it was disgusting, and you could hear the rats in the dumpsters that were even brought up in an elevator.

One day, I remember my brother and I were downstairs playing in the lobby on a pinball machine. When I think back on this story when I was a kid, it just blows my mind. As kids, we were playing this pinball machine and this couple walked up. The man was very impressed with how my brother was playing pinball. So being young, we're like, "Do you want to meet our parents?" and they're like, "Sure."

So we take them upstairs, and introduce them to our parents. Well, this very night, my parents let me go with this couple back to their hotel. They're names were Robert and Bobbie Rock---. They let me go and stay at the hotel with these people! It was a man and a woman, so I wasn't as scared as maybe I could've been if the wife had not been there. I stayed the night, and the next morning, we came back to the Cecil Hotel, picked up my family, went to the storage unit, grabbed all of our stuff, put it up on their '65 Ford and we started to drive. We went across the country. We went touring the United States I guess, and we would do it by hustling churches.

Robert and Bobbie would pretend to be my parents and at some point, I became closer to them and wished I was theirs. My brother and sister would be with my mom and dad. I sat in the front seat between the two of them; my mom and dad sat in the back with my brother and sister. I would go into these churches with them and I would hear what they would say. They would say we were trying to get about 200 miles down the road and our car broke down. We ran out of gas. We're hungry and we just can't drive any farther. Using stories similar to that is how we got around the entire United States just by getting put up in different hotels from time to time, getting a meal and getting a fill-up on gas. The only area we didn't hit was up in the New York wing, but otherwise we went through everything else. We got down to Florida, and then we made our way back to San Jose, which is where we ended up for about nine months before we moved to Portland, Oregon, which is were where I jumped off at 14. I was a runaway for a long time. After my father hit me and I left, he turned me in as a runaway to make things harder on me, even though he told the police to keep me.

Woody Woodward:
Honestly, your story is amazing. And then when you ran away, your life did not get easier. Help the readers understand what you went through at age 14.

JoAnne Kell.:
Well, when I ran away, like I said, it was when my dad punched me.

I had met a friend when I was only there in Portland for about three months. And, by the way, all this time I never did get put back in school because there was no place that we ever stayed long enough for me to get back in, so the last grade of school that I ever did see was the fifth grade. When I left home, obviously there was a lot of situations. When you live on the streets, there's not a lot you can do. I stole to get by. I didn't have any place to keep anything so I couldn't steal a whole lot. I didn't steal and resell stuff. I just stole what I needed.

My dad actually started me smoking when I was eight years old. He gave me my first pack of cigarettes, and it was Camel Straights and I smoked them watching *Hee Haw, B.J. and the Bear* and *CHiPs*. I smoked a whole pack. I was kinda sick, but it wasn't enough to make me not smoke, and so I ended up quitting smoking when I got pregnant with my daughter when I was 16, but I stole cigarettes because that's what I did. I smoked. I would steal food, clothes, cigarettes, whatever it was that I needed. I would have to break into houses to have a place to sleep that was safe. I had been raped several times while I was a runaway and held up and shot at.

There was no way to avoid it, and a lot of these things happened in the daytime, so there wasn't a safe place. But when it was nighttime, I would usually go back to a house a couple times. I would break in. I'd break a window and I'd try to break one that was down low, because I remember feeling bad that I had to break and destroy something that someone else had to pay to fix. When I would go in the house, I knew that they had running water and they had heat if they had a "for sale" sign on them, at least back then. And so I would sleep with my back up against one of the heat panel boards on the far wall, that way, if I heard something, I could get away hopefully soon enough. If I'd seen somebody coming towards me, I could get up and run and get out.

I eventually met my daughter's father, who was extremely abusive. He was a member of the Bloods gang, and back then, it was very aggressive between the Bloods and the Crips. In California right before we moved to Portland, there was something called "pulling Murphy." It was basically where you pretend that you're a prostitute. I remember never wanting to get in with a guy that was younger than me because he could probably run faster, and I would get scared and my knees would quit working. At least, that was my fear. I knew I had to be able to run faster than the person that I was trying to take the money from. "I need to see the money," I would tell him and then he would give me the money and I would take off running.

I did that a couple times, and even though it was scary, it was a way to get money, and I didn't feel bad about it because I thought the guys are gross anyway and deserved to get robbed. When I got to Portland, my daughter's father's brother (my daughter's uncle) had a girlfriend who was a prostitute. I remember feeling so bad. I felt really bad for her, and so I would try to show her how to do it without having to do anything sexually with the men. Then I started showing my friends, the runaway girls that I met. We kind of all hung out together. I ended up getting shot at a couple times, knives pulled on me, even cut a few times, and it was because I was trying to show these other girls how to do that without having to have sex with these men.

This is what I did until I got pregnant with my daughter. When my daughter was about 6 months old, Russell, being as abusive as he was, tried to punch me and knock me down a flight of stairs while I was holding my daughter. That was when I left. I felt so compelled. This little baby, my daughter, could die because of him. I think it was like I was obsessed with her. I didn't want her in a baby stroller because it was too far from me. What if somebody came and took her from me or maybe a car pulled up too close and hit her? I was so scared. I would put her in a front pack or before I had anything like that I had a bag I would put her in to stay safe. I left the hospital and I think it was because Russell had a friend that came to pick me up with a car seat.

When I left the hospital, I had no place to go. Russell and I weren't together at the time or we kind of were, but he had another girlfriend to keep who also had a baby. He'd find a place for me to go and I would stay with his friends for a day or so, here and there. Then I would have to find a place to stay if Russell didn't come back around and I didn't know where to go. I would figure it out. I would put her diapers in this pink duffel bag I have it to this day; I will always keep it. I would put all my stuff in, put her diapers down, I'd roll her up the way the nurses taught me to in the hospital. A tight swaddle and I would place her down on her diapers, pull up the straps, throw her over my shoulder and off I'd go with my baby inside. I think about that to this day. I mean, I never wanted to be a mom, but I have motherly instincts that have kept me very protective in a way.

Even though I never wanted to be a mom, and to this day, I honestly think if I could go back and do it over, I would definitely undo it. It's such a responsibility to protect and to care for children, and I feel like there are people on the planet that do it alright and raise beautiful people. But there's so many things that your child can encounter and there's nothing you can do about it. To watch your child hurt is worse than any other pain you could ever experience, not even your spouse. Watching anyone hurt is very difficult, but when you see your child hurting, it's excruciating. And when there's nothing you can do about it, it's even harder. When I think of my son in his condition, I can't tell you how many times I have to say, "I'm sorry, honey. I'm sorry, honey," and it gets very difficult to not be able to fix it, to not be able to do anything except for say "I'm sorry."

There are a lot of things I can't protect my daughter from, and I wish I could. I understand people have to make their own choices, and I used to feel very, very guilty about my daughter's case. I was a single mom, how could I have done better at that time, but you know what? I wasn't just a single mom; I was an extremely abused homeless kid with no one to turn to. I did the best that I could, and I loved her immensely. I had my own apartment when I was 17. I got my driver's license and my GED while I was 18. There were things that I set out to do and I did them. I wished, however, I would have been more capable at the time I became a mother. I also wish I would have been able to make an educated and willing choice to be a mother like when I was 25 or 30. That would've been great. I love my children and I love my grandchildren, but the pain I have suffered over the years as a mom, under the same circumstances, I do believe most people would rethink it as I have.

Woody Woodward:

Your story's incredibly inspiring, and we haven't even covered the rest of your life, but how do you keep the mindset to keep going?

JoAnne Kell:

When I was a little girl, I have to say, for some reason, I felt very different, and I know it wasn't because of the abuse that I was dealing with on a very regular basis. I felt different when I would do things like go to the grocery store and I would try to shop differently than my mom would because we were always hungry. I was only 10 years old I would go through store and push the cart around to get what I would get for my family. I would put everything back where it came from when I was done.

I would dress up in hand-me-downs and at times they were women sizes. When I would wear them I would stand away from my parents at the bus stop and I would just know people would think I was on my way to work, and that I was not with that group of people over there (my parents, brother and sister).

I want to give credit to everybody who ever said to me when we would be out and about and my parents would introduce us all and they would say, "Are you sure this one's yours? Are you sure she's from the same parents? I don't know about that?" And there would be comments like that throughout my entire life, and I swear that has to be where I get the idea I am not like them. I am not like the family I had growing up. I am so much different, and that kept me going, and hearing that, I didn't look like them, I didn't act like them, and I certainly did not think like them. As I got older and I take in more information and I process it all, I was very different. I am now like my spiritual family.

When I first watched *The Secret*, it was about three years ago, and I could not believe that. I felt like throughout my life I had used it (the Secret) and didn't realize it. I didn't know I was doing it, but I did it. Prior to seeing *The Secret*, I felt like I lived in a fantasy land my whole life. It was not really a fantasy land; I was just applying the secret. I was pretending that everything around me was different than it was, and I would live as if that's the way it was. I was doing that on a very regular basis so when I learned that it was an actual process that you could do, I just try to implement it in different ways now.

Many times throughout the years when I have been spiritually weak, I think *The Secret* and my children are the reason why I've done things the way that I have and been able to keep my wits about me and my sanity, because sometimes stress has been almost to much to bear, and honestly, they say what doesn't kill you makes you stronger. There were places in my life where I think that has got to be the stupidest thing I've ever heard because, I mean, sometimes I have been on my emotional and mental deathbed, and I'm like, "How in the heck is this ever gonna make me stronger?" But what happens is that when you go through so much turmoil and you actually have a reason to keep going, there's nothing you can do about it except change the way you think and feel about it. When I pondered that I was the spiritual head for my children to guide them, every time I hit a low, that is what helped me not give up, but what made me move forward was *The Secret*.

For instance, when things got so bad with my husband, it's not that I didn't care; I just put it in a different place so that I did not internalize it or take it personally. If I'm not going to change it or I cannot change it, then I have to think differently about it or I would let it kill me.

I went home one night and my husband was drinking. I would say he was drunk by the way he was treating my son and the way he responded to me when I got home. There was nothing I could do about it. He was never going to change that; at least, he wouldn't do it for us. I tried not to fight with him about it after time because it did not change anything and I was tired of the "sorry" that would come later. I can't say I never did, but we got to a point where I never fought about it. If he was going to drink, I just said, "Give us space." But out of guilt, he would treat us poorly. I would leave the home. There were times I spent the night in the car with my son at the time recently, severely disabled because of it, and I was not gonna do that with my grandson.

When my grandson came along, I knew if I did not leave, my grandson would have his first few years in life experiencing what my first two children went through. I could not be stronger for my two, but I was not going to see this little life so innocent be hurt by all of the negativity that we had lived prior. My grandson has never heard an argument, has never heard a fight, and as far as I can help it, he never will.

The night after my husband had been drinking was the night his family came and helped him to leave.

Woody Woodward:

When you felt down and depressed, what books did you read to pull yourself out?

JoAnne Kell:

I would say the *How to Win Friends and Influence People* is one of my favorite books, and I also would say Stephen Covey's *Seven Habits of Highly Effective People*. I want to say it's one of my favorites because I did love the book, but I tell you what. It put me in a real big turmoil for a while. I second-guessed everything about myself with that book. I did grow a great deal from it, although I hit a little depression with that book. I really started thinking, "Who am I?" So, those two books really had the biggest impact on me. I also had my friends as great life coaches. I went through Tony Robbins' series when I was twenty three and then when I got remarried to my second husband, I had my second husband do it with me. So I've been through Tony Robbins' series twice.

Woody Woodward:

Do you think your soul-searching of "Who am I?" helped propel yourself to move forward?

JoAnne Kell:

Absolutely. I feel like in really trying to be different than my family growing up, as I spent my life trying to do, when I read the *Seven Habits of Highly Effective People*, it really made me pluck out the habits or flaws that would stop me. Not that I don't have flaws still, I do, I really do, but it really made me rethink traits that even as a Christian, I did not realize I should change. Had I not read that book or referred to it over time, I probably wouldn't have gone through what I've been through in the last fifteen years successfully. During the last fifteen years, I have been through many situations with my second husband, my children; daughter leaving home early, son's disabling disease, losing my home, building and losing my business, my husband and I were sued by the state of Georgia in the prior industry we were in. I had a friend who worked in my home shortly after we met she was a consultant for my company. We worked together. We worked out together. We shopped together. We did everything together and became very close. So close to our family that she was also the secondary caregiver for my son. If he needed to do something or just wanted to hang out, whatever to help him, she would do it. My son loved her and her husband so much. He wanted to go with them if anything ever happened to me. This friend was unbelievable to me. There was probably not a friendship in the world that was closer than I was with her in the year and a half it took us to become that close. She was like my little sister. She looked up to me. I wanted her to experience everything I did. If she didn't have money, I didn't care I paid for everything. Whatever we did, wherever we went, I paid for everything. I would take her on trips with me and I would put her in the lead just to give her that feeling of success. I was happy to do that. I wanted her to feel that success.

We went to Kentucky a couple times, and I sent her in the lead just to develop that relationship with the law firm. I wanted her to experience that.

She was an in-house consultant but then her husband moved to

Utah for his work. She was going obviously with him. I thought, "how am I going to do this? She's 1099. She's an outside rep. It's a little different. How am I going to tweak things?" It put me under a lot of stress because I was already dealing with so much stress, but we worked it out. I had another friend that I had also brought in-house as a consultant. The two of them together, I thought, I love them both, they're going to be very close. They're going to love each other because I love them both. They're funny. I love to be around funny people, and these two girls are going be great.

When my friend left for Utah, I received an e-mail that went out, and found out that she had opened up her own company and was filtering my company's lead source, that was set up by her family, who owned a marketing and design business. We spent $30,000.00 with that company to build two websites and get our branding, our name, and get all this together for the two companies that we had at the time. She was using the marketing that her family's business had built for us. We spent $17,000.00 a month on leads to come in and she would take those leads and filter them to her own company. At some point I thought, "Here's this girl who turned in 20 cases a month and now she's only turning in 3. Something's wrong with that," and when I realized what was happening, it blew me away. I absolutely could not believe it.

Had I not plucked out some of those flaws that I had, I would've probably handled it differently. I was very, very hurt. It took me a year-and-a-half to put that behind me. There was no way of understanding it. It was absolutely unacceptable, unbelievable, and it was quite the blow. I do not carry any resentment now, but I can never forget the pain it caused my family. Although I did get through it, that could make somebody pretty angry. I wouldn't have had the tools, had I not been motivated throughout time with books like *Seven Habits of Highly Effective People* and *How to Win Friends and Influence People*. I don't think I could've managed those types of turmoil without having a good foundation. I have always been a spiritual person, but life can get really painful and people turn their backs on God and people because of that pain. As imperfect people, reasoning can just become excuses and after so much pain, you can turn your back on humanity, Gods creation, therefore, turning your back on God. These books took the principles we learn from the Bible, and help us put it in perspective. When you see people and understand that they are going through their own set of circumstances. Life is not just made for you and your journey but for others as well. Some have it harder and some not as hard. It helped me to not be so angry at other people.

Woody Woodward:

You're the true definition, in my opinion, of a top achiever. You've come literally through hell. You've changed your life. You've taken accountability for your life and you've moved forward. What would you tell someone who is depressed and does not feel their life is on the right track.

JoAnne Kell:

I would say, that in my life at the moment—the biggest thing is, that when people get so caught up in their moment, the cloud is all around them, it doesn't have to be that way. They may get so stressed out because they don't know how they're going to pay the bills the next month, they may have three months' worth of living in the bank and no money coming in or whatever stops them from sleeping at night. They're stressing out and they're worried about it. Remember all the times when things worked out in just the nick of time. It has happened to all of us probably several times. We may or may not have known how it was going to work out, but it did. No matter how bad a situation, they all will work out; maybe not the way you want or need at the time, but then think about all of the times you can go back to and notice the ones that, if they had went the way you wanted, where you would be today. Maybe you would not be with the love of your life, or living in another country, or in a different line of work. Whatever it is that causes you stress, understand that if you take a deep breath, be flexible and don't sell yourself short for instant gratification, IT WILL WORK OUT! Things will work out with or without the stress. Use your energy for troubleshooting, not stressing. It will work out better without all the stress and turmoil that you put yourself through. You will also work it out with positive energy which is far more powerful than negative. You also have the satisfaction of creating your life instead of being whipped about by life's changes.

Woody Woodward:

Your scenario is so different from most people because your adulthood was thrust upon you at a very young age. From your life perspective what do you want your legacy to be?

JoAnne Kell:

More than anything I want my legacy to be about knowledge, not just money. Money is great because it helps people to be able to absorb things because they have a chance to stop and smell the roses, so to speak. Unfortunately, I have spent more time than necessary in my life getting caught up. If that happens now, I get out! Whatever it takes, Get Out! Change your scenery for a day. Make yourself get out.

Being successful is pulling yourself up by your bootstraps, getting up, and if you make a mistake, just be determined not to do it again. Determine yourself, write it down: "That's one thing I'm not going do again." But you pick yourself up; you don't beat yourself up.

I understand sometimes money is a great vehicle. It's the vehicle that I'm using because it's going to allow me the time to spend with my son while I have time. So money will be part my legacy, but more so is knowledge. Just don't give up. Always remember to that it is never too late to do the right thing.

I want to tell "The Secret" to everybody. I want people to realize that they have more power than they give themselves credit for. They have more power than they could even imagine if they could just realize and understand where that power comes from. I mean don't just say that we only use a small percentage of our brain, realize it. Don't just know something, realize what you know. Put into practice what you know. What good is having all this information and knowledge if you're not really using it?

I want my grandkids and my children to whatever money they have and whatever money I leave them, I want them to use it for the benefit of knowledge. If it makes their life comfortable so that they can stop, reflect and have time to think, great. That's what I want. I want my family to have time to reflect, time to be able to look forward to the most important things so that they can think clearly and not be in such a stressed state so much of the time that they get lost in the moment.

Woody Woodward:

How important is it for an entrepreneur to have a good foundation or to have mentors or someone to follow up with?

JoAnne Kell:

Well, I believe that in any industry that you're in, having a mentor is important. It has to be somebody who's been able to go through the bumps or hurdles you may encounter. Walking through life without a mentor is like "Oh my, how many times do you have to smack your head around before you get it?" I remember hearing a phrase -and honestly, I can't tell you where it came from—but "Smart people learn from their mistakes, and wise people learn from other people's mistakes." So we can choose to be smart or we can choose to be wise.

Kathleen S. McGowan

Kathleen S. McGowan is a woman of deep faith, kindness and passion. She is a Keynote speaker, Trainer, Nutrition Expert, and Mentor. Kathleen is also a Songwriter, Vocalist, Author and Humanitarian. She has dedicated more than thirty-five years of her life to helping people and animals.

Kathleen is a woman that through her crushing life's experiences, physically and emotionally, has been able to gather the courage to internalize those experiences and incorporate them into the natural gifts she has been given, both spiritually and via education. She offers to people that are ready a way to understand, accept and incorporate into their lives a process to integrate all of the seemingly disconnected internal and external parts of their lives into a unified, peaceful, healthy new life.

Kathleen has traveled the world lecturing and in her capacity as Health Advisor to celebrities, athletes, and extreme endurance personalities. She is a Co-Creator of the Functional Health Analysis Profile™, an analysis tool that affectively helps people accurately assess their own "functional" health and then monitor their process as their health improves.

Kathleen S. McGowan is a woman who can help people integrate the deep callings of their *Body, Mind and Spirit* to become the person they were created to be. She is passionate about helping people in *"Finding their voice, telling their story, and journeying on towards Gaining their freedom."*

Woody Woodward:

Kathleen, you've been very successful for thirty-plus years in the health and nutrition world. You've now expanded your public speaking and assisting people in "finding their voice, telling their story and journeying on towards gaining their freedom."

How do you go about doing that?

Kathleen McGowan:

Woody, in answering your question, it's necessary for me to address two elements. The first is vital to my being a catalyst in assisting others effectively. This vital element is the state-of-being that I need to be in for actual enlightenment and healing to be manifested through me. The second element is the tangible delivery methods that I use to convey my message for people.

In addressing the first element, let me begin by saying that I genuinely strive to allow myself to be led by the Spirit of God in all aspects of my life. This is of central importance of my work in helping others. I do not put God in a box for if I did, I would be placing a limit on my faith and in my thinking. Such limitations would inevitably restrict me from providing inspiration to those individuals who are in need of recapturing hope. I strive to remember at all times that I am solely a conduit of God's Light; I ask God to fully utilize me as a tool to facilitate healing wherever and whenever it is needed.

The predominant theme of my work is in assisting people in discovering who "THEY" truly are... their God-created being. This discovery allows them to become further empowered as they journey the path to their Higher Purpose.

The paths that God uses to heal and guide us to our Higher Calling are limitless. In understanding this, I constantly seek to remain in a state of awareness. It is vital to have this awareness and to understand and accept that our Body, our Mind and our Spirit, are all connected.

Now, to directly answer your question how do I assist people in "finding their voice, telling their story, and journeying on towards gaining their freedom"?

I utilize the platforms of private group and public speaking engagements, seminars, conferences, retreats, and numerous segments of media communication. I sometimes combine my speaking with my vocal music performances.

If the engagement lends itself, I also incorporate other selected artists who specialize in the areas of inspiration and healing music. In addition, I make myself available for individual sessions in the areas of nutrition, natural health and healing.

From being a speaker and vocal performer for more than thirty-five years, I have found that when I genuinely share with my audiences certain aspects of my life's journey and how I gained courage to transcend restricting barriers that once held me prisoner in my own life, an "opening of the heart" transpires in those seeking healing.

Through freeing your voice and telling your story, or in other words, allowing "Light" to be dispersed onto darkness, I have learned that one of the many empowerments derived from doing so is gaining your freedom.

Each of us MUST continue to search and ultimately discover who we really are, the "child" that God created. We must learn how to love this creation, respect this creation, set healthy boundaries to protect this creation, and learn how to empower this creation, or we will never gain true freedom. We cannot live as chameleons and expect to have our gifts shine to their ultimate brilliance, or to ever be truly free in who we are.

In my life and in my work I believe in unconditionally loving others. This is why I help people find their voice and tell their story, which ultimately gives them the gift of gaining their freedom.

Woody Woodward:
A lot of times people have to take risks in their lives. What is the greatest risk you have taken and was it worth it?

Kathleen McGowan:

In answering this question, I'd like to first look at the basic definition of the word risk, because "risk" can mean a lot of different things to different people. If we look at the basic definition of this word, it means the likelihood of suffering harm or loss, and it can mean danger. It can mean the exposure of injury or loss, the probability that a specific adverse event will occur in a specific period as a result of a specific situation.

So to answer this question, I need to start by saying the greatest risk that I've ever taken was in having the courage to initiate the actions needed to find and to reclaim "myself" and "my" life. I had to choose to take the journey to reclaim "ME."

Having the courage to transcend the barriers that I was allowing to hold me prisoner from being myself and stepping out from denial into a growing empowerment, although very scary and difficult, has led me on an absolutely amazing journey and has been the catalyst in allowing me to move forward in gaining freedom from bondage.

So if I am to answer this question from the perspective of using the basic definition of the word risk, then this for me becomes a question of immensity and a subject matter that exposes self-vulnerability. I say this because in answering this question, I'm choosing to share matters about my personal life. I choose to do this in the hope that some part of my story may help someone who currently feels lost in their own life become unstuck and gravitate forward on their path to be set free.

In relationship to answering "What is the biggest risk that I've ever taken," the abridged story goes like this....

From childhood forward to the not too distant past, I would have to say that I lived in risk. I say this because I learned at a very young age the likelihood of suffering harm or loss, and the probability that a specific adverse event would occur if I did not do everything I was told or was forced to do.

This childhood was rooted in fear, betrayal, control, deception, confusion and lies. It created an aftermath of events that continued to play out in my adulthood, an aftermath which I believe happens in many people's lives. Part of this aftermath's "role" was played out when I permitted myself to be treated in any manner that anyone wished to treat me. I had allowed myself to become a victim. Somewhere along this journey, I got locked-up and buried somewhere deep, deep inside myself.

This suppression of self continued until I arrived at the point that I felt absolutely nothing, at least not for myself. In reflection, I now recognize that I actually over-cared for others, meaning that I allowed myself to be abused for the sake of trying not to ever "rock-the-boat," being fearful of what the repercussions of doing so might bring about.

I could have won an Academy Award in the way I was able to portray that I was just fine. All put together, immaculately functional, successful in every aspect of what most people would consider in the material world to be of importance.

So, from the outside what did this all look like? Well, it looked like I had the life that most people can only ever dream about. I was a multi-millionaire through both my former marriage and my own business success; however no one knew that I was not living "my" life. Oddly enough, even I didn't know it. Instead, I had become only a character in another person's life, and just as I had learned as a child, on a conscious and subconscious level, since living in the present was just too painful, I would escape from it in any way that I could. In my case, I escaped by striving to be perfect. "Perfect," I learned, is not only a tall order; it is subjective. You end up walking on eggshells in order to try to please whoever it is that you fear, and one of among the many senseless things about doing this is that there is no pleasing them, no matter how hard you try!

At some point in time, I knew that "my light," my God-given light, was vanishing; in fact, it was actually nearly dead. I finally arrived at the point of accepting that no matter how difficult the journey would be to try to reclaim my life back, it couldn't be more difficult, or more painful than the way I felt on the inside by allowing others to continue to abuse and control me.

So, Woody, my bottom line answer to your question is this: no matter how great a risk starting my life over in my fifties was, leaving all that I knew, and all that I owned behind in order to discover and recapture who "I" really was.

The far greater risk would have been in NOT beginning on this journey to free my voice, tell my story and work to gain my freedom. To not have grown deeper in my trust in God so that the Divine could lead me and heal me. For if I had not taken this journey, I would not be able to share with others and possibly be a conduit for their healing. This journey and its "risk" have been definitely worth it!

Woody Woodward:
If you could do anything and you knew you would not fail, what would you do?

Kathleen McGowan:
I need to answer this question by first saying that I don't look at things with the mindset of "Will this fail?" I do not have this mindset because I believe that it is only through failure that we learn. If we don't have failure, then we would not have any success. I believe that success and failure go hand-in-hand, as in the illustration of how light and darkness go hand-in-hand. Without one, there is not the other. I believe that there are lessons to be learned in everything we do.

In direct response to your question... I am already doing exactly what I want to be doing; I simply want to be doing more of it.

I trust God's timing in opening further doors that will allow me to devote the majority of my time traveling the world more extensively than I have already been blessed to have done. Wherever I am, it is God who allows me to be a conduit for Divine work.

I desire to be of greater effectiveness in helping others who are in pain and captivity by providing inspiration and hope and by helping them free their voices and tell their stories; this, as well as being a resource for sharing means of tangible help and guidance.

Woody Woodward:

What does it take to be a leader?

Kathleen McGowan:

I answer this question by beginning with reciting a verse from the Bible. The verse is Matthew 23:11. This verse says... "The greatest among you will be your servant." I believe that this verse beautifully states what is at the core of being a true leader.

In outlining my description of a true leader, I will identify several qualities that I believe must be present. I will also describe several characteristics that I believe a person who is not a true leader exhibits.

First and foremost, I believe a true leader has a pure heart. This heart understands, and exhibits unconditional love under all conditions. The source of this quality is the origin of love.

True leaders understand at a deep level that love is not a weakness; in fact, it is the opposite of weakness. They understand that it is the most powerful energy and strength that exists, yet although they possess this understanding, they do not use it to victimize or force people with this power. Instead, they lead by allowing the brilliant light of God to shine through them. A leader is not afraid to display this knowledge, even if this means standing alone, without others, for what is pure.

True leaders genuinely care for others. They respect others and they respect themselves as well. True leaders have traveled the difficult journey that has led them to the understanding of who they truly are.

This understanding must be not only from the standpoint of the external world, but more importantly, from an internal, or spiritual state.

I often say that "People don't really care how much you know, until they know how much you genuinely care." A true leader understands this. I believe that a true leader allows him- or herself to be a conduit of the Divine and draws upon this Divine innate strength in all situations.

I believe that true leaders not only give to others in joy, but they have also learned how to receive with thanksgiving, gratitude and pureness of heart. They have learned that by allowing themselves to receive in this manner, a new depth in the knowledge and appreciation of giving is experienced.

To be a true leader, it is necessary to learn the importance of solitude and embrace it when needed. This type of leader has learned what aloneness is and understands when it is needed. He or she has learned to embrace both of these areas with peace.

I could not give my description without stating that true leaders naturally just lead by example. They understand that courage is not the absence of fear and they move to transcend the restrictions of fear.

Great leaders have learned the skill of living in the moment. They are humble and learn from past mistakes. Yet, they also possess the creativity needed for building the future. Such leaders understand that they must be thankful for the little things first, for in doing so they will then be put in a leadership position over greater things. As a dear friend and confidant of mine once shared with me… "Just as in building a house, how one nail at a time, one board at a time, and one brick at a time creates a big beautiful house… as it is with anything in life that is significant and beautiful. It takes these seemingly little things needing to be put together first or the bigger masterpiece can never be built."

I would not be able to define what a true leader is without also describing what I believe a true leader is not. Although the list of these characteristics is extensive, I will list only a few of these traits. I will begin by starting that true leaders are not bullies. They do not manipulate by means of malicious force or fear. A true leader is not judgmental. Nor is a true leader a liar, a narcissist, a sociopath, or a dictator. True leaders are not shallow people.

I believe genuine leaders are not selfish or what I define as "external people," attempting to gain control and power from external means for self-promotion.

Woody Woodward:
One of the characteristics you described in your definition of a leader

that I especially liked is that they need to understand how to be alone. I find this a very important point because a lot of times, as leaders we are alone and we are trying to tap into our true potential; I know you help your clients do that, but when times are tough for you and you are alone, what do you do to stay focused?

Kathleen McGowan:

I've had a lot of experience with tough times in past years, so I'm rather knowledgeable and aware of how I stay focused during such times.

First, I remember to breathe. Breathe correctly and breathe deeply. This is very important. When having exceedingly difficult times, I go even deeper into prayer than my usual, which since I am already a prayer warrior, that is a tremendous amount of focused prayer. As I always do, I continue to pray for God's guidance and I remind myself that everything that happens has a purpose. I do not believe in coincidences so I always look deeper into situations than what appears to be solely on the surface. I allow myself to be conscious of what possible things I am supposed to be learning from the experience.

I always remember that God does not work within the confines of a box. It gives me great peace to know that although I may not see solutions to a situation at a particular moment in time, I can have peace in my spirit knowing that God has an unlimited reservoir of solutions to resolve my perceived problems.

It is one of my core beliefs that faith the size of a mustard seed can move mountains. Although I take time to be by myself so I can hear the innate voice within, I also know when to reach out and connect with others as to not isolate myself. I think that this is very important. There are times in life when we as humans have the tendency to isolate ourselves when in great distress. In fact, many times this is really the worst thing we can do. Sometimes, this isolation can lead us to believe that there is a great deal more darkness in the situation than actually exists in reality.

Another way I stay focused is that I may feel it wise to discuss a situation that is bothering me with close trusted friends in order to gain other insights that I may be temporarily blinded to.

In addition, I go very much into my creative side, meaning that I sing, play the piano and write more. I allow myself to spend more time in nature, and my all-time favorite way to get focused is to hike in the mountains.

My "get focused" criteria would not be complete without my writing out a list of what I need to be grateful for in my life. First and foremost, being thankful for life itself. I think this is very important. I believe making such a list helps put things back into perspective.

I wisely follow my intuition. I think out-of-the-box and I always remind myself that "this, too, shall pass."

I think it is vital to face the truth. I recognize the power in understanding that "the truth shall set us free." I no longer allow, as I did for many years, a situation to paralyze me. Instead, I say a prayer that is very special to me—"The Serenity Prayer."

"God grant me the serenity to accept the things I cannot change, courage to change the things I can and the wisdom to know the difference."

Woody Woodward:
What is the secret combination to finding success in your business profession?

Kathleen McGowan:
The definition of success in my opinion is subjective. What means success to one person may not necessarily be what it means to another. It is like the meaning of the expression "Beauty is in the eye of the beholder."

My belief is that the secret combination to experiencing success, not only professionally but with everything in life, is a collection of an ever-evolving source of innate and learned knowledge, abilities and qualities. When these elements are combined, this collection embodies all aspects of who we are. They encompass our body, mind and spirit, our lives personally, professionally and spiritually.

The following statement is a partial depiction of what the secret combination to finding success is to me:

"Knowing who you truly are; Respecting yourself and having healthy boundaries in your life, as well as respecting the boundaries others set for themselves; Living from the internal state and continuing to strive to mature in your Higher Purpose; I believe that being successful requires having genuineness of heart and unselfishly helping others, first and foremost by resonating unconditional love towards them; I believe there is no success found without sharing your God-given gifts with the world."

If defining success looking from an external standpoint, I measure my success by how greatly I unconditionally love others and by how I am loved in the relationships that I create and nurture.

In reference to my profession, the secret combination for me to be successful is vast. First, my genuineness is vital for my success, not only in my personal and spiritual life, but most unquestionably, in my professional life as well. I allow myself to be an instrument that provides inspiration and hope to people. I am a conduit to help heal people and their lives. I could not be successful in doing this if I were not genuine.

Although this is a partial list of the secret combination to what I believe allows for success, I must include one more crucial component: persistence. No success is ever gained without persistence. A persistent forward movement, no matter what challenges, heartbreaks, disappointments, or aloneness we may experience, is crucial for success. We must be alive!

Life is movement… death is no movement.

We must never, never, never, never give up! We must be true to our God-created self and be unwaveringly persistent in following the path to our Higher Purpose.

I am successful because I trust in God. I never give up no matter how tired, hurt, or how broken I may be. I have never given up and I never will. This action is based in faith and persistence is a part of that faith. Success is available to everyone who follows in these footsteps.

Woody Woodward:

What inspired you to get into the profession you've chosen?

Kathleen McGowan:

If I had to answer this question using only one word, I would need to choose the word "pain." In short, the origin of me entering my profession was the pain, both physical and emotional that I experienced as a child. I simply wanted to help others not to have the pain and confusion that I had. I wanted to do all that I could to achieve this purpose.

Then in my adult years, I realized that the survival through such a childhood was one step; however, dealing with the aftermath that such a childhood creates is another. I knew that I was to expand the ability I have been given of touching hearts through my voice, both speaking and singing, to address the whole person.

The connection and integration of the body, mind, and spirit must be addressed in order for a shift to occur and healing to transpire.

Being an instrument to help people in healing is the essence of who I am and what I do in my life. As a child, it became a learned behavior to be scared, even of my own shadow. I learned what being afraid was all about. I learned how fear paralyzes. I also learned what not knowing how you were going to make it through to the next day was like. This prison, in combination with my innate being is the foundation to the absolute passion I have in helping others.

I knew that I had a calling and in my later teenage years, I entered the allopathic medical profession. I become a co-partner with a medical doctor and also helped doctors become established in their medical practices. I saw many patients returning to these practices month after month solely to obtain prescription refills, yet in many cases they never seemed to be healed.

When I was twenty years old, my father passed on from a massive heart attack. He was only 63 years old. When the emergency room physician came out from the E.R., he told me that I should have expected my father's death would come in this manner and at his age because every man in his family had died the same way and at the same age. At that moment, although I understood genetics, I felt that there must be something that I didn't know in relation to the possibility of being able to alter the outcome of genetic predispositions to some degree.

It was at that point in time of my life that I opened my mind and opened my heart, and although I continued in the medical field for several years, I also began my education in nutrition, naturopathy and eventually energy healing. For more that thirty-five years now I have been helping people with their health.

I have now expanded my work from helping people with their physical health through nutrition into helping them free their voice and tell their story, which helps them gain their freedom.

I have learned through personal experience that it is not possible to obtain health if we are not free to be who we truly are.

Woody Woodward:

You deal with a lot of people who struggle with the feeling of failure. We all have those emotions where we feel like we've failed at something. How do you define failure?

Kathleen McGowan:

As I previously mentioned, I do not have the mindset that perhaps many people have and this holds particularly true in regards to the subject of failure. I believe that it is only through failure that we learn. If we don't have failure, then we would not have any success. I believe that these two events go hand-in-hand, as in the illustration of how lightness and darkness go hand-in-hand. Without one there is not the other. I believe that there are lessons to be learned in everything we do.

I am deeply saddened when I see a person who has gravitated into a paralyzed state, having become paralyzed because of perceived failures and fear that they have experienced. This is genuinely a tragedy when it occurs. I personally know this state far too well because I spent many years being in such a condition. Not being "me." Not living "my" life.

We must not allow the negative perception of failure to discourage us and extinguish our God-given light. We need to be vigilant and recognize the root purpose of such a force. The nature and intention of this type force is to blind us and slowly separate us from feeling the passion of our Higher Purpose. If this blindness and separation succeed, we will stop trying to climb higher. Therefore, it is absolutely imperative that we remain in an aware state and recognize what is happening energetically and spiritually when we feel like we have failed at something.

Failure is the opposite of persistence.

Woody Woodward:
A lot of people analyze their failures and they think "Well, I can't take any more risks, so they go into a state of fear. How do you channel fear into productivity?

Kathleen McGowan:
I'll begin by saying that fear cannot be left unchecked. Fear, among an array of other disabling factors, can paralyze. In addressing fear, the steps I take are:
- Pray
- Recognize the fear for what it is
- Breathe correctly and deeply
- Recognize the purpose of fear
- Analyze the fear and locate the true root of it
- Put the fear into perspective
- Reflect
- Make a wise game plan
- Convert the fear into creative emotion and activity, which then can result in productivity

Recognize that Courage is not the absence of fear; however, it is the understanding that something is greater than the fear which is trying to paralyze me... that greater something is my God-given "Higher Purpose."

To explain more expansively on the process and dynamics involved when I initiate action to convert fear into productivity, I wish to share the following...

My first action when I feel fear is to pray. I then look at the fear and recognize it for what it is. This is of significant importance. Recognizing that we are attempting to function from within a state of fear sounds simple; however, I have learned that many times we actually are not aware that we are attempting to do so and we fall into a state of denial.

After additional prayer, I then consciously become aware of my breathing. Breathing in through my nose and out through my mouth. Continuing to breathe correctly is vital under all circumstances and particularly when dealing with fear.

After recognizing that what I am feeling is fear, I remind myself what the purpose of fear is. In most cases it is to paralyze, to stop the healthy flow of breathing, and to cause a hindrance from moving forward in a positive creative manner.

I then begin to work on analyzing the fear. I search within myself to locate the root of it. Is the fear a physical threat? Is it an emotional fear or threat? Is it a fear stemmed from a violation of my emotional fingerprints, or an invasion of my boundaries? It is a fear of the unknown? A fear of perceived loss? Fear of change? Fear of financial ruin?

Once I locate the root, I remind myself that the root of fear always is of a spiritual warfare nature. Its function is to be a weapon of paralysis for the purpose of trying to stop us from moving forward from being who we really are. If we give into it, it works to prevent us from allowing our God-given light to shine out and onto others, and it works to encumber us from achieving our Higher Purpose.

It is important to be wise in understanding this dynamic of fear. Otherwise it can easily blind us, control our actions, paralyze us, and make us essentially dead, yet still breathing.

After I have located the root, I put the fear into perspective and in recognizing its purpose a natural manifestation transpires that removes or at the very least, greatly diminishes fear's strength.

I continue to focus on being in a state of awareness and I work on not giving the fear strength. I feel it imperative to point out that if there is a condition where an actual physical threat is present, the situation needs to be understood, assistance needs to be obtained and the situation dealt with the awareness and sensitivity that is necessary.

The next course of action I take in dealing with fear is in retreating to a very peaceful location that resonates with me. For me, this place is the mountains. Such a location lends itself to allowing me to feel even more closely connected with God. When in this place, I listen to the gift of my inner voice. I then can convert the fear that is attempting to afflict me into creativity.

Once this fear is converted to creativity, I am able to think more clearly and make wise decisions that allow me to move me forward and out of the paralysis of fear.

As I continue to pray, I gather more courage. This courage allows me to transcend barriers that I have allowed fear to place on me. I refocus on my Higher Purpose and remind myself that "Courage is not the absence of fear; however, it is the understanding that something is greater than the fear which is trying to paralyze me. That greater something is my God- given "Higher Purpose."

Woody Woodward:
What do you want your legacy to be?

Kathleen McGowan:
I choose my legacy to be that "I am forever a boundless conduit for the brilliant light of God, radiating unconditional love, for only with such love is the healing of all things possible. I choose to resonate all of the manifestations of God's love.

I choose that my life is one that giftedly inspires people worldwide with a message of hope and courage and that this message serves to help heal lives by facilitating the transcending of all barriers that hold people captive and in pain or torment.

I choose to be a catalyst for freeing voices, for providing platforms for people to tell their story, and share their gifts. To be greatly instrumental in helping people be free, claiming who they truly are—God's creation."

Annette Mease

Annette Mease is a leading expert on entrepreneurship, money, marketing and sales.

Annette helps business owners increase their self-worth and their net worth by becoming successful, thriving entrepreneurs. Her marketing expertise and training programs have helped hundreds of business owners start and grow financially and spiritually rich businesses.

She is the creator of numerous training programs, including *The Breakthrough Money Archetype Training, MMSI Expanded Group Coaching, Comfortable Conversation Sales Training, Money, Marketing* and *Sales Live Training and the Marketing and Sales Boot camp*.

Annette is the winner of the 2012 NPWA Idaho Business Woman of the Year Award and a 2013 Who's Who of Idaho Women.

As a master coach, speaker, author and workshop leader, her work has touched the lives of over 100 business owners throughout the nation. She happily leads a successful, six figure coaching company delivering the message that making money is part of your spiritual path and giving you the mentoring and marketing and sales tools you need to be financially successful via an exciting, thriving business.

www.unlockyourbrilliance.com
info@unlockyourbrilliance.com

Woody Woodward:

Annette, you've had a lot of experience with money. You've been broke, you've been rich, and you've been broke. You know what it feels like to have it, to lose it, to make it back. Why do you think so many people struggle with money and the concept of money?

Annette Mease:

I think one of the reasons that people struggle with money so much is because they don't have... number one, a positive money story. A lot of people believe that God doesn't want them to be wealthy. They believe that money is evil. They believe that it's a sin to be rich. They have this idea that only the rich people are greedy and the rich are not close to God. Most people want to be close to God. They want to be able to live with Him again. They want to be in heaven. So their thought process is that if I'm rich and greedy, I'm not close to God. That's not what I want to be so I'm going to live in poverty. This is the way God wants it and the poorer I am, the more that I reach out to God, and the more that He loves me.

Woody Woodward:

Was that your childhood experience? Is that where you felt that you didn't deserve to be rich as you grew up?

Annette Mease:

Absolutely. That was totally my experience and it's crazy interesting how, when I talk to people and ask questions about their first experience with money, so many have had that same experience. They believe that God won't love them if they're rich.

Woody Woodward:

I find that interesting because I've interviewed over 2500 people in my career and I have found that to be a commonality, where a lot of people feel that it's a sin to be rich. I know of a lot of people who are multi-millionaires and they had many years of struggling to come to grips with their wealth. Why do you think we get so stuck as a society with that because there are other people that have no problem? Money doesn't make a difference to them but there is a group of people where it definitely has a negative impact. Why did you think that is?

Annette Mease:

I think because most of the people that have that experience are Christian because, again, they look at having money as greedy and they don't want to be thought of as being greedy. They don't want to be thought of as having more than someone else. It even shows up in business and in sales conversations. They don't want to take money from people's mouths or food from people's mouths; they just don't like the idea. I've researched this a little bit. People think that it's a sin to be rich; that's what a lot of people say. It's wrong to be rich; it's a sin. But if you go back in the apocrypha, where they wrote in the ancient scripture thousands of years ago, the definition of sin was that you're missing the mark. So for me as I teach this, I let people know that the true definition of sin is that you're missing the mark. The truth is that you're missing the mark if you actually believe that God is sitting up there saying, "You get to be rich. You get to be poor and that's the way it is," because that's not the way it is. People struggle with that and it's just in their mind. It's this thought that they're not going to be loved. Everyone wants to be loved, especially by God.

Woody Woodward:

You have a great view about the abundance of God. Will you explain that to me?

Annette Mease:

Absolutely. If you were to take a look outside and you were to take a look at all of the trees and all of the flowers, you have to know that God did not create this world using coupons. He didn't create this world saying, "Well, I can only put a tree there because I can't have another tree there because they're too close and that's too many trees." So when you even take a look at nature and you take a look at the world, there is no way that you can think that there's no abundance. There's an abundance of everything. We have enough trees. There's enough to go around. The problem is we see with our physical eyes rather than our spiritual eyes. When you take a look physically around you and you see people lack, there's this lack. They're losing their job or they're losing this other thing. We forget to see with our spiritual eyes that there's stuff that's happening in the background that's coming to us that's full of abundance and you know that most people have experienced that. They just don't realize that there was stuff going on behind the scenes and then they received abundance. Does that make sense?

Woody Woodward:

It makes complete sense. I love your childhood story of growing up in poverty and being on welfare and food stamps and then making millions of dollars with your husband in the real estate industry. Tell me and our audience what it was like after you had that money, your confrontation and being able to deal with it and then what happened next.

Annette Mease:

Okay, so my confrontation and being able to deal with it was not a very healthy one because I started to feel guilty for having more money than the people that were our renters. And so I started to really become empathetic towards their stories. If they didn't have the rent, if they didn't have enough, I would pay for their rent. I would take care of them. I even felt really guilty one day when we got new carpet in our home and one of our renters came over to pay rent. I opened the door and she looked at me and with a very sarcastic tone in her voice she said, "Oh, you guys got new carpet." I seriously bent over backwards trying to explain to her why we got new carpet and why we needed it. I mean it's just insane how my thinking is that I felt so guilty that I got a piece of new carpet when she didn't even have money for rent. So I felt bad for having when others didn't. What happened was we ended up becoming enablers. With that experience, we started giving our money away in the form of paying rent, taking care of the properties, and then we just were spiritually, physically, and mentally drained. We thought, "We cannot keep doing this." We were losing our savings so we ended up selling the properties and any of the equity that came with those properties were given to the real estate agents. So, truly, we were left with nothing. We were left with what we went in with, which was nothing. It was very a devastating experience and then I started reliving...I literally freaked out. I remember I was sitting on the floor in my kitchen because my husband had called me, and he said, "I think I might not have a job tomorrow." So I'm thinking,"Oh my gosh, I can't handle this. We just lost everything and now this." I literally remember sitting down on the floor and then laying down in a fetal position. I just sat there and sobbed and cried and cried because I didn't know what to do. This experience was taking me back to when I was a child and we had nothing. This is when I went into my depression, actually a mental breakdown. I stayed there for about two years in hiding and not even wanting people to see me. Then I started coming out of it and that's when I found the coaching industry.

Woody Woodward:
So what pulled you out of that depression?

Annette Mease:
You know what? I honestly don't know if there's one thing. We had just adopted a little baby when I had my breakdown. I still attended church. I still would read good books off and on and I think that time and just feeling the spirit of hope and God a little bit, feeling uplifted... it was a process. It was not overnight. Absolutely, it was a process that I just got to a point where you know what, I really need to get out of this and I was able to.

Woody Woodward:
What advice would you give to a client or a friend who is suffering similar to your experience with money or depression and they just don't have that hope and faith? What would you recommend for them to do?

Annette Mease:

Well, one of the things that I do that I wasn't aware of at the time and it really helps me when I feel discouraged and upset is I use what I call tapping; it's an emotional freedom technique. I don't know if you've heard of it. It's EFT. I get on YouTube. I look for YouTube videos on depression, anxiety, stress, and I tap on it and energetically it shifts me. Every one of my clients and the people that I talk to, if they're open to energy work, I always encourage them to do that because it helps them get out of their stuff.

Woody Woodward:

Great. Other than EFT, what else do you recommend?

Annette Mease:

Good books, going outside. One of the things that I think is one of the best ways to get out of discouragement and have help is to literally, even if it's in wintertime, to go outside and look at nature. I mean you know even when it snows and it's the first snow and you're going out in the morning, it's clean, it's crisp, it's clear, it's quiet. If you go outside in the summertime and you literally take off your shoes, put your feet in the grass and just stand there, feel it, be with nature, I think that's one of the best ways, ideally. My personal belief is that nature is the angel for us.

Woody Woodward:

Since you have experience with not having money, having money, losing money, I know that you coach a lot of individuals on the spiritual laws of business. What kind of spiritual laws are there?

Annette Mease:

Well, there are six spiritual laws that I teach about and train on. It's the law of non-resistance; the law of faith, the law of ask and receive, the law of love, the law of creation, and the law of belief.

Woody Woodward:

Let's walk through each of those six. What is the law of non-resistance?

Annette Mease:

Okay, so the law of non-resistance really is about not resisting what is. Many times, we have experiences and we take them on as "Oh, this is negative" or "This is positive." The reason we take them on as negative or positive is simply because we start comparing it to something else or we compare it to someone else's experience or what's going on in their life. The truth is that it's just an experience, it's just an event, and it just is. So I train on helping people understand that things happen and this is the way it is. There's not a lot you can do to control it so don't resist it. The more you resist, the harder it is. It's almost like pushing against a brick wall and nothing's going to happen. When you let go and you stop resisting, then it lets the flow of life happen. I mean if you were to take a look at a spring coming down a hill and coming down to the river going to the ocean, when it's starting at the top of the mountain, when it hits a rock it doesn't stop and say, "Oh hey, I think I'd better gather myself so I can move this rock." It goes on and it takes a different path and it moves around it and it goes forward and it eventually finds its way to the river. It eventually finds its way to the ocean. That's the way I train. Don't put it as positive and negative. Just put it as "This is an experience. What do I get to learn from this and how am I going to work around it?"

Woody Woodward:
What is the law of faith?

Annette Mease:

The law of faith is not only just believing because there's a difference between a belief and faith. The law of faith really states that you know that something's going to happen so when you ask for something or you want something, you absolutely know, regardless of what is going on around you, you can stand in faith and know that you can have what it is that you want. The key is to do it even if you see someone else losing their job or you see the world losing itself or dying whether it has to do with financial health or whatever's going on. That's faith. It's knowing even though you're seeing other experiences, you know that what you want is going to happen to you. That's really what the law of faith is.

Woody Woodward:
Does that tie into the law of ask and receive?

Annette Mease:
It does because there's a gap when you ask and you receive. In between asking and receiving is really taking action. When you ask, it's really important for you to know what it is that you want and why you want it. A lot of people run around and say, "I want this and this is how much money I want" or "I want this particular thing" but they think that's what they want based on what other people have told them. Then they get it and they really don't want it. It's not what they really wanted. The law of ask and receive is really about knowing what you want and then knowing why you want it and then being open to receiving. Acting as if you're going to receive it, acting as if this is going to happen by having faith. Now, the key with asking and receiving is I would say 90 percent of the time when people ask for something, there is an expectation. The expectation is never met in the way they think it's going to show up. Most of the time, it shows up in a totally different way but the result is what they wanted.

Woody Woodward:
What is the law of love?

Annette Mease:
So the law of love is really about acknowledging your own brilliance, loving the truth of who you are. Everyone has a shadow side; every one of us has a secret or has something that we would be horrified if anyone knew because we don't like that about us, right? But that's a part of who we are and that is the piece that needs to be loved and accepted. When you love yourself and you love your clients, everything flows. When you love your family, when you love people, life flows together. So if you could walk around and look at people and act

as if they have a sign on them that says, "All I want is to be loved," and you treat them that way, then it's amazing what happens in business. It's amazing what happens in your personal life, in your spiritual life rather than comparing yourself and not liking yourself. That's what happens when you don't love yourself and it will destroy you.

Woody Woodward:
Is the law of love really based on self-acceptance and loving oneself so that I can then love other people?

Annette Mease:
Absolutely; that's the second commandment.

Woody Woodward:
That's very well put. What's the law of creation?

Annette Mease:
So the law of creation is really interesting especially in the corporate world there's a lot of competition going on. My experience with competition is not good because we tend to step out of inspiration and guidance. So the law of creation is really about staying out of ego. What I mean by that is you either feel less than or you feel better than. You cannot be creative. The law of creation cannot work when you're in ego. The law of creation is when you're out of ego, when you're totally connected to your Creator, when you're receiving guidance and inspiration, and you're following it. You're taking it in and you're taking action on what you're receiving versus being competitive. When you go to competition, you're comparing yourself. You're trying to do marketing like someone else. You're trying to live the life of someone else, and it's not true to who you are.

Woody Woodward:
What is the law of belief?

Annette Mease:
So the law of belief is before the law of faith, which it gives you hope

that you know or you believe that it's going to happen, that you put it in the ground and even though you can't see it, you believe that there's going to be a tree, that there's going to be a plant coming from it. You believe it so you water it. You take care of it because you trust and believe that that's going to happen. Now I teach what I call the belief cycle and everyone is always in the belief cycle. I don't know of anyone who's ever out of it. However, I have been told that some men are not in it sometimes because sometimes they don't have thinking going on. But the belief cycle is really about your thoughts and your feelings lead to your actions and your results and it's what you believe. Do you believe this is going to happen and what are you thinking about it? What are you feeling about it? And then you take the action and you get the result. Many times, people don't end up getting the result that they wanted because they don't believe that they can have it. And so it goes into this cycle of the feelings lead to the actions and the results are not what they want. Then they get discouraged and depressed. Then they start believing that they're not worthy. They start believing that they can't have it, and so then the thought is "I can't." The feeling is discouragement and the action is that they don't take any. The result is they don't get what they want.

Woody Woodward:
Is that what you and your husband experienced where you didn't believe that you should have money and therefore, you self-sabotaged? Because I find a lot of people that feel like they're not entitled to a good income therefore they self-sabotage opportunities that will keep them from earning extra income.

Annette Mease:
Absolutely. I did not think that I was worthy of having the money. I felt inadequate so my action was I was going to sabotage. Because I felt inadequate, I was going to take care of other people and give them what I had earned. Then the result was we had no money in our bank account.

Woody Woodward:

So if we were to have a healthy relationship with money, we would then have more charity and the ability to give more because we make more.

Annette Mease:

Absolutely. You'd have a bigger impact.

Woody Woodward:

So let's go into what's the biggest risk you've ever taken and was it worth it?

Annette Mease:

You know the biggest risk that I ever took was actually stepping into the coaching industry. When I was 30 years old, I wanted to be a speaker and a presenter. I was a teacher at the time. I was teaching in Texas, and I went up to one of the gals who was also a teacher and was a presenter. I said to her, "I want to do what you're doing and I want to learn how to do this," and she looked at me and she said, "You are never going to be able to be a speaker, you will never be a presenter, and you will never be able to do what I do." And I took it to heart. My self-esteem was so incredibly low, so I took it to heart and I actually shoved it down so deep within me that I totally forgot about it. When I found the coaching industry, my first coach said to me after meeting with me I think two sessions we had, "Annette, you are a speaker. You are a presenter." And I said, "No, I'm not," because I didn't remember anything, so I said, "No, I'm not," and he said, "Yes, you are." He said, "You need to get up in front of people," and I said, "No way. I'm not going to do that." He kept working with me and then lo and behold, I was asked to do a presentation to 150 women. I was practicing my speech and then all of a sudden I remembered what this teacher had told me. I mean it literally hit my like a ton of bricks. I started crying. I was on the floor, and I realized that this is what I'd wanted to be doing for 14 years but I had shoved it down and here I was, doing exactly what I wanted to do and I could have been doing it. I was so regretful because I could have been doing this for so long and I didn't. So the biggest thing, the biggest risk that I took was being willing to not listen to the lies that people had told me and to take it on anyway. Now, I'm an incredible speaker and presenter and it was what I was born to do.

Woody Woodward:

That reminds me a lot of the law of love because that woman who told you couldn't do it obviously did not love herself. She felt threatened by you. Who would ever be so disrespectful to another individual and say, "You're never going to do it, you're not qualified," blah, blah, blah, there's just no way but had she loved herself, she then could have loved you and saved you those past 14 years of not stepping into your own greatness.

So looking back at your vast experience as a coach and a strategist, what does it take to be a leader?

Annette Mease:

The very first key to being a leader is just to stand up, to stand up for what you believe in, for what you're passionate about, and then to move forward.

I believe that I'm a great leader. I'm also a great follower and I'm creating a movement. I believe that the key in being a great leader is to create a movement, to create a tribe of people who find hope, who are waking up, and who are moving forward, who are willing to follow.

Woody Woodward:

So what movement are you most enthusiastic about right now?

Annette Mease:

The movement that I'm most enthusiastic about is really helping people find their greatness and helping them wake up to their brilliance because everything in life, regardless of spiritual, physical, mental, financial, everything in life is different when you love you and when you know your greatness and you own and embrace your brilliance.

Woody Woodward:

So why do most people not embrace their brilliance? Why do they not step into their own light?

Annette Mease:

Because they have been programmed for failure most of their life by people who love them, and by people who didn't love them. They took on all of the lies and they believed all of the lies just like I did. I believed the lie that I couldn't do it.

Woody Woodward:

So how does someone reprogram themselves from those lies?

Annette Mease:

It's really the mental part. It's not the physical; it's really the mental reprogramming, where you bring in terminology and you literally tell your subconscious mind the truth of who you are and you tell yourself over and over again. There are tools you can use: you can use EFT, you can write down what it is that you want, get some Baroque music and speak it to yourself everyday listening to it. There are tools that you can use that you can actually just have like a prayer or a meditation where you speak to yourself the truth every day. That's what it takes. It's almost like a virus in the computer. You have to get rid of the virus and you have to be willing to work on getting rid of all the lies. You do that by changing your worth.

Woody Woodward:

When times are tough, how do you stay focused on your passion?

Annette Mease:

I give myself a break. One of the things that I do is I will sit down and watch an old movie that I love or I will go on a bike ride. I will go in the backyard; we have a great porch in the backyard so I'll go in the backyard. I will give myself a break; that's the one thing for me. I am a go-getter and I just move and go, go, go, go until I can't go anymore and then I kind of have a breakdown, kind of burn out a little bit. For me, I have to get up away from the computer, get up and go do something so that I can rejuvenate myself and that's what I do.

Woody Woodward:

You've had a lot of success as a businesswoman, as an entrepreneur, as a coach, and you've had a lot of failures as most successful people have. With your vast experience, how do you define success now?

Annette Mease:

You know success to me really is about being willing. I think that that is a very key word—being willing. There are many times when people say, "I'm ready," but they're not willing. I've said to myself, I've said many times that I'm ready but I'm not willing. So success really is you willing to do what it takes to get what it is that you want. Success is also about having peace in every aspect of your life, in the family, in relationships, in the money, in the financial and the health. I know many people experience success differently. People look at success in a different way but for me, it's just being able to know that I'm doing the best that I can every single day. When I put my head on the pillow, I feel like I've done my best and I feel like I'm getting better. I'm not perfect. Well, I am perfect in what I'm doing but there are things and actions that I take that are not perfect and so I try to do better the next day and improve myself.

Woody Woodward:

I have found in my experience that having a mentor helps you pay that price, someone who's been where you want to be and you're a mentor to many people, but when someone is looking for a mentor, what should they be looking for in that mentor?

Annette Mease:

I think there are a couple of things that are really key. Number one, do you resonate with this person? If you don't resonate with them, with their message, with what they're doing, it's going to be a challenge for you to be able to be mentored by them because there's going to be resistance. I think another key is that can they take you to where you want to go. A lot of times it sounds really good and it looks good on paper, but can they take you to where you want to go? Can they give you the advice? Can they take you to that place? And then thirdly, I think it's really key to know that when you're looking for a mentor you're not looking for a friend. You are looking for someone to guide you and that does not necessarily need to be liked by you because you want them to push you when you need to be pushed, to walk beside you when you need your hand held, when you need to get your butt off the ground, when you need to have a guide that's in front of you. So it's not necessary that this is going to be my friend, but it's really going to be someone that can actually take you to that place and do the things that are hard for you to do but they're willing to take you through that so that you can get to where you want to be.

Woody Woodward:
What was your biggest "Aha" moment in your business, when you finally realized I've made it, I'm making a difference in the lives of others? What was that "Aha" moment?

Annette Mease:
You know what? There are a couple of things. I have a lot of sales conventions and there was one person who I really, really wanted to coach because I knew that they needed it and they said "no." And I was okay with that. I had the same feeling when they said no as someone who said yes. I knew I had arrived because I no longer looked at them as a dollar sign or as someone who could or couldn't. I just realized that I was happy for whatever they chose because it's what they chose. It was what they wanted to do. I was not in control of it, and I knew I had arrived. It was so great because I knew, "You know what, I'm here for you; I'm here to be of service. If you want to work with me, that's great. If you don't, that's cool."

Woody Woodward:

What advice would you give to someone who wants to be an entrepreneur, someone who's been told "No" all of their life but doesn't have the courage or strength to get up to actually make that commitment quite yet? What advice would you give them?

Annette Mease:

Well, I think one thing is that it's critical that they take a look at themselves from within because when it comes to the end of their lives, what do they want to have said about themselves? What do they want to have experienced in their life? Too many people I believe die with a song in their heart. I would say take courage and have hope. I had the same experience. Take courage and have hope and keep moving forward because everyone has a purpose. I believe that every single person on this earth does have a purpose and there's a reason that they're here and that people are waiting in line for them to show up and they have a mess in their life. Everyone has a mess and they can create a message around it and then teach others how to get out of the same mess.

Woody Woodward:

I agree, we all have a mess in our life but you're saying take your mess and make a message about it and help other people do the same.

Annette Mease:

Absolutely. People are so lost and they really need help and that's what we're here for. We're here to be of service to others. People are waiting in line. They're seriously just waiting for people to show up.

Woody Woodward:

What books have you read or what is your favorite book to keep you on track to achieving your goals?

Annette Mease:

Some of my favorite books are *Working with the Law* by Raymond Holliwell; *You Too Can be Rich* by Robert A. Russell; the Scriptures,...

I've read so many books I could just list hundreds, but one that I use often in my coaching and in my training is *God Works Through Faith* by Robert A. Russell.

Woody Woodward:
Final question: what legacy do you want to leave for this planet?

Annette Mease:
I want to leave hope. I want to leave having helped people find their brilliance and see their greatness. I want my children to have that, for my family to experience that. Also, for the world to go back to the basics of they are loved, and they can turn around and love other people and help them.

Marc Frank Montoya

Marc Frank Montoya, aka "The Pioneer," was born and raised by his single mother, in the northwest inner-city of Denver, Colorado. Growing up, his friends and environment consisted of drugs, theft, and gangs. Luckily, right before high school, he was introduced to a skateboard that changed the direction of his life forever.

Skateboarding soon lead to snowboarding. He pioneered the sport of snowboarding, and became the first Mexican/American professional snowboarder. He has now been pro for over 14 years, traveling the world, having signature models on everything from snowboards to goggles, shoes, and boots.

Growing successfully and creating assets, leverage, and streaming income for himself, he now finds passion in exploring ideas and ventures to create more money and more freedom in other people's lives. He also speaks on health and business awareness in today's world, and coaches others to do the same.

For more information visit: Marc Frank Montoya, aka, MFM

www.MarcFrankMontoya.com • www.twitter.com/teamMFM

https://www.facebook.com/pages/Master-the-Freedom-Mindset/157438977631708?ref=hl

mfmsuccessteam@gmail.com

Woody Woodward:

Marc, you've had an incredible life. You grew up in an inner city, you did some "not so great" things to make money and survive; but then you be-

came this world-famous international snowboarder, as well as successful entrepreneur. When you were growing up in difficult circumstances, what did you do to keep hope alive?

Marc Frank Montoya:
Well first of all, I was just in survival mode and in the wrong environment. My closest friends taught me how to steal and sell drugs. None of us knew any better. We were just doing the things we knew how to do to get money. When you're young without good mentors and no plan, it's a hard life, and you don't know any better. That's just the way it was for us. We didn't do any of the bad stuff to be evil people; we just (at the time) didn't think it was so bad. I don't condone or support that ignorant behavior at all, but it's just what young dumb people do sometimes, and hopefully, they're smart enough to grow out of it. We were just very ignorant on that end, and just trying to get by each day.

The one thing I did know is that I didn't want the "normal" life that most other ordinary people were living, it seemed so boring! So, I've learned here's why people struggle: I was living in "survival mode."

My problem was, I was thinking about "ME." How am "I" going to survive today? How am "I" going to get by today? How am "I" going to get by this month?" instead of thinking about how I could help OTHERS get what they want. Here are four different types of thinking:

If you look at struggling, poor people, notice their mentality: they only focus on helping themselves. They can't help others because they can't even help themselves.

Some people are not really even poor. They're just broke, which means they "could" make it a temporary thing, if they CHOOSE to. But if they don't change what they're doing in their spare time, then they are POOR people. Poor people CHOOSE to be poor by their poor decisions every month, every week, every day, and even hours and seconds. Poor people think, "ME, ME, ME and how am I going to get by today?" They waste their time complaining, blaming others, and focusing on their own "problems" rather than focusing on helping others and taking action toward the solutions.

The working middle-class people also think "ME, ME, ME." How am "I" going to pay "MY" bills this month? They also only think about themselves, month-by-month, and getting stuck in their routines of safety and security.

Now, rich people actually constantly think, "How am I going to help somebody ELSE get what they want? How am I going to solve somebody else's problem?" Then, they will make a plan and take action to be set up the next year. If people have flat tires, they'll take a risk and start a tire shop. Or if there's a need for tacos in the area, they start a taco shop to solve people's hunger problem!

Then there's the wealthy—they have a mentality of abundance and they think about the masses. They target huge problems and choose to be part of the solution.

The reason that we have cars, televisions, airplanes, or anything else for that matter, is because of wealthy people. Anything that we have, even the phones we have right now, is because of a wealthy (mentality) person. They thought to themselves, "How am I going to help the rest of the masses get to where they're trying to go, instead of having to take a covered wagon for 3 months to get from California to New York? How am I going to mass produce these automobiles so everybody can afford it, not just the wealthy ones?"

You see, at first, only the wealthy people could have cars, but then Mr. Ford said, "How am I going to mass produce the automobile to get the cost down, so that we can help EVERYONE afford a car and change the world?"

And this is the reason why people are wealthy. He had an abundance mentality, a wealth mentality. It's not about money; it's a mentality of service to others. My problem was I was focusing on ME. It's why people struggle. They focus on "ME, ME, ME."

Woody Woodward:

So when someone's down on their luck, and there are many people that have been affected by the economy, would you recommend them to have more hope to solve a bigger problem, so you go out and create more value for the people so that they can change their lives?

Marc Frank Montoya:
YES. Not just hope, but BELIEF that you CAN. If you're struggling, you must help yourself first before you can help another person, by knowing that you can CHANGE your habits. I recommend reading the right self-development and wealth books, investing into self development seminars, and getting mentors to become more valuable in the marketplace. Then you'll be able to teach what you've learned and add value to others. Once you gain experience and master the skills to be competent enough to help others, you are valuable. The amount of success you'll have is directly proportionate to how VALUABLE you are in the marketplace.

For me, I had to decide that I was tired of being broke and tired. You have to decide that something has to change. You can't be doing the same thing over and over again, hoping for a different result. It isn't going to happen. You have to make a change, and in my opinion, go toward your PASSION, or whatever makes you happy. DO NOT take the so-called "safe & secure job" (money) route, unless you are truly passionate about it.

And, you can't change the world; you have to start with that change in yourself. To become valuable and create value for the world, you have to be valuable to yourself. How do you make yourself valuable? You have to invest in yourself. You have to invest the time and money into yourself.

And if you don't know how to do that, you have to go searching for somebody that can show you how to do that, or a book that show you how to do that, or a seminar that can show you how to do that. So, I have observed people. Most of them waste their valuable money on liabilities—like cars, houses, and bigger TVs. They try to look and feel successful, (spending money on liabilities), as they put themselves in debt, instead of investing into assets and themselves to create wealth and freedom. They go to the bar, wasting money on drinks, to escape from reality. I guess they think it's easier to "escape" than to CHANGE, but they couldn't be more wrong. Many people are so tired from work that they just want to go home and relax. They sit on their ass and watch TV, wasting valuable TIME that they can't get back. This doesn't help their situation.

It makes it WAY worse for them, and they have huge regrets when they die. Most people say they "can't afford" to invest money or time into themselves. I say they can't afford NOT to. I used to spend a lot of money and time (on a car and house payments) trying to look success-ful but I wasn't; I was in debt.

Woody Woodward:
I know you do a lot of seminars and you do a lot of coaching and teaching people. You mentioned before that you have these five laws that you teach. What are those five laws, and will you share them with us?

Marc Frank Montoya:
Yeah, sure man... or at least I can scratch the surface for now...
- The first one is to BELIEVE: Believe you CAN.
- Second one is to CHANGE: Your environment and habits.
- The third one is to TAKE ACTION: Massive focused action.
- The fourth one is to INVEST—Invest in yourself, or "skill up."
- The fifth one is REPEAT (& DUPLICATE): For leverage and abundance to create freedom.

Woody Woodward:
So Number 1: Belief. When someone does not believe in themselves, what would you recommend them to do to start learning to believe in themselves?

Marc Frank Montoya:
You want to get around people that believe in you, and get far away from the people who have the whining, complaining, and "blaming oth-ers for where they are" mentality. I had no idea at the time, but back when I was younger, my environment was killing me. It is so important to get around the people that are positive and push you toward success,

instead of people who pull you down and give you their opinion, their "free advice" that "it won't work" or "you're crazy—that's a stupid idea!"

I had so many people with scarce mentalities telling me how "that's a bad idea—that's never going to work," and at first, I didn't even believe in myself. Luckily, I changed my environment and met new people. I can't tell you how instrumental that is for your life.

I believe God put this person in my life to really believe in me, so I could go on to do the things I now believe I can do. And the only reason I can do everything I do, is because I now BELIEVE I can. One other person that always believed in me and supported my decisions was my Mom. She never instilled limiting beliefs in my mind. She ONLY told me that I COULD do things, and she would protect me, keeping me away from people with ridiculous limiting words and actions that suggested they couldn't do big things in this world.

I observe how many parents tell their kids, "Oh, that's not going to work, don't do that. Stop that, don't do that," and the kids hear the words STOP, NO, and DON'T all day every day, for the first 15 years of their lives. Can you imagine what that does to a kid's belief levels?

I truly believe that one of the main reasons I know I can do anything in this world is that my mom never put that scarce and limiting nonsense into my mental system. She always encouraged me and supported my decisions, as long as they were moral and ethical.

The other thing was, I had a friend that kept telling me how much he believed in me and would tell me I was really good at skateboarding and snowboarding, EVERY DAY. He kept telling me that I should get sponsored and that I could be a PRO if I went after it. And then finally, after years of him pouring that belief into me, I started believing I COULD! After I had belief, there was no one who could stop me from pursuing my dreams. The feeling was too strong, and now I have this belief for life.

Woody Woodward:
Your friend Kelly really did change your life. I know your mom did as well. But look at Kelly. How many years did he tell you that you were

*good enough to be sponsored in either snowboarding or skateboarding,
and you didn't believe him? But finally you believed him, and it changed
your entire life.*

Marc Frank Montoya:
Yeah. Well I actually remember, it took four to five years of being
around him, and him encouraging and egging me on, and pushing
me, and saying, "Dude, I'm telling you, you're good, man. You could do
this, you could do that. You should try this!"

Oh, man, I'll tear up just thinking about it what this guy did for my
life. The world needs more people like him, and he is why I do what I
do for people every day. I love what he did for me, and I feel obligated
to do it for others. I believe it's my purpose.

Kelly was always excited for me and always on my side. So I eventually learned to be around people that were excited for others instead
of pulling people down, you know?

You see, sometimes your friends (and even family) will unconsciously sabotage you. They don't actually even know they're doing
it—but if they see you going off in a different direction than they are,
they'll accidentally pull you down by saying little negative things, just
because they don't want to lose you as a friend! It is said they are like
crabs in a bucket—one tries to get out, but then the others unknow-
ingly pull them back down where they are, instead of pushing them
UP, and none of them end up going anywhere.

So you really want to choose who you spend your time with wisely.
Think about who's getting you into trouble or wasting time, doing a
whole lot of nothing. Who's just sitting there stagnant, not growing, not
learning, and not going anywhere special.

They say if you're the smartest one in your group, you need to get a
new group! You are the average of the 5 friends you hang around the
most. So pay attention to that. It's one of the most important things in
your life, especially if you're trying to live an extraordinary life instead
of an ordinary one.

You are who you hang around with. You tell me who you hang with the most, and I'll tell you what you do with your time, how much money you make, and where you're going.

For example: if you hang around people that hang in the bars, eventually you're going to drink. If you hang around people that do drugs, eventually, you're going to do drugs. But if you hang around people that are actually going somewhere and actively looking for ways to be wealthy and successful, then most likely you're going to do that with them. So you really have to watch who you hang around. If you hang around 9 to 5 employees who just go to work and back, making other people rich, and watch TV in their spare time instead of creating a better future, then you're probably going to do the same things with your time.

If you don't BELIEVE you can, then you're right, you can't and won't! It's funny how the fear thing affects us all. Humans fear the unknown, and so they're just so scared of everything. If they only knew that right past your fear is your total FREEDOM, in every direction. I'm telling you, its right past your "comfort zone" —your health, your money, your time, everything.

I remember the day that I started believing in myself, and now I know that I can do anything in this world just because of that one law right there. You must BELIEVE you CAN. There's a quote that says, "Whether you think you can, or you think you can't—either way you're RIGHT." Believe me, it's not just a catchy phrase!

In fact, that's your subconscious! It is 30,000 times more powerful than your regular conscious, and if you let that thing control you, it's going to run your whole life. You have to really watch out for the stories you tell yourself, out loud and inside your head. The only things that keep you from every dream you ever had, are the stories and excuses you have for why you're not there already!

Woody Woodward:
Perfect. Tell us about the Law 2 about, "CHANGE." What does that mean?

Marc Frank Montoya:

It means for things to change in your life, you have to change YOURSELF. You can't change other people, or the world. Those are things you cannot control. If you try to control others, you will be unhappy and hopeless because it is not possible. The only thing you DO have control over is YOU—your ability to respond. And you can change, to take responsibility!

Every single decision you have ever made in your life has led you up to where you are right now, so you can go around pointing fingers and blaming the world for everything that happens, but you're going to be made fun of! If you're not happy with your current situation, you must change your habits, patterns, and decisions, or things will stay exactly the same. You must create the change internally and change your internal language.

It's called responsibility—the ABILITY to RESPOND. If what you've been doing up to this point in your life has not been working, then you MUST change to something that DOES work... or at least find some people that can show you things that DO work! You must change your environment—the people you're around, the food you eat, what you do with your time, your relationships, etc.

Woody Woodward:
So does that bring us to Law 3, about Massive (focused) Action? Because you're trying to change, but don't you really need to focus in on what you want to do and take massive action?

Marc Frank Montoya:

Yes, exactly. All 5 must be done simultaneously. Numbers 2 and 3 blend together as if they are one. You can't just "read the book." You have to take action and execute the steps to produce results.

You can't just tell yourself, "I'm going to change" and then go be a pro basketball player. You have to get out there on the court and on the pavement and do the action, massive action every single day that you can. There must be actions, STEPS with focus, discipline, and determination.

You must put that 10,000 hours in. Either 10 years or 10,000 hours of practice and training is what they say, which I'll get to in the next steps.

A lot of people think that being "busy" is being productive, but there's a huge difference. Massive focused action is where you're doing the specific things needed to achieve results—specific step-by-step actions that are going to inevitably get you where you're trying to go. Being "busy" is where you're running around thinking you're doing something, but it's not focused on the core values. I used to do that. I used to be a Fireman, putting out "fires" and running around "patching things up" in my life, instead of an Architect, investing my time to create my future dream life.

I know a lot of people that run around "doing things." I see most people spending more of their time buying Christmas presents, planning their weekend BBQs, and watching their TV, than they do creating their dream life.

Woody Woodward:
Totally agree. Number 4, "INVESTMENT." What do you mean by investment?

Marc Frank Montoya:
Well, it's not what most people would initially think. It's hardly a money investment. It's TIME investment, and "skilling up." It's about acquiring "specialized skills" in whatever field you love. It's the small decisions people make every single second of their life that are more important than the "bigger" decisions.

For instance, right now: The people reading this book are making an extremely valuable time investment instead of watching other people live THEIR dreams on a TV. Are you going to sit there and invest time into watching TV or gossip about people, knowing that it does nothing for your future?

OR, are you going to invest that same exact time into reading the right book, investing in yourself to learn how to get where you're really trying to go? This would be a tiny decision, but over time, it adds up to make the ultimate decision to be successful.

There are tons of books on "skilling up" and self-development. The last one I read was *Outliers*, where it's a golden rule: You must invest either 10 years or 10,000 hours of practice and training to have the "specialized skills" in the bigger money and success in your field. There's "luck," if you want to call it that but you must realize that every circumstance can be an opportunity, depending on how you CHOOSE to look at it. You can choose to create your future, instead of being a victim to the things that happen in your life.

Let's say you get laid off. How do you know it wasn't an unknown force or the Law of Attraction that makes it a blessing in disguise in the near future, forcing you to take a new direction you were supposed to be headed in the first place? You can take those "setbacks" and make them into stepping stones, to make yourself strong, learn from your mistakes, and make money with your passions, as long as you put those hours into Skill Development.

Many people will accidentally and unconsciously put most of their time into a job that brings linear income. This means that they do the work once, and get paid once, so they will be working for a very, very long time, making someone else rich, in what is called the "Rat Race." Without much thought, they will just "do what they've been told." Many of us have learned to trade our time for money, making an hourly wage or salary. Is that really what you would call the American dream? Not for me! Most people thoughtlessly spend all of their time chasing money, so they never have any time. They constantly say they're "too busy" for other things that are important in their life!

What about your freedom? Imagine yourself being FREE financially? Have you ever stepped outside of the box to understand what that means or how to achieve it? Most people will unconsciously invest their priceless time to become skilled at something that brings in linear income, which means you trade hard work in exchange for money.

My point is you have to watch out! What are you investing your spare TIME into? What are you becoming skilled for? After I learned how important freedom really is, I invested my time into learning how to create more freedom in my life. I invested to get skilled at FREEDOM, and I can't even begin to tell you what an amazing life it is. It is very different from the "regular" world of "traditionalists."

If you get "skilled" at watching TV because you do it all the time, wow, okay, sweet. You're the guy or gal that knows everybody's name on the local professional football team. But now you must think: Is this going to help you create a better quality future? What value does that skill really bring to the marketplace or the world? You see, you've got to watch out what you're spending your time on! Your success in this world is directly proportionate to how much VALUE you bring to it. If you don't choose to be a valuable person, you will struggle, and not be successful.

So, first I got skilled at my passions—skateboarding and snowboarding. I thought, "At the very least, even if I'm not getting paid huge amounts of money, I'll be in the industry that I love, doing what I love! Then it won't really be "work" for me!" I figured if I'm happy, then that is success!

I didn't know what I did when I did it, but just because I loved snowboarding and skateboarding, I invested all of my extra time, sacrificing other things I liked, to eventually gain the "specialized skills" in that field. I ended up growing into an international professional snowboarder, and got paid tons of money and traveling the world to do what I love!

BUT, then I tasted what real freedom is—you know, like not having to show up to a 9 to 5 job any more, and listen to some jerk tell me what to do all damn day! There wasn't any way I could go back to a "regular" job or business, making the tiny wages I made before. I knew I couldn't snowboard forever, so I decided I needed to invest in myself and take risks to get skilled on the business side of things.

I invested everything I had into different businesses, ideas, and ventures for a while, and all that really did was get me really "busy!" I invested a lot of effort and money in the "traditional" world, but it didn't get me what I wanted, and actually took me AWAY from the important things in life. Good thing I've always been the type to not care about anything except for being happy. I took a step back, and started looking for other successful people that had the success, and more importantly, the freedom that I wanted. So I invested the time to know what they know, and do the things that they were doing, so I could get what they got! Funny how it totally worked out!

Woody Woodward:
How do Laws 1, 2, 3, and 4 apply to Law 5, "REPEAT and DUPLICATE?"

Marc Frank Montoya:
Well, I say "repeat" because many people think that success is the destination. Once people gain riches, or what they thought was success, it's hard for them to learn anything because they then think they already know it all! This stuff cracks me up!

The problem for a lot of people is: this world changes so fast. If you're not willing to learn and adapt to today's fast-paced changing business world, you fall behind the bubble very fast. People that do not stay open-minded to learn, or realize that success is a journey that doesn't end, and that it's not a destination, are quickly left behind, stuck in their "comfort zone," stuck with old ideas they've been taught. They have to be willing to change their beliefs, take action, and invest again. REPEAT!

Now, the duplication part: duplication creates abundance. Take franchising, for example. The problem with "smart" or "skilled" people is, it's hard to duplicate them. Small business owners like doctors, lawyers, and dentists have a hard time with this. They don't trust other people or systems to run a business. To create abundance or wealth—in money, or time, or health—there must be duplication. The way you can do that is you have to duplicate yourself.

Nothing wrong with small business owners; but if I'm owned by my business, I don't have the time to save the world, right? I mean I wish I could save the world, you know, that'd be a sweet deal.

I also believe that everybody wishes they could help others, but they can't because they don't have the extra time or money. Even I can only give so much to charity and have the time to help so many people.

BUT, if I duplicate myself and teach others how to do what I've done, using systems and different business models to create freedom, well.... duh! So, let's say I make over $200k per year. Well, either I'm going to have to give a lot of that money to taxes to spend on war, or I'm going to give it to charity! So I'm going to give it to charity, plus it's a write-off!

Well, now, if I duplicate and teach others how to make $200,000.00 or $1 million per year, I can show them how to give it to charity and write it off instead of paying it all to taxes to make bombs with! Now THAT'S how you save the world! One time, I was in a convention where we were able to raise $1.2 million dollars in two hours by doing this! It is one of the most powerful things I've ever seen in my life. I also now work with a company that has fed over 300,000,000 meals around the world. This can only be achieved through duplication.

Now, as far as franchising: I can go from getting 100 percent of ONE person's efforts (which is only my own), to getting 5 percent of 1,000 people's efforts instead. Then I have created the abundance of money and time using systems to duplicate myself. I'm not quite sure if this is making sense because I'm trying to cram it into a chapter. Let's say I work one of my businesses for 2 hours today.

Now, if I have a team of 150 franchisees that are all working on their own businesses for 2 hours today, then that's 150 people times 2 hours. That's 300 hours, plus my 2 hours. Now, that is 302 hours of work I got for 2 hours of work I did today! Can you see how that gives me an abundance of time because I've duplicated my efforts by building sales TEAMS, like every other business does? Mini-franchising is key!

Woody Woodward:

You had a successful snowboarding career and you're still a professional snowboarder. But you've also gone into investing in real estate and small companies, stock investing, movie production, etc., but also teaching other people how to be successful in business. What do you do now? What's the favorite thing that you do now?

Marc Frank Montoya:

My favorite thing is learning and growing so that I can duplicate and spread the knowledge. The world needs real education, not corrupt school systems. It wakes me up in the morning just like snowboarding does, to know I'm helping people. When you're passionate about something, life is amazing. I think a lot of people become depressed and all that crap when all they do is focus on themselves. As soon as you live your life to help others, it's funny how fun it gets!

One of the best feelings in the world—and it's actually one of the seven human needs—is contribution. It just feels so good, even just helping an old lady cross the street. When you walk away, that feeling of doing something for another person is amazing. You feel so good about yourself and have real purpose in the world, and that only comes from serving other people.

I believe life is about serving others, helping other people, not just yourself. BUT you must start with yourself and grow to overcome obstacles, so you have been there and done that. Then you can help others do the same. The learning and growing part is mandatory. It's called "failing forward." You may crash and burn, get rejection, and hit walls, but you push through them, get back up, and learn what not to do the next time. There is no "try," there's only a DO.

We're like a tree, you know. We are like anything in nature. As soon as you stop growing, you start dying. That's when life becomes boring and stagnant for people, no matter how much money you have.

When we're young and we're just out there learning new things and having new experiences, climbing trees, discovering cocoons in a tree, we're like, "Wow!" Life is exciting because we're learning, our brain is growing, and that's when life is fun. If we're NOT learning, we're stagnant and life becomes boring.

So when we grow older, get out of school and reality hits, we have to go get a crappy job. We stop learning, stop growing, and that's when we get caught in a rut and feel stuck. People caught in their "comfort zones" and it just becomes boring and drab, almost hopeless.

So I love to see when things click for people and you can see their brain working and growing. Their hope starts to grow and their life becomes fun and bright again! People who learn new exciting new things start looking forward to the future instead of being a victim to it, you know?

All you have to do is get out there on a Monday and you'll see what I mean. People are stopped at the light, dreading going in to work all day, waiting around in "quiet desperation" for a lot of their life. They look stuck, they feel stuck, they're pissed off and they don't know WHY. But when you're able to show them a way, and you see the change that happens in them, and all of a sudden, they are actually stoked on the future and they know where they're going. It's an amazing feeling to know you helped someone, and changed the course of their life.

Woody Woodward:
You've had a lot of mentors in your life and you've been a mentor in many people's lives. When someone's looking for a mentor, what should they look for?

Marc Frank Montoya:
You should ONLY look for somebody that has the life you want, or has a proven track record in the area you're looking for. Then you study them, model them—you copy them to get what they got. You study and learn and try to grow. If you don't know them personally, then find them in books. Growing up, I didn't know any millionaires or ultra successful people, so I found my friends and mentors in the books, and went searching for people that were successful in the areas I wanted to be successful in. I made new friends, and that's who I started to hang around more. I changed my environment. It is so important to understand that you are a product of your environment. A seed will not grow if it's in dry, non-fertile grounds. You have to get yourself in the right environment if you want to grow upward.

When I wanted to be a good snowboarder, I moved to the mountains where all the good snowboarders were, and I got around people that were better than me so I could get better faster. Then I knew to take a risk and move to Utah where the snowboarding was at another higher level, the kind of snowboarding that I wanted to do, which was big mountain riding. It was at a higher level, so I got better faster. When it was time and I wanted to build a business, I knew to do that with business, too. I needed to get around people that were better than me, so I could get better faster.

So, a warning… and this is one of the most important things I'll say here. You really have to watch who you're taking advice from, because our friends and our family are most of the time our worst enemies when it comes to success. Now, this may sound harsh, but it's the truth.

Most people are not wealthy with time freedom or money, but they want to give their "free" advice. Most advice is free, right?! And so you watch out; you get what you pay for!

I had a lot of people giving me advice back in the day. "Oh, that's not going to work. Oh what, are you trying to be? Mr. Mountain guy pro snowboarder?" Many times, people are actually thinking they're helping you by trying to keep you "safe," away from risk and failure. What they don't understand is that failure is mandatory to be able to learn. If you're not crashing and burning, you're not trying hard enough or taking enough risks! Those that are scared to take risks, end up doing nothing special in their life time. Those that aren't getting criticized must not be doing anything out of the ordinary, so they'll just be ordinary.

My dad loves me to death but he was giving me his opinion back in the day. He would say, thinking he was helping me, "Man, what are you doing with that skateboard? You need to go to school and get a job; that's what you need to do."

That was his advice. He was trying to HELP me and was just giving me the information that had been handed down to him, which came from his parents and influences who were not wealthy either. They struggled. So really, he almost killed every dream I ever had. I never would have lived out all of my dreams, traveling the world, making tons of money with total freedom. If I had taken that advice and gone to school to get a "safe secure job," I would have been stuck in a building being bossed around for the last 16 years, making a tiny salary.

Now, my Dad and I have these talks all the time. He is so happy and proud of me, and I love him, you know, I've helped him retire. But he was born in a chicken coop. I mean they were poorer than poor. What good advice could they hand down? He was literally born inside of like a chicken coop!

So taking different types of advice from the wrong people can be deadly. Let's take the subject of health for example: Taking health advice from somebody that's obese would not be a very good idea, would it? In most cases, taking business advice from traditionalists who are not successful in business would not be a good idea at all. It's funny to listen to a traditionalist give their advice. "No, don't try that! Are you sure you want to risk that? Yeah, instead, just go to school to learn how to make somebody ELSE rich in a "safe secure job." There you go, that's a great idea! Get taxed to death in the employee tax category and build somebody else's dreams your whole life, not your own! Yep, just sit there and work 45 hours a week for the next 45 years to retire when you're 70 years old!" RRRRIGHT.... I don't think that's the best advice you could give someone you care about! People that are struggling month-to-month, or stuck in a job they hate, should not be giving business advice AT ALL, and if they do, you should not take it! I wouldn't listen to an unsuccessful person give any business advice because they haven't really "been there and done that."

And if you're currently in that situation, you better take massive action to invest in yourself and find a way out of a J.O.B. (It means Just Over Broke!). Realize that there is no "tomorrow." Tomorrow never comes. Do it NOW. At least take the first steps and find a way to go after your dreams! Think about this: Say you're having a relationship problem. You're on the rocks with your significant other, and you have that friend sitting there giving you their "valuable" and FREE advice on relationships. They say things like, "Yeah, yeah, forget her, man. There's way more other fish in the sea." I mean come on! Should you really be taking advice from someone that's been divorced three times and is currently single? Then why would you listen to struggling, month-to-month working class people on business?

So again, you have to watch out who you're taking advice from and look for people who actually HAVE what you want, and then only take advice from them on that subject. As soon as I stopped taking advice from broke people or struggling people, and started doing what wealthy people do, is when things really started to change for me. Now the only business I do is for residual money, never "linear" income. I only do business that creates true wealth and time freedom, that allows me to do what I want, when I want, so I'm not owned by my business. By the way, wealth is not measured in money, it's measured in TIME! The only people I take health advice from are health gurus that have a proven track record, and look and feel healthy and young with tons of energy.

Woody Woodward:
You've had a lot of success in your life; you've had ups and downs. And now that you've made it to the top, how do you define success? Because we all know it's not about dollars and cents.

Marc Frank Montoya:
Yeah. I define success as being happy and free, with abundance, and no stress, with extra time to help others in need. If you're happy doing what you're doing, and it creates joy for others, that is success.

Woody Woodward:
When times get tough, as they all do for entrepreneurs, what advice would you give to someone to encourage them to keep going?

Marc Frank Montoya:
When times get tough? I would advise them to—seems like a catchy phrase or cliché—but you literally have to step back and think about, "What good can I learn from this? What valuable lesson can I pull from this?" The bad things that come your way—I believe they're put there on purpose, and you can use each and every one of them as a stepping

stone to make your character stronger, to be able to get you to the top.

It's not what happens to you, it's what you DO with what happens to you. Many people think that problems go away when you have more money but they are wrong. In fact, more money means more problems. It's not that there are fewer problems when you have money. It's that people with money are successful because of the way their mind works. They are good at making "problems" into CHALLENGES, and they make problems extremely small very quickly. Instead of "road blocks," they think of problems as road bumps! You can sit there and be a victim, but it's all about the decisions that you make on how you deal with things. You can whine and complain and point fingers at everybody, and blame the world for YOUR problems that YOU created. But whether you're successful or not, it's YOUR fault. YOU did that! Your decisions and action or lack thereof, create the quality of your life. It's a choice, every second—happy or not, free or a slave to fear or laziness.

No matter what, there will always be the finger-pointing, blaming whiners that blame everything else except themselves for where they are. But every decision you've ever made has led you up to where you are right now. So, you know, if you're not happy with where you are, it's time to start making better decisions; and you can literally use the "setbacks" as a learning tool and say, "Oh, awesome. I know not to get in that situation again!"

Sometimes, things happen that are out of your control; but what you CAN control is how you RESPOND to the things that happen. That's why they call it "response-ABILITY." There's a reason, every single time. You can choose to be the victim, and act like it was just put there to make your life horrible, OR you can make a decision to say, "Wow, that was probably put there for a reason so I can learn from it, to build me into a stronger person, and be able to help others going through the same thing."

That's also how God works: You might be road-raging and be pissed off that the light turned red and you have to sit there for the next five minutes. But you never know. What if you wouldn't have been stopped, you would have gotten in a crazy car wreck on the next intersection, but God kept you a block away? You never know why until later, when the real lessons are learned.

Woody Woodward:

What do you want your legacy to be?

Marc Frank Montoya:

I want my legacy to be that I duplicated knowledge. It's the ignorance—the LACK of knowledge, the lack of information that causes FEAR. People fear what they don't know about. They fear the "unfamiliar." So it's the ignorance that causes fear. The hatred in this world comes from FEAR, and fear is not real; it's in our imagination.

Humans instinctively fear what they don't know, and they don't know to look from other perspectives besides their own. They have their existing beliefs, and then they try to push their beliefs on other people, because they're looking for significance. Here's the funny part: they are trying to be significant so that they will be LOVED. Why do they want to be "loved?" So they will not be "alone." It's one of the deepest human fears and one of the only fears you are basically born with. So what people are actually looking for is LOVE, but how do you get real love?

You don't really get love by being significant and pushing your beliefs on other people. You get love by GIVING love, right here, right now. That's how you get real love. So I've realized to love and help people, and educate them on the things they need, so that they're not fearful, but joyful. It may be a selfish reason, I don't know, but damn, it's a good feeling. Humans don't feel fear when they actually know their environment and are familiar with it. This is why deer stay on "deer trails." Same way humans put themselves in "ruts" or routines. So if I can make the "unknown" the KNOWN, and transfer this knowledge to my kids and to other people that will spread that knowledge and get rid of a lot of the fear, that would get rid of a lot of hate and greed, struggle, and all the crazy things ruining this world.

I'll hopefully be remembered and known for helping change the limiting habits and beliefs of people, to make the world a better place. I've broken the chain of bad lifestyles that have happened in families, and hopefully, will help it carry on through generations. Not just legacies of money, but the knowledge it takes to manifest abundance. You can leave kids with millions of dollars, but without the correct values, knowledge, and information, they're just going to blow it if they don't know how to manage and manifest the things they want in their lives. It's the information, the mindset, and the knowledge that I'd like to leave.

Maria Olson

Maria Olson is passionate about freedom and believes that it can only be created through individuals and families learning and applying the principles of freedom in their own lives, and then reaching out in love and compassion to teach others to do the same. She has successfully overcome depression and anxiety in her life and has assisted many other women in freeing themselves from emotional and physical issues using The 5 Systems Approach to Personal Freedom™. She has a gift for mentoring youth and women. She has mentored some men as well. She believes that mission and business can and should intersect. She is enjoying living her passion while helping to provide financially for her family. She is dedicated to helping others do the same.

In addition to being a successful business woman, she is also devoted to her family. She has been married to her husband for 17 years and is a homeschooling mother of 5 beautiful children.

Website: www.mariaeolson.com

Woody Woodward:

Maria, you've been a successful mom and a successful businesswoman. How do you juggle both? Most parents have a tough time being one or the other. How have you managed to spend time with your children and still run your company?

Maria Olson:

I think the key for me with juggling my business and my family has been to create blocks of time where I focus on my business and then other blocks where I focus on my family. I also include a block of time for myself and my individual growth and needs. I have found that doing this has allowed me to be 100 percent present everywhere I am. Early on in my business, I made the mistake of trying to be a mom and do business all in the same time period, and it just wasn't working for me, so I switched over to this time blocking, and it has made all the difference. My kids feel more important. They feel more loved because when I'm with them, they get my full attention.

When I am with my family, I'm not thinking about my business. I'm thinking only about them. When I'm doing my business, I separate myself away from the family and I am focusing only on clients and the business.

Woody Woodward:

I think that is a great idea about time blocking. What would be some suggestions on how to time block?

Maria Olson:

It has been a process of trial and error, trying different things, moving different time blocks around until I found the right system for me. But I think what has worked the best is in the morning, when I wake up, and then right before I go to bed is my time. That's when my kids are in bed. It's quiet. I get to focus just on myself. Then, since I am a home school mother, I usually spend the mornings with my children, and also one full day a week with them. In the afternoon, typically from about 1:00 to 5:00, is my business time.

Woody Woodward:

When juggling your business and your personal life, how do you—or what do you do for your personal time? What are some things that you enjoy doing for your personal time?

Maria Olson:

I am a very spiritual person, so I like to spend a lot of time in my core book. My core book is the book that I align myself most with truth, so I spend a lot of time there. I also rejuvenate by exercising and studying. I do a lot of studying on my own. I am constantly reading about five or six books at a time and really working on my own personal development. I also do some meditation and keeping my mind clear, free and inspired.

Woody Woodward:

I find that most successful people—I would say almost all successful people I've ever interviewed or know are very tenacious readers. What books have helped you the most? Is there a certain author or a certain book that really set you on the right path that you'd recommend?

Maria Olson:

Yes, to tell you the honest truth, I love—and you wouldn't think of this as a typical business book, but it really is what set me on my path—*The Coming Aristocracy* by Oliver DeMille. In it, he talks about how we are losing our freedoms in this country and how one of the keys to gaining back our freedom is by becoming leaders—he calls it social leadership—and finding a need in our communities and filling it. Not waiting for someone else to fill it, but just taking that plunge ourselves and doing what needs to be done. I would say that book really started me on my path and really helped me understand that I needed to discover what it is that I can do to make a difference and do it.

Woody Woodward:

Books are really one of the greatest mentors I've ever seen. For you, when you started your company, you mentioned that you liked having a mentor. How did you find the mentor that helped you get on your path?

Maria Olson:

Earlier I mentioned being a very spiritual person. I am prayerful and meditative, and I am always seeking for the right mentor for me at the right time. So a lot of times, to tell you the honest truth, I have just been led to the right mentor. I am actively seeking, and that mentor just appears.

Woody Woodward:
So, it goes along with the quote that when the student is ready, the teacher will appear?

Maria Olson:
Yes! I just always set the intention that I will find the right mentors that I need at the right time, and they do show up for me.

Woody Woodward:
When you've met that mentor, how do you interview them, or what do you look for in a mentor to make sure they're the right fit for you?

Maria Olson:
For me, it's more of a feeling. I do ask questions, but it tends to be very organic. It is more just feeling a connection and resonating with that person. I think I am drawn to the mentor before I see what it is they're doing. Does that make sense? And then, if they're doing exactly what I need, then I know it's a right fit. That has worked really well for me.

Woody Woodward:
Let's shift gears real quick. What is the greatest risk you've ever taken, and was it worth it?

Maria Olson:
That's an interesting question. I think my whole life has been about taking risks. However, at the time that I take the risks, I don't usually realize that I am taking one. I tend to be a ready- fire-aim type of person. A lot of times, I will jump into things with both feet, just gung-ho and excited and then later on down the road, I'll look back and think, "Oh, my goodness, that was really scary. I can't believe I did that." But at the time, it didn't feel scary.

Woody Woodward:
What advice and encouragement would you give to a budding entrepre-

neur, somebody who wants to follow their dreams, but just doesn't have the courage to do so?

Maria Olson:

I would say go for it. It is so worth it. If you just keep going on the path, you will get there someday. It's just a process of falling down and getting back up. Just keep doing that over and over and over again. If you keep getting up, you cannot fail. That's probably my biggest advice.

Woody Woodward:

Most successful entrepreneurs I've interviewed have an interesting concept on failure. You kind of mentioned it right there as, as long as you keep getting up, you haven't failed. How do you define failure?

Maria Olson:

I define failure as giving up. I don't think there is any failure until you quit. We fall down, and we make mistakes, but we can always learn from those things. Just get back up, brush ourselves off, and keep going again. I don't believe in failure unless it means just giving up.

Woody Woodward:

You've had success in your personal life, your relationships, and your business. How do you define success?

Maria Olson:

This goes along with the answer that I gave for failure, but it's just going the distance, being willing to go all the way with something, make a commitment, and stick to it. That's what success is to me. If I have made a commitment in my marriage, then I am willing to do whatever it takes to obtain it, and this pertains to any type of goal or decision.

Woody Woodward:

When times get tough, and they do for all of us, what do you do to stay focused?

Maria Olson:

I have what I like to call an emotional toolbox. This is just a collection of tools and things that I have learned along the way to help me stay motivated and to get back up when I fall down. Some of these things are reading good books, staying around inspiring people and associating myself with them. I also use my personal freedom techniques that I have developed to stay clear and focused and to keep myself in an emotionally good place—that's been a big key for me. I also use prayer and meditation. I have so many things in my toolbox that I can just draw from and pull out whenever I need them.

Woody Woodward:

What would you recommend for somebody who is going through a challenging time? What would you recommend for them to put into their emotional toolbox?

Maria Olson:

I would say number one, even before putting anything in your emotional toolbox, is get a mentor. Get somebody who has the result or is on the path of the results that you want because chances are, they're going to have the tools that you need and will help make them available to you. Another great thing to do is to sit down in a quiet place and make a list. What are those things that uplift you, motivate you, and help you to get out of the down places that we all face and none of us are immune to? Who are the people that inspire you and help you to be accountable?

Woody Woodward:

What has been your greatest "Aha" moment in your business, when you finally realized, "Oh, my gosh. I'm on the right path, doing the right thing?"

Maria Olson:

Let's see, I would say it's having people come to me and ask me what I am doing and ask for my services because to me, that is just the ultimate sign that I am doing exactly what I need to be doing. People are actually asking me for help.

Woody Woodward:

Being an entrepreneur, a lot of us run into fear. We run into those ob-

stacles that hold us back. I know you talked about the emotional toolbox, but is there a different technique you use when you're faced with fear? How do you turn your fear into productivity?

Maria Olson:

I think that there's always going to be an element of fear when you are doing big things. I have found that I can do all of the emotional work, I can use every tool in my toolbox, but there will always be fear when I'm doing something big and I'm taking a risk. And so, the key for me has been to do it anyway. I just push through that fear because on the other side of that fear is success and results and satisfaction. You just can't get around that fear.

It's always going to be there, but it lessens and it goes away. Then we get new experiences that help us stretch and grow. I really believe that having fear is actually a good indication that you're on the right path because change and doing big things require an amount of fear. It's something different. Our bodies are meant to protect us and keep us safe, so when we change and do things that we've never done and we're not accustomed to doing naturally results in fear. We just have to push through it anyway.

Woody Woodward:
What is the best thing you like about being a mentor and helping people?

Maria Olson:

I love it when people have "Aha" moments and you just see that moment where they connect with truth. That, to me, is so fulfilling. Their eyes light up. Their voice changes. They're filled with excitement. They're filled with understanding and knowledge and light. That is so exhilarating for me.

Woody Woodward:
You have a special system to help people overcome their challenges. You're a personal freedom mentor. What is that system?

Maria Olson:

The system that I use to help people overcome the blocks that are coming up for them in their life is called The Five Systems approach to personal freedom. This is my personal method that I have learned and developed along the way as I have learned tools from other mentors, books, and other insights that I have picked up along the way. The five systems are the heart, the mind, the soul, might, and strength. I use these five systems to help people figure out what the blocks are that are keeping them stuck in their lives. The heart deals with beliefs. Beliefs guide our lives. Whether we consciously want them to or not, what we believe in our heart is going to influence the decisions that we make. The mind deals with thoughts and learning how to be in charge of our own thoughts instead of allowing them to control us. If we are not in charge of our thoughts, then they will just take over in a negative way.

The soul mainly has to do with emotions that become trapped in the body that create health and physical issues. Might has to do with all of our surroundings that support us: money, other physical resources, our relationships, and our education. Strength has to do with our inner abilities and our personal energy that enable us to do what we want to do and fulfill those dreams in our lives.

Woody Woodward:
What type of legacy do you want to leave?

Maria Olson:

The legacy that I want to leave is freedom. To me, freedom is being able to move, and do, and be without any inhibitions, with nothing holding me back.

Liz Phalp

Liz is a health coach who loves helping people discover the power inside themselves to be sexy, powerful and productive. She has a degree in Human Biology, and has experience in First Aid teaching and Natural Childbirth Education. Her most valuable experience has come from learning to feed her six children, healthy, easy meals, while staying in shape after multiple childbirths herself.

Liz's philosophy is that with a greater application of the rules that govern our bodies, we can more easily attain results that will keep us motivated long after the initial excitement wears off.

Liz comes from an anti-diet philosophy, showing that deprivation and restriction never lead to long-term benefits. In adapting a new belief system, clients will learn to enjoy eating and exercising, and the fat-loss that comes as a natural result.

The Green Smoothie Goddess • liz@lizphalp.com
lizphalp.com • powerlifeacadey.com

Woody Woodward:

You're very successful in teaching women how to overcome their challenges, how to have the life they want, and the permission to have passion in their life. What three steps do you recommend to women to take their lives back?

Liz Phalp:

I studied a lot about people losing weight and reaching those kinds of goals, and then a lot of programs, and such. I found that the very first most important step is the mindset. No matter what physical actions we take, if we don't address the mindset, then nothing lasts. Everything goes back to the way it was. So I always focus first on the mindset.

Second is skill set, or what I also refer to as habits. This is where we invest time in creating new habits—new ways of doing things. I explain to people in my program that it's an investment initially, but that will create an automatic response afterwards. So it's a little work initially; but then they have these habits and patterns that are going to build on top of that mindset, or on top of that new belief system that will keep them on that path that they have determined that they want to be on.

The third step is environment; this is all about setting ourselves up to succeed. We ask ourselves, "What can I do with my physical environment and the things that surround me to keep me supported in this task?" There are many different ways to do this with our physical environment.

When talking about food specifically, it might be having lots of healthy options available in our kitchen, healthy foods within easy reach, etc. But there's also the idea of creating an environment that's more supportive to our mindset and our habits that we've developed. We just eliminate all of the clutter, all of the things that make us feel guilty, and we replace it with things that are more supportive of this new belief system that we have created for ourselves.

Woody Woodward:
Having a mindset is one of the most crucial things. Can you go deeper into mindset? What do you mean by mindset and what do you do to help your client overcome the mental challenges that they have?

Liz Phalp:
I believe mindset really is the core of it all. I have a lot of experience in hypnosis. I taught childbirth hypnosis classes—and what we really discovered in everybody is that we all come with a mindset that is either inherited from our families or developed throughout

our childhood. Not all of them are beneficial to us. And so we've got to take some of it out and put some new stuff in, and create what we really want, and what will be beneficial.

One of the first things I focus on for shifting mindset is—when I'm working with a client, and they've determined what the goals are that they want to reach, what results they want, the first thing I ask them is, "What's the downside to achieving that goal?" There's always a downside to it; otherwise, they would have reached it by now.

There's something in their mind telling them it's not safe, or it will be too hard, or it's not worth the cost. There's something in their mind that's keeping them from reaching that. So we have to go into that and address it, and see what needs to be reprogrammed there.

Another obstacle to shifting our mindset is the judgments—our own judgments—and to be able to release these judgments we have of ourselves, of our abilities. We are all capable of so much more, but we end up making these judgments about ourselves... "Well, I can't do that much, I don't have that much time, I'm not that strong." Once we release these judgments, we are open to so much more access of empowering ourselves.

Another idea that I focus on is the importance of pleasure. This comes back to the guilt that we feel, and it sort of fits in with judgment. But it's one step farther where, when we live in this "should world" of doing all the things that we should for some reward down the line, or whatever reason it might be, we deprive ourselves of a very innate need that we have to experience pleasure in our life. And when we deprive ourselves of pleasure, our mind and our body will find that pleasure for themselves, if we don't provide it in healthy, natural ways.

This most often leads to addiction and many other problems, especially at night when we're tired. And so getting on top of that, being able to shift the mindset that giving into, or enjoying, pleasure is weakness, and instead, seeing how to incorporate pleasure into our experience with eating, and in our experiences with everything else that we do on a day-to-day basis, in that entire process of reaching our goals, and being able to find the joy in it. Once we give ourselves permission to find joy and pleasure in life, we are much better off.

The last thing I do involves my experience with hypnosis. In my programs, I actually use hypnosis scripts to help ingrain these new belief systems onto the mind, so that rather than just hearing an idea once, they are able to impress these things upon their mind and have it become a new part of them. It really does reprogram that part of their brain. For example, it's like when you read a book and you come upon an idea and think, "Oh, that's good," and then you forget about it within minutes. Hypnosis enables the person to retain this information in an intimate way. It really is an amazing tool.

Woody Woodward:

What books would you recommend for someone who wants to change their mindset?

Liz Phalp:

I guess the first one that had a big impact on me was Steven Covey's *Seven Habits of Highly Effective People*. That was the first one that really shifted my mindset in a dramatic way and opened me up to a whole world of new beliefs and ideas. For me, that was the first one. It's basic, but it's also really comprehensive and profound.

Woody Woodward:

There was a second thing you mentioned about skill set. Will you go into further detail with that? How does someone increase their skill set? Or let's say they don't have the confidence; but how does someone increase their skill set?

Liz Phalp:

So this is where action comes in. If all we do is focus on the theory of things and the mindset of things, nothing ever really takes hold. We have to get at this point where we start taking action, where we start doing something, or else all these things that we've re-trained our mind to believe are not going to stick. If we don't have some physical proof of things, some evidence, then these new ideas aren't going to stick and aren't going to create the necessary change in our lives. And so this is why the second step is this more action-oriented way of developing a skill set.

I compare this to driving. When we're learning how to drive, there are a hundred things we're thinking about at one time. It seems like so much effort and so much work to just think about all this and we can't imagine how someone could listen to the radio while they're driving. But then once our body and our mind learn these things, they become habits. We can do it without thinking at all.

And so what I do is, I take the things that have the most dramatic impact on the most common goals that people want to reach when they come to me; and then I have them practice these habits until they become part of their lifestyle. I tell them it's going to feel awkward at first, just like the first driving experience—like you're trying to think and do too many things at once. But in the end, it's going to create this magical gift for you. Once you've invested this initial work, you now have this result that your mind and your body take over and just do these things for you.

You don't even have to think about it anymore, yet you still get the results from it. So things like having a morning ritual, exercising, taking time to meditate—all those kinds of things— that are usually on our "should" list, but most people never actually invest enough time to turn it into a habit.

Woody Woodward:
A lot of times, people say that they're a victim of their environment. How do you help people look at their environment differently and put them back in control?

Liz Phalp:
The first thing is just being able to get really clear on what it is we want. Such as, "What would be a supportive environment to us?" Because if we can't imagine it, we're not going to be able to create it.

For most people, the biggest thing to do first is just to start to de-clutter, start to get rid of things. This can be done in so many different ways. For example, if we're looking at our home, and there's clutter everywhere, we become this slave to organizing and putting it away all day long, and that sucks up all our time and motivation.

The same thing can happen with our bodies. Clutter in our minds or clutter in our bodies can take many forms. One example can be from eating junk food all the time. It's just going to fill up our body with all these toxins essentially that our body has to wrap up in fat in order to protect us.

And then there's the clutter in our minds. If we are not able to say no to people and we sign up for things all the time that really aren't our highest priorities, then we're cluttering up our environment and mind with things that aren't necessary, things that aren't ours, or things that we didn't really choose.

And so the first principle is to clear some space to make some room to create what we want in our environment; because trying to put stuff on top of what's already there is simply not going to work. So if we focus on first clearing out our minds, and creating some new space, then we can go into specifics—things related to their goals. We can ask, "What do you want to be in that space now and how would you like to create it?"

Woody Woodward:
As a mom, spouse, daughter, and a friend—you've got so much on your plate. When you look at your life, what do you see as the biggest risk you've ever taken? It might have been starting your new company, it might have been selling another company. What's the greatest risk you've ever taken, and was it worth it?

Liz Phalp:
Just over a year ago was, I finally decided to really trust this voice inside me that was telling me that I needed to do more; that I needed to invest in myself to be able to take those shortcuts of what hiring a business coach could do for me, and in having the mentors and the

people around me that I need. And so I invested a large amount of money into mentoring and into coaching. This was super scary. My husband was the one providing all of the income for our family at the time, and I was full-time with the kids.

So it was scary in a couple of ways. Number one, I'm taking away these resources from the family, and investing them in myself. And second, if I'm doing this, I've got to be pretty committed now. If I don't get results, it's a huge weight to carry. I've committed myself to take this time essentially out of what I'm doing with my family, and to put them somewhere else.

So it was a huge risk, and I felt 100 percent that it was what I wanted to do and what I needed to do. I haven't regretted it for a second.

Woody Woodward:
What are the most common challenges your clients are faced with?

Liz Phalp:
My tagline is to be sexy, be powerful, and be productive. Maybe because of that, I've attracted women who are seeking more energy in their life. Energy is number one. They have a lot that they want to do and feel like they can't keep up, and they're just tired.

And the second thing is, they just want to look good and feel good about themselves. Then they want to be more productive in moving towards their goals in life.

What it really always comes down to, and what they really need is, to give themselves permission to invest in themselves, to take some time out to go to the gym or to start a new sport or hobby, to give themselves permission to enjoy their lives and to find pleasure in the things that they do—the list of things that they feel obligated to do, as well as the things that they've chosen for themselves.

So what they really need is permission to tap into that inner strength, that inner power that they have, and to give themselves permission to be true to themselves, to be who they know they want to be, and who God wants them to be.

Woody Woodward:

I know a lot of parents especially—even spouses, but parents especially—never really give themselves permission. They kind of lose their identity, if you will, in their children. So how do you help someone give themselves permission to tap into their inner strength?

Liz Phalp:

To be honest, with women who have children, I almost can't fully get their attention until I prove to them that they are not serving their children as well as they could if they were more true to themselves. It's easier for us to do something when it's going to benefit somebody else, rather than ourselves. It's how I first get them to see, "Look, you're not even serving your family like you think you are."

Woody Woodward:

I've seen that in my wife. She'll go and spend for clothes on the kids and she'll never buy herself a new outfit. And I'll say, "Sweetheart, you've got to buy yourself an outfit if you're buying the kids an outfit." So how do you wake them up to that reality?

Liz Phalp:

Really, in my very first conversation with women is when I ask them, "Why do you want to lose weight? Why do you want more energy? Why, why, why?"

When they ultimately break down, it's the point where they say, "I'm a bad mom. I'm a terrible mom when I don't like how I look, and I'm depressed, and I'm not feeling good about myself. And I don't want to pass on these same habits to my kids."

That's the most powerful motivation for them. But then once they start investing in themselves, they do start to see that they need to do it for themselves as well.

Woody Woodward:

A lot of people feel they should do something. How do you get them off their "should" list and get them on their "want" list?

Liz Phalp:

I just use those exact words and I ask them. I say, "When you feel like you should do something, where do you feel that?" And it's always outside themselves.

I say, "How committed are you to these things you feel you should do?" What's in common is that the things we tend to flake out on, the things we show up late to, are the things we never fully committed to, because they're on our should list rather than our want list.

And so I just use those words and I say, "Is this something you feel like you should do or is it something you feel like you want or need to?" I really make them decide, "Are you going to put this into the want or need category, or are you going to say it's not worth it and just cut it out of your life?" I don't even let them use that "should" anymore.

Woody Woodward:

As a successful entrepreneur, it's hard to stay focused at times. What do you do to bring yourself back in alignment when you get discouraged, when you get down, when you're on your should list?

Liz Phalp:

You know, sometimes it's just that I need a break. If I need a break, I take a break. And then I just get re-inspired. I go back to the things that inspired me in the first place. I go back to reading books, or connecting with my mentors, or even just hearing how other people, on these same topics, struggle too.

Ultimately, staying committed to my daily routines of taking care of my body, drinking my green smoothies, exercising, meditating, studying—these things that I know ultimately are going to give me the strength that I need to push through—doing those regularly, even when I don't feel like it, helps me get through those times where I lose focus.

Woody Woodward:

How do you define success?

Liz Phalp:

To me, the path to success begins when I become awakened to a possibility. And success is when I've come to achieve that possibility. It's never really an arrival because there's always a new opportunity, always a new possibility. But the path to success, I've noticed, is never what I imagined it's going to be, not even close.

And even the arrival isn't what I imagined it would be. It's usually more involved than I imagined—so much better than I imagined it. But success is just that ability to keep going as the path drifts, and shifts, and changes and not quitting.

Woody Woodward:

How do you channel your fear into productivity? Because we all have fear, we all have times where we get scared. What do you do? What techniques do you use to get yourself out of that slump and moving forward?

Liz Phalp:

This is where the action part of the equation comes in for me, because that's the one thing I know that will change my reality. If I'm afraid, if I'm scared, I know that sitting and pondering on it isn't going to do any good; so that's when I just take action.

There's this principle that happens in health, when you start doing something, that provides a huge upgrade for your body. I've noticed it the most in many of my clients when they start drinking green smoothies. Most go through a detox process, where their body is recognizing that they're getting higher quality ingredients now, so it's going to take some time to shed off all of the toxins that are in it. And going through this process, if you don't know what it is, can be really confusing and difficult.

Then, what so many people tend to do is, they start making these improvements in their lives, and then they start to experience this detox reaction where they can feel sick and tired, which is the opposite of what they were expecting to feel. So then what they do is they back off, and they stop drinking the green smoothies. Then, maybe, they come back and approach it again, and then they again start feeling that sickness from the detox event; and so then they back off, and they just stay in this miserable state for a long time.

And, for me, I feel like I have that same choice with my fears. I can approach them. Things get scary, and then I back off. Then I come back and approach them again, it gets scary, and I back off. If, instead, I just power through it and say, "I'm going to stick with this, I'm going to stick with the things I committed to. I'm going to follow through on these actions and know that on the other side of this is clarity."

So, to finish the detox example, what people experience after this detox phase—this cleansing—is both a mental clarity and greater energy; in other words, a higher level of being. I feel like it's the same with any of these mental or emotional challenges that we push ourselves through, including fear.

Woody Woodward:
What advice would you give to a budding entrepreneur who wants to go out there, but just is stuck with that fear of, "What if I take that risk?" When you look at what you had to go through to pull yourself around to fulfill your mission for your life, what advice would you give to someone who's sitting on the fence right now and is too afraid to take action?

Liz Phalp:
I would tell them to just decide what it's worth to them, how much they want it, to get really clear on why they want it, and why they can or can't live without it. Get down to the core reason of why they have no other option than to do this. Once they've decided that, there's no reason to look at any of the other things, no reason to look at any of the fears or any of that other stuff because none of that's an option anymore. Once they get themselves to that point where, "This is the only choice," then everything else can just be ignored.

Woody Woodward:
You give a lot from being a spouse, and a mother, and a business owner. What kind of managing techniques do you use to keep you on track?

Liz Phalp:

I love the idea in the book, *Eat That Frog*, which is, "If you start with the biggest, most important, usually the scariest thing first, then everything else seems to kind of fall into place."

This is how I start every day. This is how I start every project. This is how I start everything. I say to myself, "What is the one thing that's got to happen for this to succeed? What's the most important thing?"

And it usually is the thing I'm resisting the most. If I do that first, everything else after it is easy, and gets done. And so I go in this descending order of scariest, biggest, most important first, down to those other things that, you know, if I end up having time for them, I do them.

Now, obviously, with family, with children, and other responsibilities such as these, there are all kinds of interruptions, from changing diapers, to making lunch for the kids. But if every time I'm in the office or during my business time my focus is on, "Get this big thing done first," then that creates 80 percent of the success I need.

Woody Woodward:

What inspires you now? Looking forward on the horizon, what's that one project that you're so enthusiastic about, it keeps you up at night?

Liz Phalp:

One project? Wow. The vision is that I now have a very clear view of who my target is and the possibilities available for them. It's now just essentially ramping up my ability to speak to them, to be heard by them, and to show them what's possible.

Woody Woodward:

What's the most rewarding thing about what you do?

Liz Phalp:

Absolutely, the most rewarding thing is to be able to see women give themselves permission to be all of the things that they hoped were possible, and then to see them actually do it; and to see how it changes every other area of their life.

Woody Woodward:

What do you want your legacy to be?

Liz Phalp:

What I ultimately really want to give to the world is for women to see that seeking the possibilities and the successes that men have is shortchanging themselves. What is really possible for them reaching the full potential of what feminine energy can provide is so much more, and such a great possibility.

Gerald Rogers

Gerald Rogers is a professional speaker, transformational seminar leader and elite entrepreneurial coach who has worked with thousands of purpose driven business owners around the country to discover their purpose, ignite their passion and learn how to make a great income while making a huge difference in the world.

As a father of four kids, Gerald has a passion for creating meaningful change in the world and believes that awakened entrepreneurs who stand as "conscious creators" in their lives and their businesses, hold the key to the future of this country.

If you are looking to get your message out to the world and want to get paid for doing what you love email Gerald for more details:

coach@prosperitysummit.com

To download free audio and video training visit:
www.GeraldRogers.com • www.CreatorAlliance.com

Woody Woodward:

Gerald, you've had a lot of success in your life and you help entrepreneurs find that purpose driven path for themselves. A lot of people have a challenge finding their purpose in life. How do you help an entrepreneur or an individual find their purpose?

Gerald Rogers:

A lot of times people get overwhelmed when they think of this idea of their purpose or their mission in life. What I help them do is understand that there are clues around them every day, which help them to know what their purpose is. And those clues show up in the form of things that they're passionate about, causes that they're interested in, talents that they have, things that come naturally and easily for them, things that they love, books that they like to read, and hobbies that they love to pursue. Really, when it comes down to it, all of these things are clues as to what your natural gifts and strengths are that help you make a difference in the world. And really, at the end of the day, our purposes always tie back to the fact that we want to make a difference in other people's lives. The only question is what's the best way for us to do that? All of these clues help us identify what is our unique gift that we can share with the world.

Woody Woodward:

That kind of reminds me of Hansel and Gretel as they're going through the forest. It's leaving those bread crumbs to find your way back. In our life, we have these clues that show up all the time. We keep seeing them as patterns. So, when someone finds these clues that identify their purpose, why do you think most people don't take action?

Gerald Rogers:

I think that there's a lot of fear that comes up that keeps people second guessing of what they should be doing and thinking maybe there's something more. Another problem is, a lot of people don't feel worthy to live that calling or live the mission that they have. Sometimes, I think that people over-complicate it and make it too hard and don't know where to start. My whole mission is to help people simplify that path and to help them understand that there's a way that you can take your gift and your passion and your purpose and to make it so it's a central part of your life and even a place where you get to make money. And my belief is the more money you make, the more you can amplify that gift and purpose, but there's a lot of fears and a lot of subconscious doubt and limiting beliefs that hold everyone back and so one of the big pieces is helping people learn what those blocks are and helping them move through those fears so they can live that purpose courageously. But it all begins with decision and a commitment to do whatever it takes to move forward.

Woody Woodward:

A lot of people, because of the economy's ups and downs have had a tough time either in their business or in their relationships. How do you help someone transition from one area of their life that they feel is failing, to a more positive, more grounded area?

Gerald Rogers:

It begins, I think, by redefining what failure really is. Let's face it, in our lives sometimes, things don't work out the way we want them to or the way that we think they should. Heaven knows, I've had lots of times in my life that I have struggled, that I've had pain, where I've had things that fell apart.

But what is failure really? To me, failure is nothing more than giving up and as long as I keep moving forward, as long as I pick myself up every time I fall down, then it's impossible for me to fail. And so when you make that decision to do whatever it takes, when you make that decision to keep picking yourself up, when you make that decision to stay positive and to focus on the possibility rather than the problem, then miracles will continue to happen in your life. And when you're in the midst of those challenges or problems or those transitions that you don't like, when you're in the midst of what might seem like a failure, it's just really important that you raise your perspective, you raise yourself out of the problem, and consider what is the gift of this opportunity in my life and how can I create something new?

My belief is all of these problems come into our life because of decisions that we make. If we can learn how to make better decisions in the future, then we've learned and we've gained something valuable from that experience. If we don't learn from those challenges or problems, then we're doomed to repeat them.

Woody Woodward:

I heard a great quote that a lesson is repeated until it is learned. There are a lot of times in my life alone where I've had those ups and downs. I feel like I'm repeating those lessons over and over again until I finally learn them. What techniques do you use or is there a book you recommend that really helps people change their perspective?

Gerald Rogers:

For me, all change in perspective comes from three core things. The first is change your environment to get around new people, new conversations. This is one of the reasons why education is so important, why reading books is so important, why having uplifting friends is so important. It's because when you can change your environment and get new inputs coming into your life, new information from your life, it automatically will help transform your "outputs" and what you're creating with your life. So it's critical to make sure that you've got positive information and that you're in a positive environment.

The next key is to ask powerful questions. The quality of our life is based on the quality of the questions that we ask ourselves. So when we are asking ourselves questions like, 'Why is this so hard?' or 'Why is this so challenging?,' or 'Why can't I ever figure this out?,' then we're doomed to get lousy answers in return and we're doomed to get lousy results. But in order to change our perspective, we ask ourselves powerful questions and say, "Okay, what's great about this situation? How can I get this new result? What do I want? How could I do this more effectively? If I had solved this problem already, what would I have done?" Questions like that help us to shift the way we see things.

And the third key is shifting the way that we see ourselves. This is really fundamental to all of our success. There is a great book, called *Psycho-Cybernetics* by Maxwell Maltz, which is kind of a foundational book if you want to understand the psychology of transformation. His whole concept is built on the idea that the results of our life are based on our own internal self-image, the way that we see ourselves. If we can begin to see ourselves for who we are, as divine, powerful, inspired beings, if we can begin to see ourselves as confident, as capable, successful, powerful and compassionate, then all of the sudden, the results in our life begin to reflect our new internal self-image. So the third key, which is probably the most important of them all, is to begin to shift the way that we see ourselves, change our perspective to believe that the new results in our life are not only possible, but that they are destined to be our results because it's built on who we really are. If our self-image is limited, our results are going to be limited. But if the self-image is positive and powerful, then all of the results in our lives will work like that as well.

Woody Woodward:

I have to admit, this is very profound and I hope the reader understands this, because I've studied human behavior for the last 20 years, I have never seen it packaged this way. Selfishly, I want to go into further detail with this, so number one, changing your environment. When someone's going through a transition, it could be a bankruptcy in a business, it could be a divorce, it could be a child who has got an illness, how do you help them change their environment? What advice would you give for them to tap into a new environment or create a new environment?

Gerald Rogers:

So, the first is to really look at the people that you're surrounding yourselves with and ask yourself, "Are these people that I'm surrounded by, are they encouraging and do they support this new self-image that I want to have?" Everyone's heard this idea that your income is the average of the five people you spend the most time around. Well, think about that in other areas of your life, too. If you're around people that are constantly pulling you down or talking negatively or they don't want to see you change, they don't want to see you grow, and any time they do, they discourage you, then it's going to be very, very difficult to change.

So the first key is really looking at who are the people that you can be around that do support this new change, that do support this new possibility in your life, and to focus on those inspiring and uplifting and meaningful relationships that you can build and nurture.

You may ask, where can I find people like that who will support me in changing? If you are someone like me, who is driven to learn and to grow and with passion about education, then going to workshops and seminars and places like that, you will find a lot of like-minded people, who also share that interest. And there are other places, like meetup.com or Facebook groups and just all sorts of other different places where you can find like-minded people, so go search for them. What you seek, you will find.

Sometimes, the change in an environment means getting away from people and just having time to be with yourself. Maybe it is a very simple thing, which you just go up into the mountains or into the forest for an afternoon and just have some quiet time to just be in nature. Maybe that means taking a week and just going on a sabbatical by yourself. So there are lots of different ways to shift your environment, but you really need to look at where you are spending time and who are you spending that time with. Those are the two biggest factors that will determine whether or not you're able to maintain this positive change in your life.

And I would have you also look at even the environment within your home. There are so many triggers around us all of the time that reflect back to us how our life is, and if you live in a house where there's a lot of clutter here or there's unfinished projects here or you've got things that are broken down here, it will naturally anchor back to you the limits that you've been experiencing. So, maybe one of the keys is to go and declutter your house to change your environment. Maybe it's to go and finish those repairs or finish those unfinished projects. And by doing that you'll automatically feel this great accomplishment and momentum that happens in your life, because you've literally changed your environment.

Woody Woodward:

I like what you said there because people often say, "Well, it's my environment and there's nothing I can do." Of all the people you've interviewed and studied, the people I've interviewed and studied, the environment has never held anyone back. Otherwise every poor person would always stay poor and every rich person would always stay rich. We know through history that's not true. Our environments change. People change. They change the outcomes of their lives.

The second thing you talked about, which I really want to focus on, is asking powerful questions. I'd like to use the analogy of Kennedy in the '60s. You know, they asked a question, "Can we put a man on the moon?" The researchers found out, yeah, we probably could do this. They made a declaration and by the end of this decade, we'll have a man on the moon and they did that. I think our entire lives change when we ask powerful questions.

So, what are some questions that people aren't asking that they need to start asking?

Gerald Rogers:

That's a great question right there and that's a perfect example. You see, in our mind we have this portion of our brain called the reticular activating system. That is the goal-seeking mechanism of our brain and there are some people that doubt that they're goal achievers or that they can achieve their goals at all. But the truth is, you are constantly, constantly achieving goals. Unfortunately, most of the time they're unconsciously programmed goals. And so people ask themselves questions that say "Why is it so hard?" or "Why can't I do this?" or "Why can't I do that?" These thoughts and questions are what program this goal seeking part of your brain. It's like the reticular activating system is striving to find validation for your limits. So the big key is to look for questions that empower you, the questions that strengthen you. Rather than focusing on "Why is it so hard?" ask "Why is this easy? Why am I able to accomplish so much? Why am I so great?" Those seem like such vain questions, but by asking those questions, your mind has to find the answer. And those answers then support you in achieving more in your life.

And then there's the how-to questions, which is like, "Okay. How can I be more productive today? How can I serve more people with my product? How can I be more effective at sales? How can I live my purpose more fully? How can I be more influential? How can I develop deeper relationships?" Whatever challenge you're facing that you want to find solutions to, just continually ask yourself the how questions that enable you to activate your ventricular activating system to find the answers; and the reality is your brain contains all the answers that you're looking for very deep within the files of your brain somewhere is the answer that you need.

And what's great, if the answer isn't there, you will attract into your life whatever solution of your answers you need. This is one of the great secrets of the law of attraction that when you're asking these powerful questions and you have this positive focus in your life and you're looking for these things and believing that you'll find the answers, then all of the right books, all of the right information, all of the right people will be drawn into your life, because your brain is actively seeking those answers. And whatever you seek, you shall find. What you focus on expands.

Woody Woodward:
This brings us to the third part: shifting the way we see ourselves. We can ask all the greatest questions in the world and we get phenomenal answers from our brain, but if we don't shift the way we see ourselves, we remain stuck. So go into more detail about how to suddenly shift the way they see themselves.

Gerald Rogers:
So, from the time that you were born, you're constantly given input from all of these different people and all these different situations

in your life that helped define and shape your self-image. It's when your mom told you you were bad for taking a cookie. All of the sudden you have this belief that you adopt that says, "Well, I'm not good enough" or, "I'm not lovable," or "I'm not worthy" or whatever it might be. And as you're growing up, you're constantly getting input from your parents, family, friends and other people. The challenge with this is we adopt so many negative, limiting beliefs and patterns in this negative self-image and then that negative self-image is what holds us hostage as we grow up.

So it really becomes a conscious effort of really defining and "re-aligning" with the truth of who you really are. And the truth is that you ARE powerful. The truth is that you ARE divine. The truth is that you ARE inspired. The truth is that you're creative and you have a whole set of unique truths about you that are absolutely amazing and empowering. Part of being a 'conscious creator' is learning how to reinforce those new beliefs into your life.

So there are a lot of tools and a lot of ways to do that. One of the main things is just identifying who is it that you want to be and creating these affirmations and being able to recite them and repeat them and integrate them emotionally into your experion. I had heard about affirmations for a long time and I thought they were totally cheesy to be honest. I thought that is ridiculous. You know, "I'm good enough, I'm smart enough and gosh darn it, people like me," whatever the Stuart Smalley thing was on Saturday Night Live. I thought they were so cheesy and it's like I asked why would you do that?

But then I had a mentor whose name was Chet Holmes who was one of the top coaches for Fortune 500 companies and would go in and help these companies double their income over and over again. And this guy made multi, multi-million dollars every year in what he did and I remember how he talked about how much affirmations changed his life. And he shared about his process and how every night he would listen to these affirmations about who he was and what he was creating and what he was doing and he said that every year for five years his income doubled that he did that. And I was like, "Whoa! If it's good enough for him, then it's probably good enough for me." And so I started creating some affirmations about me being a confident and powerful, inspired leader, me being a master of communication, me being someone who stands tall and strong with a clear vision of who I am and where I'm headed. All of these different affirmations, which, at the time that I wrote them it's like, "Yeah. Right. This isn't who I am. I would like to be that person," but I really didn't see myself that. I felt shy. I felt awkward. I felt inadequate in some of the areas.

But what was interesting was as I began listening to those affirmations, after about 30 days, the resistance started to disappear and I started to feel more and more in alignment with that. And I noticed myself being more confident, and more passionate, and more powerful in what I did. And within six months, I remember having this major breakthrough where over the course of one weekend, I made over $100,000.00. I stepped back after that and was like, "Whoa! I never imagined that would be possible for me." But then I thought, what shifted? And one of the things that had shifted is the fact that I suddenly felt worthy and able to receive this abundance in my life, because of these affirmations that had been going through my mind and going through my head in the time leading up to it. So it's like as you're listening to these affirmations, as you're telling yourself these things. It's like planting these seeds and nurturing the seeds and growing these seeds. At the same time, you're weeding out all the weeds in your garden that say you're not good enough, that you're not worthy, that you don't deserve money—whatever those limiting beliefs are.

So, my invitation would be, number one, figure out what it is that you want to have in your life. Ask yourself what would you need to do to achieve those things in your life. Then ask the question, okay, "What would I need to believe in order to do those things?" And the final question is, okay, "Who do I need to be in order to receive these?" So that's really kind of the process that you go through to really figure out the beliefs and then it's just a journey of reinforcing those beliefs and speaking from validation, speaking for support for those new beliefs, to rewrite those old patterns and beliefs that are in the past. And to be kind to yourself and know that it's a journey and it's something you've got to continue to work on, to be committed to the journey and be committed to the process and you'll get there.

Woody Woodward:

What is on the horizon for you right now that has got you so excited it keeps you up at night?

Gerald Rogers:
I am launching some marketing campaigns nationally for a program I call the Creator Alliance, which is a program to help empower people that have a mission, that have a passion, that have a voice, and they're just trying to figure out how to get it out to the world. They want to be able to create that financial freedom and success so that they can live their purpose and passion every day, but they're just not sure how to do that. So I'm excited to be able to take my experience and my voice and my expertise and help empower these people to be the coaches, to be the speakers, to be the experts that are out there making a big difference in the world and getting paid a lot of money for it. So that's what's turning me on and driving me. For me, it's getting my message out to more people to empower them to live the life that they've been dreaming about, but haven't known how to create.

Woody Woodward:

You had a mentor in Chet Holmes. I had mentors in my life. What you're doing right now is really building a nationwide mentoring program to help people take these great concepts, these great passions that they have and bring it to the masses. How influential have your mentors been in your success?

Gerald Rogers:
How could you ever create success without mentors? I often think

that if you are looking for the hardest, most painful, and time- consuming way to achieve your dreams, then do it on your own. I remember when I first started real estate investing years ago. That was my path. I was like, "Oh, you know, mentors are too expensive. Coaches are too expensive. I'll just figure it out on my own." And that led to so many painful, expensive mistakes that I never would have had to go through if I had someone to hold my hand and lead me through the process. And so I'm a huge advocate for education. I'm a huge advocate for finding powerful coaches and mentors, finding people that have created what you want, and to follow them. That's why I coach personally, it's because I know that if someone works with me, I can save them three to five years off the learning top and, you know, help them create way more success than they ever would have otherwise. And so I'm a massive, massive advocate of having the support that you need and creating the team that will support you in getting the results as fast and quickly and easily as possible.

Woody Woodward:
When someone is looking to hire a mentor, what should they look for? What attributes? What skill set? How does someone go about finding the right mentor?

Gerald Rogers:
Number one, look at their experience and results. Are they living what they teach? Do they do what they talk about? Have they created what you want to create?

Secondly, are they authentic? Do they care? There are a lot of people that maybe have experiences out there, but they don't really fully invest themselves into the results of their client. They're just looking to get paid. So you want someone who cares and is sincere about your success.

The third key is a skill set. There is a unique skill set that is required to coach people through the process of getting you results and it requires intuition. It requires the ability to help create breakthroughs. It requires the foundation in understanding the psychology, as well as the knowledge and skill set for success and you want the coach that can deliver those things for you.

Do understand that different coaches will have different strengths, so one mentor may serve you in helping you overcome your limiting belief. Another mentor might help you with implementing a Facebook ad word campaign to grow your business. So, make sure that you hire coaches specifically built and based on what it is you want to create.

Woody Woodward:

I've got a dear friend, Tony Magee. He said it takes a team to stream your dream. And I think that's exactly right. There is not one mentor who is going to be everything for you. You've got to have your Facebook mentors, your Twitter mentors, your social media, and your mindset— whoever it is. So thank you for that advice. I think that's very profound.

How do you define success now? You've had the ups. You've had the downs. You've transformed people's lives. You've had a great impact. You get back in sharing your philanthropic work. How do you define success?

Gerald Rogers:

For me, success is just about enjoying and embracing the journey and doing the very best you can. I am not a believer that you will ever "make it." I believe that there are so many cycles to life. There are ups and downs. There are times where you'll have lots of money and times where you won't have very much money. There are times where you'll have passionate relationships and times that you won't and for me, success is being in the journey and to not judge the journey, to just be in the process and just to do the very best you can on a daily basis.

Woody Woodward:

When we do have those times along the journey where we're fearful and we're scared, what advice would you give and what have you personally done to channel your fear into productivity?

Gerald Rogers:

Number one: I acknowledge the fear and sometimes I allow myself to, you know, take time to heal. I think oftentimes we judge the pain and we try to hide the pain and we try to ignore the pain and in doing that, we don't have the pain ever heal. So for me, it's just acknowledging and embracing it, asking myself, okay, what can I learn from this? And then constantly coming back to the question and saying, "Okay, what do I want to create from here and how can I find the support in my life to create that?"

So you know, when I've been going through painful transitions in my life and when things are broken down or I've experienced major letdowns or upset, I need to step back, allow myself to heal and clear and get confident in terms of where I'm going. And when it comes down to addressing fear, there comes a point where your vision has to be more important than your fear. And when it is, the fear will almost dissolve, just because it has no other choice but to give way to the vision that's bursting forward from you. So to really connect deeply with your vision and purpose and passion, if there's enough strength there, then whatever fears you're experiencing will fade away.

Woody Woodward:
What advice would you give to a budding entrepreneur, someone who's starting out right now? They've identified their passion. They know what they want. What encouragement would you give them to keep them going forward?

Gerald Rogers:
This might sound like a funny thing to say, but I would tell them to expect things to not work out like they're wanting them to and to be okay with that, because any time you're beginning the journey and you've got this idea of where you're headed, when you're actually in the journey things are going to shift. Things are going to fall. It's always going to be different than you expect. And the great thing is when you understand that stepping into the journey, then when those upsets, when those disappointments come you say, "Oh yeah, this is what Gerald was talking about."

And then to constantly come back to the anchor of the why that motivated them in the first place, because the 'what' and the 'how' will change. It will evolve. It will. There's no way for you to see at the beginning of the journey the same perspective that you'll see half-way through. Things will just change. But if you constantly anchor back to the why and continue to move forward and have that commitment to bring the best team in possible, to get the right education, and to keep moving forward no matter what, as long as you have the commitment, you can create amazing, amazing things.

Woody Woodward:
You had a phenomenal career in changing many people's lives. What do you want your legacy to be?

Gerald Rogers:
For me, I want to live the type of life where people think, "Wow! My life is better because Gerald was in it." Whether it's my clients, whether it's my family, whether it's my friend, whether it's a person I meet at the grocery store for five minutes, I want to be the type of person where people think, "Wow! My life was better because I knew that man."

Derek Rollins

Derek Rollins is an entrepreneurial mentor and trainer. He has produced two audio CD's and has held over two hundred trainings. As a dedicated learner he has invested over 3500 hours in self improvement in learning to become a mentor and trainer.

He has earned a black belt in Tae Kwon Do.

Derek has two adult sons that are his pride and joy.

Feel free to contact him by email: derekhasanswers@gmail.com

Woody Woodward:
Derek Rollins is a successful mentor and entrepreneurial coach. He's had incredible opportunities of working with large medical factories and even with Hostess. As an entrepreneur, it wasn't until he was 41 years old did he go out on his own. So Derek, what is the greatest risk you have ever taken and was it worth it?

Derek Rollins:
Okay, the greatest risk that I took was when I deliberately got myself fired from Hostess because I felt like I couldn't just quit. I did something stupid and got myself fired and then I felt free from work-

ing at that place. So I was out of work for about a week and I just didn't know what to do. I wasn't getting very much sleep and so I was kind of losing my mind in some ways. It's just really weird to explain what happened. Late at night after midnight, I was just walking. I walked past a bar and outside there were four cars, three cars that were pickup trucks and they were just running. I was thinking that it's kind of weird that people would leave their vehicles out, four of them, and they were running. I just walked past it and I continued walking. I wanted to run away and the destination that I wanted to run away to was about 600 miles away and I was determined to walk. It didn't make any sense. However, I had already given my car to my son. I wrote a note to my son saying, "You can have my car. I don't need it anymore." But the thought in my head said, "You'd better take a car because you're not going to make it to your destination alive." So I took one of the cars and I drove from Layton to St. George. When I got to St. George, the thought in my head said, "Okay, you need to turn here and turn here and turn here and go to this place." I drove to Deseret Industries where I had the feeling to give the car to them. So I stopped there. They were outside and I said, "Hey, you can have this car. I don't need it anymore," and I walked away. Then the thought came to mind, "You know what? You've got to turn back and turn yourself in." And so I went back and I said, "Do you have a manager here?" and they said, "Yeah." So I talked to the manager and I said, "You know what? I need to turn myself in. I took this car last night and I drove all night to get here." So they called the cops and they took me to Purgatory, which is a Washington County facility. I stayed there for 57 days.

Woody Woodward:
So what lesson did you learn?

Derek Rollins:
Oh, I learned that you get sufficient sleep so your mind or subconscious

doesn't take over and you do things that will get you in trouble. My subconscious was fully running the show. Consciously, I wasn't in control at all. My subconscious totally was controlling everything that I was doing without me realizing what I was doing. I don't know if that makes any sense or not.

Woody Woodward:

It makes complete sense. We've all had our subconscious take over. However, I'm sure there are many people reading this chapter who didn't do what you did, but we can all relate to having our subconscious do things that we don't recommend doing ourselves. But now having learned that lesson, what do you do to stay more focus and more conscious so that you don't make future mistakes.

Derek Rollins:

Okay, so what I do now is I have a vision board that I focus on three minutes in the morning and three minutes in the evening at least. Then I focus on one. When I receive that item off my vision board, I replace it with a different item. So that has really helped me focus and I've created personal declarations of what I want to become and what I want to do. I get really intense with my declarations. I yell it really loud out in a field and I whisper it and so that helps me keep focused as well. And another thing that helps me be focused is if I have a lot of negative energy, then I write it down and I burn it. Can I give an example?

Woody Woodward:

Please do.

Derek Rollins:

An example is like, "I feel frustrated because..." and then I just write whatever thing that comes to my mind of why I'm feeling frustrated. I can write 15 pages even though sometimes it's hard to read because I can't even read my own writing sometimes. I write it down on paper and then I burn it. I burn all the negative emotions that I put on paper and then that helps me get rid of it. Then on the following day, I write something causative about me, like for example "I feel happy because..." and I just write all the things that bring joy and happiness in my life. So I alternate from day to day. What helps me remember is that on the odd day, like the first, third, or fifth, or seventh, I write the negative stuff on the paper and then I burn that. On the even days like the second, fourth, sixth, or eighth, I write the positive stuff and that helps me keep really focused on the direction of where I want to go.

Woody Woodward:

Let's go back to the vision board for a second. What is one of the things on your vision board right now that you are trying to accomplish?

Derek Rollins:

Okay, so one thing that I have written that's on my vision board right now is to have a club list and a book that I guess is called a New York bestseller. So I want to be published in a book that's a New York bestseller. Another item I have on my vision board is to become a phenomenal mentor and receive a grand compensation for my mentoring services, to mentor very successful people who know where they're going. Through mentoring, they can become even greater and more phenomenal in their endeavors.

Woody Woodward:

Who has been a mentor in your life and what lessons have you learned from them?

Derek Rollins:

So I have hired a mentor and learned many wonderful, phenomenal things from him. His name is Kirk Duncan, the Founder and President of 3 Key Elements. The mentoring tools that I have learned I have applied to my life, which has helped give me a more clear direction as to where I want to go and realize that I can accomplish the dreams that I have for me. Before, I really was in a place where it was very dark and I couldn't see clearly. I had a very low self-esteem. When I decided to hire an awesome mentor that has helped me literally turn my life around and give me clearer focus, I realize now that I can accomplish any dream that I have and just to go for it. Don't hold back and just run.

Woody Woodward:

When you mentor somebody, what key areas do you like to focus on?

Derek Rollins:

Key areas is I ask the mentee what their dreams are and then to see that they have clear understanding of where they want to go. It could be like in terms of what financial dreams they have, what they want to accomplish. Then I look into their eyes and see if there's a tool, a mentoring tool that can help them. Their essence will tell me that they need a tool that will help them. I explain and write it down. For example, I'll say, "Well, do you have a vision board?" and if they do not, I'll suggest creating a vision board. The tool is looking at it at least three minutes in the morning and three minutes in the evening before they retire for the evening. And then they hold themselves accountable to me that they will actually do that step. What good is a tool if you don't use the tool? If it just sits there, then it doesn't do any good so that's one example.

Woody Woodward:

What other tools besides vision boards do you like to use to help your clients get results?

Derek Rollins:

Creating their own personal declarations. There is a way to create declarations that will continue. Create many declarations like every two weeks or every three weeks or every four weeks. Create a new one and totally ingrain that declaration into their subconscious. Create another one and then add that to their being so that it's always new and fresh. There's a process to do that.

Woody Woodward:

What does it take to be a good leader?

Derek Rollins:

To be a good leader, I believe, takes a person who decides that they must first be a great follower. Follow a great leader first and then they will become more like a great leader by following that one. They themselves will turn into a great leader.

Woody Woodward:
So to be a good leader you must first know how to follow and then learn those lessons from a leader and then take them to the next step. Is that correct?

Derek Rollins:
Yes, that is correct.

Woody Woodward:
When times get tough, how do you stay focused? We all have problems with social media and our work schedules, so what do you do to stay focused?

Derek Rollins:
What I do is I journal. I journal and write down things. For example, I will write, "I desire to stay focused because…" and then I write everything that comes to me why I desire to stay focused. I just write all this positive stuff down and then I follow what I write. It's different for everyone. That's the basic step.

Woody Woodward:
How do you define success?

Derek Rollins:
I define it by feeling self-worth. When I feel that I am very valuable and I can contribute great things while I exist on this planet and I can help millions of other people do the same thing; that's one form of success.

Woody Woodward:
When you get discouraged, what techniques do you use to pull yourself through?

Derek Rollins:
The technique that I use is I go out to a field and I yell and scream and have a tantrum out in the field instead of on another human being. I find a tree and I yell at the tree and tell the trees why I am

feeling really discouraged and I get all of that negative energy out in a field away from people so it doesn't hurt anyone. That really helps me get over those discouraging, negative energy feelings.

Woody Woodward:

What is the secret combination to finding success in your line of work? So what I mean by that question is what makes a good mentor? What makes a good entrepreneurial mentor in your line of work?

Derek Rollins:

Hiring an amazing mentor and following what they suggest, to actually use the mentoring tools that will help the person become even more creative than they are and do more. Another thing is having a higher power. If they don't have a higher power, I suggest they find a mentor that is following the higher power as well. Does that make sense?

Woody Woodward:

How do you define failure? We all have ups and downs, but if you're coaching someone and they say, "Well I'm just a failure," how do you help them get through that?

Derek Rollins:

Well one mentoring tool that I refer to is they can write down, "I am afraid of failure because…" and their own soul will tell them what to write. They just write down all the stuff as to why they feel they are afraid of failure and by doing that, they can find their own answer to that question. Then they can just write the opposite like, "I want to be successful because…" and they just write everything that their soul is telling them as to why they want to become successful.

Woody Woodward:

When someone is finding a mentor, what should they look for in that mentor? How does someone find the right mentor?

Derek Rollins:

All right, so my feeling is they need to look for a mentor that has high levels of integrity and honesty, with tools that will actually help them get unstuck and move forward and upward and onward.

Woody Woodward:

What's the greatest "Aha" moment you've had in business?

Derek Rollins:

The greatest "Aha" is for me to realize that I myself have great value and I can accomplish anything that I put my mind and soul and heart to and become very successful and help millions of other people on this planet do the same.

Woody Woodward:

How do you overcome fear?

Derek Rollins:

I write down on paper, "I want to overcome fear because..." and then I just let my heart and soul write. I write and I write and I write to answer that question. It puts my subconscious mind to work to find the answer and I just write and write and I find the answer in what I've written down. That helps me to answer those questions.

Woody Woodward:

What do you like best about what you do? What's the most fun thing about being a mentor?

Derek Rollins:

The most fun thing is seeing the beautiful light in people's eyes, see how their lights radiate and they want to move forward and do wonderful things while they're on this planet to help their fellow beings, help mankind or men and women and children, the human family because we all share this planet and I believe we are all one family, the human family, and so we have that connection. I like to call it brothers and sisters you know from a spiritual sense and just working and having fun. This planet is place to just play and we're all grown children and act like children sometimes.

Woody Woodward:

What type of legacy do you want to leave?

Derek Rollins:

What I want is to be known for is doing good, for being able to rise from a very dark place to a place and known for helping millions of lives adjust and change for the better with righteous, good causes and feeding the hungry, clothing the naked, and liberating the captive.

Woody Woodward:

What's the greatest challenge you've had to overcome?

Derek Rollins:

Oh, the greatest challenge I have overcome is my own wickedness. I had to overcome my own wickedness and selfishness and I guess myself, me. It's a personal battle to overcome the flaws of the natural man and become more unnatural and more like... becoming more superhuman. Does that make any sense?

Woody Woodward:

That's one of the best answers I've ever heard. If you could share any advice with someone, what would it be?

Derek Rollins:

Oh, my advice would be for people to hire an awesome and amazing mentor and follow their suggestions and actually use the mentoring tools. That would be my advice.

Matt Schultz

Matt Schultz has spent the past 20 years as a "serial entrepreneur." His ventures have evolved from owning a small vending business, all the way to serving as a director, and officer of multiple publicly traded companies. Matt has been instrumental in the startup, funding and development of more than two-dozen businesses. He now spends his time as a volunteer youth coach, a consultant to other entrepreneurs, and is developing and implementing accelerated marketing strategies in high-end real estate. Matt and his wife Sherree enjoy an extremely active lifestyle, and he is the proud father of six children.

Woody Woodward:
Matt, you've had a very interesting background. You've owned several million dollar businesses. How did you get into oil & gas and alternative energy?

Matt Schultz:
The energy business kind of happened by accident. Back in 1999, I started a financial public relations firm that assisted small-cap publicly traded companies in raising money. It was really a glorified website and email list of people that were interested in what I had to say. Subscribers were actually paying me to find them undervalued investment opportunities. I found companies that needed money, and in-

vestors that were interested in the specific businesses, and I brought them together. That business gradually evolved into a boutique investment firm, and through a prior business relationship, I was invited to visit with a group in Texas that owned a small oil company. They were buying undercapitalized oil leases, and then working them over to increase the production. That type of business is pretty capital intensive, so they asked if I could help them to raise money. As I got more involved with the funding aspect, I became passionate about the business itself, and ultimately, with a group of partners, took over the company. As I learned more and more about domestic energy production, and especially how oil wells are very similar to real-estate investments, we began to package oil drilling programs and offer them to investors.

It's hard to imagine that I started by working with companies to more efficiently and effectively communicate with their shareholders, and very quickly I was the president of a company doing nearly $20M per year. I learned a lot. We became a brokerage firm. We created 'syndicated offerings' of oil investments that we shared through a network of brokers. Soon, I found myself being invited to speak to high net-worth investors at wealth development conferences throughout the country. I have been on the same stage as Tony Robbins, Donald Trump, Rudy Giuliani, and Suze Orman.

Woody Woodward:

A lot of times our greatest successes are things we haven't planned. How did your relationships with people you network with help you build this vision?

Matt Schultz:

I would say that relationships played the single largest role in going from a start-up to a $20 Million business. I have been so fortunate throughout my career to have been mentored by people that had achieved great successes in their own businesses. I was taught at a young age the value of "modeling." Modeling is basically an NLP term for identifying what successful people do, and then duplicating it. I'm a pretty passionate guy, and there have been many occasions that I found myself reacting to a situation, rather than being proactive. I'd say that relationships and mentors provide the greatest value, at least for me, in times like that. When the pressure is high, and I feel like I'm alone on an island, my choices weren't always the most prudent business decisions. Calling on mentors, mastermind groups, former colleagues, and even competitors, I often found a different perspective. It's amazing that if you literally stop and look at a challenge from someone else's perspective, how clear things can become. As I began to see other possibilities, solutions to challenges just became automatic. When I would look at creating new ways of doing business, instead of how I could more aggressively compete, it generated a lot of momentum. Once you have momentum, it's easy to enroll other people into the vision you are creating. Doors open, introductions get made, calls are answered, and it all happens as a result of being in alignment with my vision, and then sharing that with those close to me.

Woody Woodward:
I know a lot of readers who are reading this chapter are saying, "Well, gosh, I want to make $20 million a year and I want to make more money." And what a lot of people don't understand is how crucial relationships are to success. How do you network, how do you connect with people? How do you really tap into a resource of people and information?

Matt Schultz:
I'm glad you asked that. I was involved in DECA in high school. DECA was terrific for me in realizing the value of relationships, and ultimately, it was DECA that sent me to college. I remember specifically we were tasked with developing a full business plan. Our plans had to be complete with financials, pro-forma income statements, competition, equity distribution, and even fund raising. I was discussing the project with my grandfather, who was very successful in his own right. As I was putting together the list of officers and directors for

my 'imaginary' company, I remember him telling me that in business, "it's not what you know, it's who you know." So, as I put my team together, I went big. I put the most successful, most powerful, most persuasive people I knew on my board of directors. Of course I didn't actually do it, but for the purposes of the assignment, it was basically swinging for the fence.

The project then shifted to equity distribution. Basically, how much of MY company was I going to GIVE away? That's the exact attitude I had as I started that task. He then shared another pearl of wisdom with me... this one I use to this day with my clients. He said to me, "you can't do it all alone, and even if you could, it would kill you"... then he continued by saying "I'd be happy to give up 99% of Joe's Shoe Store in exchange for a quarter of one percent of Chrysler. I make people my partners."

Throughout my professional career I've dealt largely with companies that either were or later became publicly traded. The value I found in either owning or consulting with companies that used shares of stock as currency is this: People care more when they are an owner. Think about it. Would you be more inclined to invest your time, your relationships, and your rolodex in a business in which you actually had an ownership stake? Many of the mentors and advisors that I've had in my career had this same mindset. I've found that by sharing in the successes I've had, people are more willing to invest with me. I use the word invest, but I'm certainly not referring only to money

I'm a big supporter of the JOBS Act and the new mechanism of utilizing crowd funding to build a business. I firmly believe that as you enroll others to participate in your business; you develop a network of people fully invested in assisting your success. You literally create a group of partners all pulling towards a common goal. I'm not talking partners from the standpoint of having a set of keys to the building but somebody that may have a fraction of a percentage ownership in your company that can fire off an email and say, "Hey, have you ever considered this?"

As I started building my businesses, I got involved in industry groups, networking organizations, different masterminds, and was invited to assist other entrepreneurs. The thing I found was that as I began to share with others and as I was able to make a contribution to someone else, the value I received was infinitely greater than what I perceived to be my own contribution. I was invited to participate on community organizations, as a director or even an officer of other companies.

Woody Woodward:

When a new entrepreneur starts there are a lot of fears. It is difficult to network and get out there. But then when we start having some success we believe our own stories of our own greatness, there's also external temptation. What life experiences have you had on both sides at the beginning and at the end of this huge success?

Matt Schultz:

Well, as we discussed earlier, I've had some amazing opportunities in my professional life. I've been fortunate to have surrounded myself with very successful mentors. I've literally had businesses in more than a dozen different industries. I've sold air. I've loaned money. I've financed infomercials. I've owned an oil company and drilled wells. I've been a consultant. I've been a public speaker. I own an alternative energy business. I've owned an investment banking firm. I've been in the automotive business, and several other ventures. I've been called a serial entrepreneur. I find that I love the challenge of creating something new, something different, something exciting. When I was younger, I didn't care about risk. My biggest fear was that I wouldn't take action and someone else would, and I would have to live with regret. That was much more stressful than any financial gamble. I found that I had to literally 'burn the ships' behind me. I had to create a white-hot belief that I would succeed, and then go all-in. If that meant maxing out a credit card and letting go of whatever was holding me back, then that was the step. No excuses. As I became committed and passionate about what it was I was creating, it became contagious, and then it was easy to enroll other people.

Conversely, once I achieved "success," I stopped doing many of the things that got me there. I thought that the Black AMEX, the Jet, and the Range Rover were "success." These things, the external image of "success" literally took precedent in my life over many of the fundamentals that composed my core values system. I began to see myself as invincible. I believed that I was 'above' many of the things that I used to do, the very things that created the financial abundance in my life. I perceived "success" as material wealth. Throughout this period of my life, I began to lose, and lose a lot. I made bad decisions on investments. I made bad decisions in my companies. I made horrible decisions in my personal life. I was so caught up in the "success" that I very nearly lost my own family. I wasn't operating with clear intentions…I lost my "why." I didn't trust my instincts, and I certainly wasn't living my life in integrity. And then I watched as all of the "success" began to go away. And I literally held on by my fingernails to keep my family and to keep my marriage together.

What I learned through that process is success is far more than the number of digits to the left of the decimal in your bank account. Success is about creating balance in your life. It's about being in absolute integrity. The most important relationship for me to maintain that integrity is my relationship with myself. I had to rebuild my self-esteem. I studied myself, studied my actions; I learned that esteem comes from the Latin word aestimare, which means "to add value." So self-esteem is to add value to myself, to hold myself in such a way that anything less than my best is abject failure. The beauty in this belief is that I'm only competing against my own best self. When I'm in absolute integrity with me, all of my other relationships are automatic. My marriage, my children, the sports teams I coach, and the businesses I run, and even my friendships, they just work. When I operate from that place, when I'm very clear on my 'why,' I seek out people that support and encourage that part of my belief system and that part of my life more so than people that just contribute to the dollars in my bank.

Woody Woodward:

Thank you for being so transparent. A lot of times when someone's reading a chapter or a biography on someone, we always talk about our positive attributes instead of the reality of, "You know what, I failed like you failed. We all have our mistakes." So I appreciate your transparency. I also liked how you talked about your why. Talk more about that. How does someone identify their why? Because I agree with you, as soon as you know your why, you can endure any amount of how.

Matt Schultz:

Absolutely. For me, what I've realized is that it's that tiny little voice inside, that little feeling, that prompting. I literally feel compelled towards taking some type of action. I've found that my instincts don't mislead me very often, so I get very clear on my intentions. I write it down. I imagine what it might feel like, what I might see, what I may hear once I've achieved the desired intention. From that point, I trust the instincts I have on what the next steps might be. When I've got a clear intention, and a pretty good feeling about how to start, I take massive action. I'm not talking about baby steps; I'm talking grab the bull by the horns and shake stuff up. When I get stuck in my ego-driven mind to make decisions, those decisions are generally competitive; they're generally about winning, about having 'more than' and they're not necessarily in alignment with my why. I have a system that I created that works for me about the way that I identify and build my purpose, and I rely heavily on my instincts. I really believe that as entrepreneurs, we often sabotage our own success by being paralyzed... by being afraid to act. I know that when I feel that certainty, I'm clear with my why, and I can certainly endure any challenges to the how or what.

As we experience the initial resistance that inevitably arises when we step outside our comfort zone, it's super easy to regress to old behaviors. It's just an effect of a new action... but it can challenge us to question our own why. Sometimes when things aren't immediately easy, like many people, I start second-guessing myself. I start trying to "figure out" ways to work around the results, how to minimize the problems. One thing I've learned is that you'll never be able to change effects if you're working on effects. Every result we experience has a root cause. It's our nature to focus on the effect and try and manage around it. If the effects aren't working, addressing the cause, getting down to the core, trusting ourselves, that's where we get clear.

I sometimes share the story of the defective auto-fill system on my swimming pool. The system told the control panel that the water level was low, so the faucet continuously would turn on to adjust to the proper level. The overflow to my swimming pool went into a gravel pit that was adjacent to my house. Once that pit became saturated it began to flood my basement. I have pictures of my basement with all the carpet ripped up, with the drywall ripped out and all the furniture gone. We resealed the entire basement of my home with a tar-like substance, and put it back together. Within a few days.....the flood was back. Everything was soaked again! All the new drywall was trashed. I've got pumps in my basement and contractors all over the place. Once I took the time to look for the cause, as opposed to dealing with the effect, the problem was solved. Shut off the damn water. I know it's obvious, but sometimes, in the heat of dealing with results, the cause is so easily overlooked. As an entrepreneur, I can't begin to tell you how many times I "ripped the carpet" out of my companies. And in every instance, the simple answer was just like my basement... shut off the water.

As long as I follow the three inputs of being very clear on my intention, trusting my instincts and maintaining absolute integrity, the outcome is predictable and positive. My ability to influence both myself and others, to inspire them to invest their support, time and energy towards my 'why' becomes automatic. I've found in my career that once I create momentum, as long as I continue to live in alignment, the opportunities that present themselves can be described as nothing short of magic.

Woody Woodward:

When you woke up the day after and I'm using this as an analogy but the day after where you realized, "Oh my gosh, I have messed up my life. I've potentially sacrificed my family; I've sacrificed my business potentially." What was your first step to taking your life back? And I think the reason why this question is so important is all of us at times have sacrificed too much for an outcome that was too little. So if a reader is at that stage right now, what would you tell them to do to pick up their life and keep going?

Matt Schultz:

You know, for me I had really reached a very, very low point in my life. I had been to a retreat and I had the opportunity to work with some incredible mentors and coaches. I was given the task of creating my own obituary. The purpose for this exercise wasn't very clear to me at the time. To be honest with you, I still—even though my life had been reduced to chaos, I was still living from my ego. By participating in this exercise of creating my own obituary, that is, not as though I died today, but at the end of my natural life, I got to ask, how was I remembered? Who was I remembered by? What was I remembered for?

That simple exercise allowed me to take a look at who I was becoming, and how that differed from who I am. Once I got a little bit clear about who I am as a man, as a husband, as a father, as a coach, as a mentor, as a friend and as a business person, as I discovered who I was, who I am, I created the shift. I literally chose to put the proverbial oxygen mask on me first. I had to save myself before I could give, do, or be anything to anyone else.

Woody Woodward:

What is the greatest risk you've ever taken and was it worth it?

Matt Schultz:

The first time I left the 'being an employee' mentality and I started my own company. I had three young children at home. I maxed out credit cards and I started a business. I had no health insurance, no retirement, and as a young father, I had very little savings. I literally went all in, and I did whatever it took to make it work.

I joined organizations where people were involved in similar businesses. When there were areas that weren't being served by existing groups, I helped to begin new ones. I was the founding Vice President of the Utah Consumer Lending Association. We created the organization to assist people that were involved in financial services in effectively managing, and properly protecting their businesses. We brought together all of the 'competitors' to create a united voice as we dealt with myriad legal challenges that faced our industry. Over a decade later, the association still exists to serve the members that participate.

All of this came as a result of trusting my gut, going all in, jumping head first into a business within an industry in which I had no prior experience. I have no regrets. That started me on my career path and it taught me—literally it taught me how to make money. Not how to just exchange my time for a specific amount of dollars. This taught me how to MAKE money, how to create wealth.

Woody Woodward:
What you're doing now is very fascinating I think because you're dealing with a lot of very wealthy individuals who are selling their multi-million dollar homes but yet you're doing it in a very unique way. Tell us some more about that.

Matt Schultz:
I was approached by someone whom I've known for over 25 years. He's a friend, business associate, and mentor but mostly just a buddy. He was interested in getting involved in real estate. This guy, you'll have to meet him, he's the consummate promoter. He has relentless drive and, good or bad, has no filter. He was telling me about an industry that was fairly new within our local market. We identified a company with the proper licensing and a strong track record, and we affiliated ourselves

with them. We create an accelerated marketing program for high-end real estate, yachts and aircraft. We utilize several different methods of attracting buyers to properties that have a very finite sale date. We create massive urgency. We create excitement. We flat out move property.

A week ago, we assisted a homeowner to sell a home that had been on the market for years. We literally brought over 1,000 people through open houses, and then we set a specific date, time and place that the home would sell. Because there was urgency, because there was excitement, because there was no 'tomorrow,' this home sold for nearly seven million dollars.

Woody Woodward:

Tell us a little bit more about the house, how large of a home, what kind of land was it on?

Matt Schultz:

It's beautiful—this home is certainly one of the nicest in the state. It sits on over six exquisitely landscaped acres. It has over 20,000 square feet. It was a showpiece from the imported roof tiles, all the way down to the multimillion dollar landscaping.

Woody Woodward:

So what is it that drives a buyer to purchase a home that has sat on the market for years?

Matt Schultz:

Urgency. For me it's all about creating and telling the story properly and having the right people in the right place at the right time and creating that urgency. And once you do that you can move mountains.

Woody Woodward:

How does that same principle apply to regular business? A lot of people who are reading this book obviously have their own companies. How does that translate?

Matt Schultz:

Deliver value. Give people more in use value than the cash that you take from them. Exceed the expectations of the people that choose to do business with you. Work harder than you think you can. Be passionate. Burn the ships. Take away the chicken exits. Go all in. Trust yourself. Invest in your relationships. Show up for other people. Be a giver. Promote other people. Make introductions. Joint venture with people you like. Share your passion. Become a magnet.

What I've found is the most successful for me is networking. I first find out what it is that I can do to assist other people. When I invest in the success of others, whether it's mentoring them, sharing advice, or maybe referring somebody to their business, I add value. Those people are then magnetized to do the same for me. I would say that being focused on providing service and value to others is infinitely greater than being focused on money, because that takes care of itself. Once you're very clear about your purpose, everything else becomes automatic.

If anyone in your industry has been successful, so can you. If anyone in your area has been successful, so can you. If you've made money before, you absolutely can get it back. It's like a magnet. Bear with me for a minute, but I think you'll see my point. If you take a piece of steel, and you put it next to a magnet, the steel becomes 'magnetized'. Literally the molecules are lined up in a particular order that create an energy that pulls it towards a similar material. Now, if the same piece of steel is 'demagnetized,' the magnetic field hasn't gone away, it's just that the molecules are moving in a random order. I believe, that as people, as entrepreneurs, we are also magnetized towards success, or demagnetized from it. Either way, it's just a function of reproducing the actions that we took to get us to a point of success initially, or modeling the actions of others that have achieved the results we desire.

Woody Woodward:

When you look back on your life and you look forward, what legacy do you want to leave on this planet?

Matt Schultz:

You know, as I experienced a low point in my life, the question that I asked myself was this: If someone 20 years from now met one of my kids on the street and they said, "I knew your dad," what would they say about me? When I build from the perspective of leaving a legacy that my posterity would be proud of, that's where I find my ultimate why. When I'm living in alignment with that, when I'm balanced, when I'm on purpose, focused and present, I can create more than I ever dreamed was possible. I want to inspire people. I want someone to say to my kid, "Because of your dad, I didn't give up."

Rebecca Yates

Rebecca Yates is a published author, licensed insurance broker, consultant and owner of Ark Insurance Solutions, LLC. She has been working in the health insurance industry since 2004. Before starting Ark in 2010, Rebecca worked for a diverse range of organizations including insurance brokerages, aerospace engineers, emergency medical suppliers, and technology consultants. She received a Bachelor of Arts degree from Westminster College and is currently serving on their Alumni Board, along with various committees at the college. She is also actively involved with Business Network International, Corporate Alliance, and most recently has joined the board of Women in Insurance and Financial Services (WIFS).

In her spare time she runs a small, custom clothing line, a health insurance general agency and a property and casualty insurance agency. She loves to read, improve her home, and travel. She has a beautiful family and was recently blessed with another girl.

Contact: Ark Insurance Solutions

rebecca@ark-ins.com • www.utahinsuranceexperts.com

Woody Woodward:

Rebecca, you've been successful in two different industries, insurance and retail. Based on your experience in those industries, how would you define a leader?

Rebecca Yates:

I believe that a leader is somebody who builds a good team. If you don't find the right people, you can never succeed no matter how many leadership tapes you listen to or classes you take. Your team is what defines you as a leader.

Woody Woodward:

How do you find the right people to join your team?

Rebecca Yates:

One of the best ways to find people is to use your network. Start meeting people and even if there's nothing that you can help them with presently, develop relationships with them. Spread your reach everywhere so you can pull people when you need them.

Woody Woodward:

As an entrepreneur, what is the greatest risk you've ever taken? Was it worth it?

Rebecca Yates:

The day I left a previous employer, I was told I would be sued and that they would "destroy me." In spite of the tremendous risk, my business partner and I decided to go down our path anyway. We endured the legal chaos and were able to build a business the way we wanted to build it. It all worked out in the best possible way.

Woody Woodward:

That is an inspiring story. Many people are afraid to take risks. What has been your approach to weighing risk?

Rebecca Yates:

With any opportunity I've been presented with, I look at what the best case and worst case scenarios are. I ask myself if surviving the worst case scenario would be worth it in order to achieve the best case scenario. I write down a list of pros and cons for each scenario. I seek out advice from other professionals to supplement my own knowledge and experience.

Woody Woodward:

How do you stay focused in difficult times?

Rebecca Yates:

When I'm struggling with something, I will listen to self-improvement CDs on my computer. Hearing someone else, even only as background noise, giving encouraging words keeps me motivated and focused. I keep pictures of my children all over my office and when I see them in front of me, I remember why I'm doing this. That way I can stay focused on making my time productive.

Woody Woodward:

A lot of top achievers have different techniques to beat discouragement. What techniques do you use to keep the right perspective?

Rebecca Yates:

My secret weapon is keeping a good team around me. When I'm feeling discouraged or unable to focus, I lean on them. I jokingly tell my assistant that she is my personal cheerleader. I'm not afraid to turn to the people in my life. I lean on my friends, my team members, and my partners for help in keeping the vision.

Woody Woodward:

What is the secret combination to finding success in your specific line of work?

Rebecca Yates:

I believe that one of the most important secrets to success is discovering who you are serving. You need to have this so clear in your mind that it vibrates down to your toes. For me, in the insurance industry, I serve people that will have a life-altering illness. I believe with every fiber of my being that what I do saves lives.

Recently, we had a client with an employee that chose not to purchase the insurance. As a result, she did not have her annual exam done. At the age of 44, she passed away due to a heart condition that would have been detected and corrected in an annual exam. She left behind her children and her husband and died far too early. I succeed because I know that what I do will save lives every single day. I also believe that creativity, no matter the industry, will turn into success. Be your own creative force!

Woody Woodward:
What inspired you to get into this line of work?

Rebecca Yates:
I had a very personal experience where health insurance saved me from bankruptcy. I had recently gone through some very difficult personal problems. Just as I was beginning to recover, my soon-to-be ex husband was in a horrible accident. As I stood in the ICU watching him on the breathing tubes, the nurse called me aside and asked how I was going to pay the bill. It was $150,000 so far that day and was expected to be up to a million dollars. He had not taken the insurance he was offered so it was falling on my plate. I truly felt hopeless. My father-in-law called his insurance broker and they were able to negotiate with the insurance carrier. The entire bill was covered.

Woody Woodward:
Wow.

Rebecca Yates:
I had been offered employment in the health insurance field. I was convinced it was filled with greedy, scummy liars and wasn't sure I would be able to work in that environment. Then I had this experience and I thought "All right, I can do this. This does help people."

Woody Woodward:
I find that tragedy often breeds triumph. Has experiencing tragedy helped you?

Rebecca Yates:
Absolutely! It has given me the gift of perspective. I know that most

of the time the choices I have to make are not fatal. Once you realize that, life is much easier.

Woody Woodward:

In our lives and work, we need people to help us. Mentors keep us on the right track. Have you had a mentor in your life? What did they do to help you?

Rebecca Yates:

I have been blessed with several mentors in my life, both officially and unofficially. I hired a coach that did a lot to help me with the organizational structure and vision. I have a wonderful friend that is my unofficial mentor and she helped me see that I can march to the beat of my own drum and still succeed. It's very easy to start to conform and I believe that will hold you back. Be who you were meant to be.

Woody Woodward:

When someone is looking for a mentor, what specifically should they watch for?

Rebecca Yates:

First, you should look for people that are accomplishing what you would like to accomplish. If they haven't done it, they can't coach you on how to do it. My mentor is not in my industry, but she has become the leader of a very successful business. That is my goal as well. You also need to find someone that is willing to invest time in you.

Woody Woodward:

As you have succeeded in life, can you share a time when you had an "Aha" moment? Specifically one where you realized "Ah, I've made it" or "Oh, I need a change" or "Yes! I'm on the right track?"

Rebecca Yates:

One of my favorite "Aha" moments was my first conference call with the leadership team of a Fortune 500 company. We were discussing my newest product. The conversation was about them trying to determine how to change their product to fit into my mold. I was completely amazed that a giant, successful company would be willing to change for a simple girl from Idaho. That's when I realized I was on to something. It was a lot of fun to experience that.

Woody Woodward:

I believe in relationships to riches. Riches are not defined by dollars and cents. It's about relationships to resources. We don't know who we don't know. We need to meet other people through our friends. How does someone give a good referral? How does someone be a good referral?

Rebecca Yates:

The best way to give a good referral is to really listen. Listen to what they're looking for. Sometimes, it's best to bluntly ask "What are you looking for?" Once you know that, you can focus in your other conversations and start connecting dots. I went to breakfast with two companies just this morning. Their relationship won't benefit me at all at this time, but in our discussions, I realized that they were perfect for each other. I love to connect people in person. Then, I have the advantage of listening to their conversation and finding out who else are they looking for. If you are always looking to help other people, you will naturally give good referrals.

Woody Woodward:

You have a lot to manage in your life. How do you stay in control?

Rebecca Yates:

I lean very heavily on the people in my support system. American society has gotten away from that. We've developed an "I can do it all, and do it on my own" culture. It's no wonder that stress-related diseases are so prolific now. It was a hard lesson to learn for me, but now I can say "I need help." I do my best to return the favor when they need it. I think of it as the barn-raising principle. In pioneer times, everyone needed a barn. Rather than let each settler struggle to build their own, or only have their immediate family help, the entire community would chip in. It turned into a party. The work was done quickly and there was time for dancing and joy. When the next neighbor needed help, it was the same. I try to have a network of barn builders.

I also try to be forgiving of myself. I can't possibly control it all. If I didn't get my house spotless before I had a contractor come in, I just have to say, "Well, I accomplished the things that are important. This doesn't matter." My mother always used to tell me that she would rather spend time with us than have a spotless floor. I really subscribe to that theory.

Last, but not least, I try to make my travel time productive. I don't mean productive in making calls or checking email. I mean that I turn the car into my mental/emotional/spiritual development time. That may be listening to self-improvement CDs or talking through a problem that I'm struggling with. If I can get that work done, I am much more productive and focused when I arrive.

Woody Woodward:
Who has inspired you along the way?

Rebecca Yates:
My mother. She would not be defined in traditional terms as successful. She's never had large amounts of money. She's never had huge accomplishments listed under her name. But she does get up every day, despite her chronic disease, and work hard at everything she does. She isn't afraid to do the right thing, even if it is at the risk of her own life, and I admire that greatly. My mother has succeeded in ways that I only aspire to.

Woody Woodward:
What recommendations do you have for people who are struggling mentally, emotionally and physically? What would you recommend to inspire that person to keep going?

Rebecca Yates:
I would encourage them to remember that nothing lasts forever. The difficulties and trials that you are experiencing will end. Just take

tiny steps forward every single day and that is enough. You don't have to move a mountain today; you just have to pick up a pebble. Tomorrow, pick up another pebble. Pretty soon you will look back and see the mountain has moved. Find the things that bring you joy and do them every day. For me, taking my children to the zoo has gotten me through many difficult trials! The greatest things in life are accomplished by moving pebbles and finding joy.

Woody Woodward:

Most people don't know the details of your story. You've suffered severe tragedy in your life. When did you develop your optimistic attitude? When did you realize "I own my own life? I control my life. I'm taking it back"?

Rebecca Yates:

I have had horrible tragedy, but I have been very blessed as well. There were many days when I felt discouraged, times when I felt ruined and hopeless. There was an entire year of my life that I lost to depression. I remember my mom saying to me "Well, you have to keep going because your only other choice is suicide and that is not an option." It was during this time that my dear friend came into my room and physically pulled me out of bed. He pointed out that I was missing out on my life and on my daughter's life. Between the two of them, I had my perspective shift. I realized that the choices I was making were not only harming me, but my child as well. That was really powerful for me. I started to make different choices, little ones at first—something as simple as deciding not to lock myself in a dark room after work, but have dinner with my family instead. I consciously changed just a few little choices, then a few more. Pretty soon, my life looked completely different.

Woody Woodward:

How old were you when you were at that point of depression?

Rebecca Yates:

I was 22 years old.

Woody Woodward:

Once you made that choice, what actions did you take to get your life where you wanted it to be?

Rebecca Yates:

I started spending a lot of time outside. I started exercising more. I started eating healthier. I started serving others whenever I could. I also spent a lot more time with my daughter.

Woody Woodward:

For people that are ready to take the leap and start their own company, what advice would you give them.

Rebecca Yates:

Don't be afraid to ask questions. Ask everyone. My clothing line was on the verge of not becoming a reality when I was referred to a local clothing store. I was having difficulty seeing the relevance of what she was doing and what we were doing, but decided to visit with her anyway. When I arrived, she wasn't there. I was feeling frustrated, but decided to check next door and see if they knew when she would be in. The women tending the store asked me what I needed with her next-door neighbor. The next thing I knew I had a manufacturer in Sri Lanka, which was the exact piece we were struggling with. If it is what you believe in, don't be afraid to put yourself out there and talk to everyone about it. You never know who is going to be able to give you the missing puzzle piece.

Woody Woodward:

What is the last bit of advice you would give to lift someone's spirit and encourage them to keep going?

Rebecca Yates:

Life happens to everybody. Nobody escapes it alive. You get to find the joy in it. No matter what is going on, look around and find the beauty. Look with the eyes of an artist. It's easy when you see something every day to miss how beautiful it is. Stop today, look at the view. Imagine turning it into a beautiful painting. What would the highlights be? Which pieces would be the center? You will find a new appreciation in the things you see every day. Take that joy and then pick up your pebble.